Early praise for *How Champions Sell* by Michael Baber:

"This is an outstanding book on professional selling! It is loaded with page after page of immediately usable ideas that any salesperson can use to get more and better sales results that very day."

—Brian Tracy, Chairman, Brian Tracy International
Author of *The Psychology of Selling*

"Michael Baber's book, *How Champions Sell*, is the most complete, thorough treatment of sales available today. Read it and reap. It's great!"

—Bill Brooks, Chairman, the Brooks Group
Author of *You're Working Too Hard to Make the Sale*

"Congratulations on the terrific job you did in writing *How Champions Sell*. Your approach of focusing on the advanced, unique strategies top performers use was refreshing. Thank you for the great ideas."

—Michael Price, COO, Sales & Marketing Executives International

"Of all the sales books I've read, *How Champions Sell* is by far the most truly strategic in nature, and does the best job of showing an experienced or inexperienced salesperson how to greatly improve long-term sales results."

—Dr. Peter Johnson, Director, Strategic Performance Institute

"Mike Baber's book, *How Champions Sell*, should be titled *The Complete Encyclopedia of How to Sell Into the Year 2000*. The book is much more than enlightening. Its reference format provides a critical resource tool for day-to-day planning and decision making in the real sales world."

—Bill Daughtery, Director National Accounts
Garlock Sealing Technologies—Coltec Industries

"Your ideas to sell more effectively in *How Champions Sell* have been critical to my developing ideas that enable me to sell to my strengths as a person and to the true strengths of the organization I represent."

—Eric P. Barnett, Account Executive
UST, Inc.—The Business Marketing Group

"The results from Baber's championship sales training were beyond our fondest dreams."

—Roger Huber, Executive V.P., MidAmerica BancSystems

"How Champions Sell is extremely well thought out and structured for ease and use."

—Jim Cathcart, author/speaker

"An absolutely great book! Great idea. Solid advice. Guaranteed to help anyone who wants to become a champion salesperson."

—Nido R. Qubein, Chairman, Creative Services, Inc.

"The Book, *How Champions Sell*, shows how we plan to sell in our company to serve customers mightily and expand business greatly. We have purchased a copy for every manager and are purchasing copies for many of our nonsales, frontline people."

—Robert Lancaster, President
Cascade Rehabilitation Counseling, Inc.

"How Champions Sell gave me new insights into how to sell and how to effectively manage a sales force. It contains the essence of selling success, presented in an easy-to-read format. The chapters 'Personal Presence, Power, and Passion' and 'Grasping Critical Issues' alone make the book worth reading."

—Don Lowery, Vice President-Marketing and Sales, AVSCO

"The most useful book on sales I've ever read."

—John Potter, Senior Vice President
Liberty Mutual Insurance Company

"This could well be the most comprehensive selling book on the market today. Reading *How Champions Sell* will give you the *different* foundation you must have to prepare for the year 2000!"

—Tom Reilly, author of *Value-Added Selling Techniques*
and *Value-Added Sales Management*

"A trully excellent book that will make every salesperson who reads it a champion with their company and their customers."

—Dr. Tony Alessandra, author of *The Platinum Rule*
and *Collaborative Selling*

"I found *Cross-Marketing* to be a brilliant book—loaded with scores of useful, implementable ideas! You've gone *Service America* several times better. Your new book, *How Champions Sell*, is equally great."

—Jeff Davidson, author and business book reviewer

"Captures the key points of successful selling and consolidates them into a very readable format."

—Lou Atwood, Vice President-Marketing, Alltel Supply, Inc.

"This book is a gigantic accomplishment. It's fun, easy-to-read, and jammed full of ideas and ways to get business."

—Jack Brown, Division Purchasing Manager, TRW, Inc.

"I greatly enjoyed reading *How Champions Sell*. Your B^2 formula makes eminent sense. You have a powerful grasp of the literature and practice of selling, and tap into a motherlode of powerful techniques. Your book will meet with wide acceptance I feel certain."

—Richard J. Allen, Ph.D., Director, Executive Resource Center
The International Centers for Excellence™

Baber's clients have responded enthusiastically over the years:

"Your program was the best we have seen in a very long time. The follow-up actions by our management team to your presentation have been outstanding."

—Mark L. Braunstein, President, National Data Corporation

"You have done things for AT&T no other consultant has been able to do."

—Jim Olson, CEO, AT&T

"Both your vast background and knowledge in marketing and business development and your ability to work well with people were apparent as our group moved forward rapidly to meet our objectives under your prodding and guidance."

—Frank Topping, Manager of Engineering, AT&T

"Your performance as a featured speaker on championship selling was one of the key reasons for our having such an outstanding national convention."

—Jack I. Criswell, Executive Director
Sales & Marketing Executives International

"As a result of your time with us, we have successfully entered a new marketplace and trained our branch managers in effective sales and sales management."

—John A. Young, Sr., Vice President, MidAmerica BancSystems

"We really received rave reviews on your presentation on 'Keys to Championship Selling.' You presented many really meaningful and usable ideas and concepts while still making it so exciting and interesting."

—Thomas H. Garcia, Jr., Manager, Membership Services
National Tooling & Machining Association

"Our results from your program and follow-up were outstanding."

—B. Charles Millner, Vice President, Citicorp Real Estate, Inc.

"As a result of your process, for the first time in the 18 months I've been with A&M everyone is hitting their quota on a regular basis."

—Mike Rayfield, Sales Manager
A&M Roofing and Construction Company

"Michael, you are one of the most knowledgeable management consultants we have had the pleasure to work with.

—Doug Coleman, Department Manager
McDonnell Douglas Corporation

HOW CHAMPIONS SELL

HOW CHAMPIONS SELL

Michael Baber

AMACOM
American Management Association

New York • Atlanta • Boston • Chicago • Kansas City • San Francisco • Washington, D. C.
Brussels • Mexico City • Tokyo • Toronto

This book is available at a special
discount when ordered in bulk quantities.
For information, contact Special Sales Department,
AMACOM, a division of American Management Association,
1601 Broadway, New York, NY 10019.

This publication is designed to provide accurate and authoritative information in regard to the subject matter covered. It is sold with the
understanding that the publisher is not engaged in rendering legal,
accounting, or other professional service. If legal advice or other expert
assistance is required, the services of a competent professional person
should be sought.

Library of Congress Cataloging-in-Publication Data

Baber, Michael.
    How champions sell / Michael Baber.
        p.   cm.
    Includes bibliographical references and index.
    ISBN 0-8144-0371-9
    1. Selling.   I. Title.
    HF5438.25.B243   1997
    658.85—dc21   96-23715
                                            CIP

Printing number

10   9   8   7   6   5   4   3   2   1

Contents

Foreword

Every business and salesperson seeks to improve sales performance. While businesses have poured billions of dollars into sales training, marketing systems, and sales bonuses, no one seems to have found the magic bullet that can convert an average or good salesperson into a championship performer.

Does such a magic bullet exist? Michael Baber says there are several magic bullets. You have to determine which fits your situation. My experience with him says he's right.

Michael has an unusual background for a marketing and sales consultant. After graduating from Virginia Tech and University of Delaware, he proceeded to work as a manager in the five major functional areas of a large corporation: research, production, finance, sales, and marketing. This gave him a unique insight into what a business wants and needs from a vendor to perform profitably and competitively.

He was Assistant Vice President of Corporate Planning for Reynolds Metals Company and Manager of Market Research and New Business Development for Monsanto Company. He then started, sold for, managed the sales force, and was president of two million-dollar corporations.

Michael started part-time as a sales and marketing consultant in 1972 and became full-time in 1986 when he published the first of his four books, *Integrated Business Leadership Through Cross-Marketing*. Cross-marketing is a business concept in which "everyone in the organization works effectively as a member of a team focused on better serving the customer." It involves marketing, customer service, and sales—all at the front line. It is the forerunner of "Frontline Marketing," a chapter in this book.

Most marketing and sales managers and trainers focus on ways to help poor and average salespeople and marketers become more effective. Michael's primary focus is on how to help average or "very good" salespeople and marketers to become "great."

This started in 1986 when Michael headed up a study of a number of the nation's top salespeople. Out of this came his presentation, "Six Keys to Championship Selling," which he has given repeatedly to sales organizations, large and small, in and outside of the United States.

For the past nine years, he continued in his consulting and research to further differentiate between the "good" salespeople, the 20 percent that generate approximately 80 percent of the sales or sales results, and the "truly great" salespeople, those who far out-perform the "good." This book encapsulates the best approaches and case histories Michael has found.

How Champions Sell offers 27 different strategies and skills in six categories that championship-performing salespeople have used to achieve sales results that far exceed their peers and competitors. Actually, champions usually don't have peers or competitors in the normal sense of the word. What they do, how they do it, and the results they achieve, are so different from the norm it is as if they are from another planet.

I had the opportunity to lead the sales and marketing turnaround of two mid-size corporations. The second effort was with Michael Baber's assistance. His assistance, and his knowledge of how champions sell and market, made the second turnaround much easier and more effective that the first effort, which was without him.

In all, Michael spent 15 months helping our company, AVSCO, improve its sales and marketing performance using concepts presented in this book. Our sales and profitability increased markedly and we received numerous letters of congratulations and thanks from customers and vendors alike.

When Michael first came to address our sales and branch managers, most of them were skeptical. In a matter of hours their skepticism dissipated. After the first two day session with Michael, one of our top sales managers came to me and said, "The way we have been selling is entirely wrong. We must change immediately." We did, and the verifiable results are a matter of supreme pride to me today.

In this book Michael gives you the unique opportunity to learn what we learned—how champions sell, and how you can achieve championship results.

A few years ago, baseball slugger Jack Clark joined the San Diego Padres baseball organization. The *San Diego Tribune* newspaper quoted Tony Gwynn (a future Hall of Famer) as saying that when Jack walked into the locker room the first day, "We all felt like standing up and cheering!"

After you read Michael's book thoroughly and apply its strategies and skills to your selling, it won't be long before your company's management, your family, and your friends will feel like standing up and cheering when you walk into the room—because of your "championship" sales results.

Good selling. Good championship performance.

> Jonathan Ottens
> Former President, Aviation Service Corporation (AVSCO)
> President, Harman Paint Company
> Atlanta, Georgia 1996

How to Use This Book

The Introduction to this book explains how champions sell. The 27 supporting chapters explain how you can become a sales champion.

Each chapter describes a different strategy or skill that selling champions have used to achieve extraordinary success. Most people want to know the one "magic bullet" that they can use to achieve greatness. There isn't one magic bullet. There are 27 magic bullets. You have to determine which one or very few fit your gun.

Following Baber's Law, described in the Introduction, your objective should be to determine which few of the chapters are most important to you. Then concentrate on how to use and implement those few strategies and skills with excellence.

It will benefit you greatly to read the entire book. Some of the chapters may seem to be of little interest to you. But the "A" sections are easy to read, and all the chapters contain information that can be very helpful, at least by giving you a broader and deeper perspective. And some of the information in non-key chapters and the Appendix will be helpful in understanding and implementing the ideas in chapters that are key to you.

But your primary focus should be on determining which few strategies and skills will be most helpful to you. And then on what the book says about those that you can use both short term and long term.

Each chapter is divided into three parts. First is the title and a short definition of that strategy or skill. Then comes a short "A" section titled "Illustration and Rating." It further defines and describes the approach, and illustrates it with experiences of selling champions. It concludes with a quick rating exercise to help you determine whether that particular strategy or skill is highly applicable to you. If it is, you might want to read the third "B" section of that chapter right away. If not, you might want to skip to the "A" section of the next chapter and come back to the "B" section later. The "B" section is titled "Implementation" and describes what you can do to perform that chapter's strategy or skill with excellence.

If you are busy and are looking for an interesting, short, easy-to-read book which describes 27 different ways to be highly successful in selling, then read through all the "A" sections first, and come back later to sift through the more detailed and weighty "B" sections and Appendix.

The Appendix presents a host of creative approaches to the fundamentals of selling, plus additional helps and supports. Many of these fundamentals and helps are used by the selling champions we studied.

Book Organization

Less is more. This book contains a huge amount of valuable information. But it is divided into small units that can be easily digested.

The 27 chapters are divided into six major categories of strategies and skills, Parts A—F.

Each chapter can be thought of as a very short book. The "A" section of the chapter tells you what the "book" is about and why it is important. It gives you a tool to evaluate the "book's" importance to you. The "B" section explains what you can do to substantially increase your effectiveness in that area. It doesn't include everything that has been written or used in that area. But it includes enough to make a huge difference in the effectiveness of most readers. Most of the presented ideas and approaches have been used by salespeople to increase their selling effectiveness.

The chapter titles themselves are significant. For instance, in Chapter One the word "passion" is in the title. To be a selling champion you must be "passionate" about what you sell. Believing in it is not enough. Nor is being enthusiastic. Selling champions change and improve what they sell until they are "passionate" about it. Chapter Two is titled "Really Listening," not just listening or effective listening. The same type of observations can be made about other chapter titles.

Read the definition of each chapter's strategy or skill carefully. It may be quite different from what most people think of when they hear the title. For instance, "Building Partnering Relationships" is not relationship building or relationship selling. It is more. And sales consulting is more than just consultative selling.

There is a tendency for very important, but more basic, strategies and skills to be presented in the early chapters, and more advanced and more complex approaches to be covered later.

Strategies and Skills

There are probably 1,000 sales improvement ideas in this book. Of these, 500 may be important to you; ten may be key; and one may (should) change your world. A selling friend of yours in another company may find 400 of your 500 to be important to them. Only two of your ten keys may be key for them. They are likely to choose an entirely different chapter, or strategy or skill, for their emphasis. It is likely that you and another sales associate in your company or department will find many of the same ideas and approaches to be important. But you still may choose an entirely different strategy or skill for major emphasis. This is because of the difference in your product/service line, in your key customer segments, or in your personal experience and strengths.[1]

Some of the discussed strategies and skills are more helpful in some industries than others. And some more in one type of selling than another.[2] Some have lost or gained importance with time. However, if you do them "far" better than your competitors, and effectively apply some of the methods described, an "out-of-favor" strategy still could be the key to your success. For example, in some industries consultative selling has lost favor. Customers have tended to get all the free consulting advice they could from as many salespeople as possible, and then go out for bids looking for the lowest price. The problem in this case may not be with consultative selling. It might be with how and with whom it is done.[3]

Some of the 27 strategies and skills are totally foreign to the knowledge base of most salespeople. It still will benefit you to read about and understand them. This is true, even if you don't choose them for focus and concentration. They will give you a perspective usually held only by upper management and skilled marketing professionals. This gives you a decided competitive advantage when meeting with, planning with, and planning for calls with upper management and sophisticated business people. Also, it might help you to emulate the performance of the AT&T sales engineer described in Chapter 24. Thus, like him, you might think of an idea or ap-

---

1. Nick DiBari is discussed in the Introduction. Nick had two highly successful salespeople reporting to him. They both sold consultatively and they both attempted to develop partnering relationships. However, one concentrated on consultative selling because he was highly technical and felt comfortable developing great technical expertise. The other concentrated on developing personal relationships, because he was highly skilled at cultivating and influencing friends, and he was very social, belonging to a country club and owning a large boat that could be used to take out customers on social occasions.

2. An internal study at IBM indicated that different skills and personality characteristics were needed to be successful in each of three major types of selling: (1) to data processing departments—these huge, long term sales needed patient salespeople who develop close partnering relationships, (2) computers to mid-sized and small corporations—these required energetic, persistent salespeople who could prospect and sell assertively, and (3) office products—these required flexible salespeople who could sell programs to upper management and at the same time maintain friendly contact with the first level workers who used and often chose the equipment. Different material in this book may be highly important to each of these three types.

3. Concerning "with whom"—usually it should be done at a higher level than it is. Concerning how—consultative selling often should be upgraded to the "sales consulting" that is described in Chapter 18.

proach that could mean tens of millions of dollars in extra profitable sales for your company. Entrepreneurial attitudes and skills (Chapter 4), pull-through marketing assistance (Chapter 23), and new business marketing and marketing assistance (Chapters 24 and 25) are examples.

Most chapters can be read on a stand-alone basis. If particular chapters or sections are of special interest, or if they directly pertain to a current challenge you are facing, feel free to read them first.

ILLUSTRATIONS AND CASE STUDIES

Many of the supporting illustrations come from our nationwide studies. Some come from the author's training and consulting experience. Sometimes names were changed slightly to protect the guilty. Some illustrations, but not the main points, were altered slightly to protect confidential information.

Selling is different in different industries. Some practices that work well in consumer sales are inappropriate to business-to-business selling, and vice versa. However, the principles are the same. Therefore, a basic approach that helped a champion to be successful in one industry or type of business might well be applicable to you in a different industry or situation.

For instance, Keith Dillon sells mortgage financing on straight commission to or through real estate agents. You probably don't sell mortgage financing. And you don't sell to real estate agents. You may be on salary plus bonus instead of commission. But you still can "leverage your selling" using the approaches that Keith used, described in Chapter 15. Keith increased his take-home income from $50,000 to more than $250,000 in slightly over a year by focusing on leveraging his selling.

I'm not suggesting that all the readers of this book can earn more than $250,000 per year. Many can. Some can't. But I am suggesting that you can greatly improve your selling effectiveness, regardless of your situation.

BEYOND SELLING FUNDAMENTALS

This is not a book on the fundamentals of selling, despite the information on creative fundamentals presented in the Appendix.

But as a professional salesperson you should know and use the fundamentals.

Your character is important to your selling success, and character is more fundamental than the strategies and skills presented in this book. However, doing something helps you to be something. And implementing some of these "right" strategies and skills will help to build the character of a champion, such as honest interest in the customer's welfare, drive to achieve and succeed, unwavering focus on important objectives, and self discipline.

Have a positive attitude. Believe in yourself. Believe in your company. Believe in your products and services. Demonstrate those beliefs to your customers. Then customers will have confidence in you and in your products and services. They will be more likely to buy. They will give you the benefit of the doubt when something goes wrong.

Be enthusiastic. When you are enthusiastic—when you demonstrate your strong belief in your products and services and how they benefit your customers—then customers feel that. Again, they are more inclined to buy.

Know the benefits of your products and services. Talk in terms of benefits and values rather than just features.

Develop evidence to prove that what you say is true. Evidence includes testimonials, supporting statistical data, and stories of people who have successfully used your products or services.

Be professional. Dress professionally. Be dependable. Don't waste the customer's time. Plan and be organized. Have professional literature and demonstration materials, not dirty or dog-eared materials.

Be reasonably assertive. You can be low key and laid back. But at the same time you can have an aura of confidence and even a slight pushiness. This is because you believe so strongly. You believe that you are going to really help the customer. This is because of the value of your products and services.

Manage your time effectively.

Know the steps to the selling process, and how to present each step effectively, plus how to prospect effectively.

Develop empathy with the customer.

You should be of sound character. And you will be more effective if you understand and use the fundamentals of selling. If selling is your profession, you'd better. But even if you slip up on the fundamentals occasionally, you will sell much more if you can effectively employ one of these 27 championship selling strategies and skills.

They are grouped into six sections or "parts" by type. The first part is titled "Champions Have Personal Power." It starts after the Introduction and begins the main part of the book.

SALES LEADERSHIP AND CONSULTING

If you are a sales manager, leader, trainer, or consultant, this book and its approach should be extraordinarily helpful to you in evaluating the overall selling effectiveness, strategy, and plans of a salesperson or sales organization.

If you are thoroughly familiar with this book's material, you can analyze a selling situation and the appropriate strategies and skills will "jump" into your head and fall into place. Thus, the case for repeated reading and study. (I just completed such an analysis. I found that reviewing the table of contents beforehand helped the "jumping" process.)

Additional materials to support implementing this book's concepts are available either from the publisher or from Business Development Institute. These include video training assistance tapes and an action guide. The action guide was designed to be used by a sales manager for a series of sales meetings. It can be used to design effective sales training. It can be used by an aspiring sales champion (individual book reader) to more effectively implement the concepts, strategies, and skills discussed in this book.

Appendixes E and F present additional helpful information on how to use this book.

Acknowledgments

There are so many people I am indebted to for assistance, advice, encouragement, and partnering over the years, related to this book, that I couldn't possible include them all. But I'll try. First, my associates during the initial study that identified the keys to championship sales performance. Tony Alessandra, Phil Wexler, and Jim Cathcart were very helpful to me during this time. As was Dr. Peter Johnson, who continues to be an advisor to this day.

My special appreciation to those sales champions who talked with me, as well to those who performed so effectively as to be written about in the press.

The following are some of those who have worked with me as partners and clients during the past few years. I thank them all: Doug Coleman of McDonnell Douglas, John Thompson of Christian Hospitals, Dan Isom of Parkway School District, Ernest Launsby of Barnes Hospital, Len Hart and Frank Topping of AT&T, Harry Scott of Monsanto Company, Irving Roberts of Reynolds Metals, John Potter of Crawford & Company and later of Liberty Mutual, Jim Murphy of Wang Laboratories, F.N. "Redd" Storey of Dale Carnegie Courses, Kathy Storr of Siemens, Anthony Summers of National Food Stores, Jim Hasemeier of Kroger, George Rancilio of DuPont, Jack Conner of MediService, Armand Diaz of Washington University, Les Crider of the State of Missouri, Don Hanna of the YMCA, Dan Vogler of Anheuser-Busch, John Young of Missouri Savings, Ron Neverman of State Farm, Charlie Milner of Citicorp, Richard LaReau of Metropolitan Life, Jack Brown of TRW, Keith Bierbaum of Square D, David Chichester of American Express, Roger Huber of MidAmerica BancSystems, Nicholas Franco of Pennsylvania Life, Mark Braunstein of National Data Corporation, Don Lowery of AVSCO, Greg Klapp of Missouri Equipment Company, Perry Murphy of Sales & Marketing Executives, Tom Kimmel of Hardie Irrigation, Pam Schuknecht of La Jolla Bank & Trust, Debbie Caly of St. Paul Insurance, Tom Garcia of National Tooling & Machining, Kathleen Davis of Automotive Satellite Television Network, Mary Jane Bradley of Pharmacia, Deen Seedorff of General Mills, Joan Weber of Small Business Development Centers, Phil Hunsker of University of San Diego, Alex Martell of Eli Lilly, Michelle Poisson of Best Western, Bill Gambro of United Jersey Bank, Bob Dorr of Brown Shoe Company, and Vice Howcroft of Indal.

I also appreciate the special encouragement of Jon Ottens, president of AVSCO, Nido Qubein, and Jeff Davidson. And a special thanks to Jayne Smith, who has been a special inspiration.

Some others I feel indebted to are Patricia Ball, Larry Baker, Peter Drucker, Tom Peters, Stan Davis, Karl Albrecht, Tom Garcia, and Jim Olson of AT&T.

I appreciate the time and efforts of all those who reviewed and discussed the book manuscript with me, especially Tom Reilly, Stan Scioscia, Bill Brooks, and Greg Moore.

I thank Becky Craig for her ideas, design, and computer expertise.

To my children, Gayle, Karen and Donna, and their husbands, Dean and Matt, to my mother, Inez Baber, to my brother, Dale, and my sister, Carolyn, I give my thanks for their love, encouragement, and ideas over the years.

To those who should be listed and weren't, I thank you more than you know.

HOW
CHAMPIONS
SELL

Introduction

"Great thoughts put into practice become great acts!"

William Hazlett

How do champions sell?

We know the answer. Salespeople and sales managers can thereby increase their selling effectiveness far beyond what most people think is possible.

Ten years ago I led a study on highly successful salespeople to determine why they achieved results far better than those of their peers, even those considered to be "good" salespeople. The study identified key attributes and actions of the selling champions.[1]

I continued to study selling champions and work with salespeople and sales managers of varying abilities and achievements. Some achieved phenomenal results. Over time, I found an even more accurate answer to the question, "How do champions sell?"

> Sales champions sell something "entirely" different, or in an "entirely" different way, or in a "far" better way than do other salespeople, by which they provide "extraordinary" value to "high potential" customer segments.

Sales champions find ways to generate great value for customers, even when others don't think it is possible. They position themselves powerfully, with the result that customers see them as being in a different and higher category than other salespeople. They are highly effective, doing things

---

1. The seasoned salesperson will quickly recognize from a first review of the book's table of contents that most of the key aspects to being successful in selling seem to be covered. So is this a book on *championship selling* or on how to become a really effective, "good" salesperson? It is both, as can be seen from referring to the earlier section in How to Use This Book, "Sales Leadership and Consulting." However, a more thoughtful review of the contents turns up phrases that are unfamiliar to most seasoned pros; phrases like "critical issues," "business cases," "commitment to a concept," and "pull-through marketing assistance." The book's emphasis and uniqueness is on providing the "good" salesperson or sales organization a clear pathway to becoming a selling champion, which sells far more than the average "good" salesperson or organization.

other salespeople don't like to do to generate great results and use resources well. They exhibit a positive personality, demonstrating both their character and a passion for the value they deliver to customers. Many of them find ways to generate new business and new sales through some aspect of "new business development."

There is so much difference between what most salespeople do and achieve and what they could do and achieve, that it is mind-boggling. That probably includes you.

Once you know what the champions do, you can select and implement those things that fit you and your situation. This will help you to sell much more effectively, and perhaps become a champion. Helping you do that is the purpose of this book.

There is a reason that the words "entirely," "far," "extraordinary," and "high potential" are surrounded by quotation marks. Those words are key to understanding the difference between the champions and the just "good" salespeople.

Some capable salespeople and managers just don't "get it." They don't grasp the real meaning of the difference between selling champions and other salespeople even when it is explained to them. Some reasons they don't "get it" are that they don't see, don't believe, or don't understand the significance of those four terms. Or they are blinded by their past reasonable success using traditional approaches. Understanding the importance of those five words will help you to "get it," and as a result improve your performance many-fold.

In this book, you will read case histories that demonstrate how selling champions carried out each of the five parts of this answer. You will get ideas and approaches you can use to sell "entirely" differently, not just differently; and "far" better, thus providing customers with "extraordinary" value.

Everything seems to be changing about us. The world's situation is changing. How and what your customers purchase is changing. How they are organized is changing. How your company operates is changing. Or it soon will be. While how an individual champion sells in particular may change in the future, because their circumstances may change, how champions sell in general does not change.

HOW CHAMPIONS SELL

Sales Champions Sell (1) Something "Entirely" Different

There are three different ways, or approaches, that champions use to provide extraordinary value to high potential customer segments.

One is to sell something that is "entirely" different. They sell a "product" or "service" that is very different from what their competitors and peers sell, even peers in the same company or department.

For example, average insurance agents sell insurance. The "good" insurance agents, the top 20 percent which generate 80 percent of the results, usually sell security or peace of mind. (They sell insurance, of course, but they emphasize these two important benefits of the insurance.) Joe Gandolfo initially became a very "good" salesperson by selling security and peace of mind, aggressively following the selling procedures laid out by his company. But later, he became a sales champion by selling tax shelters. As explained later, Joe eventually sold more than 100 times as much insurance as do most "good" insurance salespeople. But to do this his approach became entirely different from that of most others. He packaged insurance as one component in providing tax shelters to higher income customers. What he sold, and the emphasis of what he talked about (tax shelters), was "entirely" different from what most other insurance salespeople sold (insurance, security, or peace of mind).[2]

Or (2) in an "Entirely" Different Way

Most people who own a home do so through a home loan or mortgage. Most mortgage financing salespeople make frequent sales calls on real estate agents. They try to get them to encourage their clients (new homeowners) to place their home mortgages with the salesperson's mortgage company. Almost all mortgage financing salespeople sell the same way. They call on real estate offices. They attempt to develop relationships with real estate agents and stay visible. This is so the agents will think of them, and contact them, when they are placing mortgages for the new homeowners.

One mortgage financing salesperson was very successful selling on straight commission in an "entirely" different way.

Keith Dillon, who is discussed in Chapter 15, formerly sold the way described above. Then he developed a short seminar on creative approaches to home financing. He gave the seminar to two large real estate offices. It was so well received that he was invited to give it to other offices. In a short time, he was so busy handling phone questions from seminar participants, consulting with them on creative financing, that he didn't have time to make personal visits to real estate offices. However, whom do you suppose the agents who called him placed their mortgages with? In just over a year, his take-home income increased from $50,000/yr. to more than $250,000/yr. And it has remained at the higher level for years.

2. Many insurance agents today have evolved to being tax consultants and financial planners. But Joe Gandolfo initiated his "different" selling strategy during the 1970s and early 1980s, before most tax shelters were eliminated in the mid-1980s. Today, Joe has evolved his approach to include selling differently. He is a celebrity consultant, selling through seminars—like Keith Dillon.

Or (3) in a "Far" Better Way Than Do Other Salespeople

Nick DiBari earned more than $8 million in commissions in six years as a salesperson and sales manager for Comdisco. Comdisco distributes computers and computer leasing out of Chicago. Nick also led the salespeople who worked with him to be highly successful.

Nick sold in a "far" better way than did his peers and competitors.

He was highly expert in the use of computers for increasing productivity and effectiveness of business processes. He didn't just know how computers work. He knew how they could help prospects in major ways to accomplish what prospects wanted to accomplish. And he knew how to explain this to the managements of his prospects so they would understand what computers were all about and how they could use them.

Nick developed a method of researching prospects before he called on them. Then he prepared a list of questions to ask them. The answers he got told him whether or not they were high potential prospects, and what the potential was. He would refuse to leave the prospect's office until he got all his questions answered. He had the ability to generate great enthusiasm in himself and in his prospects, because of what his computer systems could do for them.

Nick used a number of the strategies and skills discussed in this book. He used them with excellence. He used them in a "far" better way than do most other salespeople.

By Which They (4) Provide "Extraordinary" Value

Joe Gandolfo helped wealthy clients to substantially reduce their taxes. Would it be of "extraordinary" value to you to cut your income taxes in half?

Keith Dillon helped his real estate agent clients get home loans for their customers (new homeowners) that they otherwise wouldn't have obtained. All they had to do to accomplish this was to attend his seminar and then phone him when they needed consulting advice. He helped them make sales and earn large commissions they otherwise wouldn't have made. And he helped them do this in much less time and with less hassle. This reduced their stress, and left them with more time to make other sales or to spend with their families.

Nick DiBari helped company owners and top managements to clearly understand how they could run their companies more productively using his computer products and services. This made their jobs easier, and substantially increased their company profitability and executive bonuses.

To (5) "High Potential" Customer Segments

Joe focused on high income prospects. According to Joe, "It is easier to sell a million dollars worth of insurance to a millionaire than $30,000 worth to the average person." Joe selected specific industries and invested time and money, becoming well known and even a "celebrity" in those industries. One industry he concentrated on was owners of automobile dealerships.

Keith concentrated on working with the two largest real estate agencies in his city. He worked with others, but he focused his time and energy on becoming a partner with the management and the individual agents of the largest two.

Nick had a system to determine who were his largest prospects, and he concentrated on those. He focused more on some industries than others. But his primary focus was on larger companies of all types that needed and could afford computer productivity improvement.

Figure 1 is my favorite cartoon, and that of many salespeople.

Your competitors battle with the equivalent of spears and swords. You can battle with the equivalent of a machine gun—by employing the strategies and skills presented in this book. And you will provide your customers with great profit-generating value. They also will have the equivalent of machine guns—while their competitors are using spears and swords, and wishing they could find someone like you to bring them machine guns.

PARETO'S LAW

Pareto's Law states that there is an inverse relationship between the percentage of anything and its importance. This is frequently known as the *80/20 rule.*

Figure 1. "No! I can't be bothered to see any crazy salesperson, we've got a battle to fight!"

For instance, in any large group of salespeople the most successful 20 percent generate about 80 percent of the results, or sales. We define the top 20 percent as the "good" salespeople. (Also, 20 percent of customers represent 80 percent of total sales. Using the "best" 20 percent of the ways to improve selling results generates 80 percent of all the potential improvement results.)

Shown in Figure 2 are two graphs demonstrating Pareto's Law.

Mathematical calculations on Pareto's Law, assuming the 80/20 relationship, present some startling results. Each of the top 20 percent of a large group of salespeople (the "good" salespeople), on average, sells 16 times what each of the remaining 80 percent sells. From this you could conclude that if your company has 100 salespeople and the company has sales of $100 million, the top 20 sell about $4 million each and the remaining 80 sell an average of $250,000 each.

But experience and common sense say this is not what happens. The 80 do average about $250,000 each. But most of the top 20 average between $500,000 and $1 million. Then how does the company's sales get to be $100 million? The answer—a few salespeople or executives make major deals or develop major market arrangements that move $10 million or more each. Those are the selling champions who often sell an order of magnitude more than even the "good" salespeople.

How do they do it? By following "Baber's Law."

As a result, they sell something "entirely" different, or in an "entirely" different way, or in a "far" better way than do the other salespeople, by which they provide "extraordinary" value to "high potential" customer segments.

Think about it. Look at your company's results, and those of a few others with which you are familiar. Isn't this what always happens? The question is, how can you make it happen?

Figure 2. Graphs of Pareto's Law.

BABER'S LAW

If you can identify the very few (often one to three) most important selling opportunities or approaches available to you, and perform them with excellence, you can make it happen. You can become a selling champion—who sells far more, maybe an order of magnitude more, than the average "good" salesperson.

That demonstrates Baber's Law, which states:

> "In any large group of actions taken to accomplish a total result, focusing on implementing the few most important achieves by itself a large part of the total result."

For sales this could be stated as follows: "List every approach you can take to increase selling effectiveness in order of priority. Then choose the one, or very few, most important and implement it, or them, with excellence." As a result, your selling effectiveness will skyrocket.

Baber's Law is the foundation for this book and how it is recommended that you read the book. It is distinctly different from Pareto's Law. It is a mind jump forward. And it is critically important that you understand the difference.

By following Pareto's Law you can learn to do fairly well the most important 200 or so of the 1,000 different things available to become a "good" salesperson.

By following Baber's Law you will do with excellence one or a very few of the critically most important things, and become a selling champion.

KEYS TO CHAMPIONSHIP SELLING

Our initial study not only identified a number of selling strategies and skills used by champions. It uncovered "Six Keys to Championship Selling." These relate to and support all of the 27 chapters in this book.

The first key, as you might expect, is "being different" in a positive and effective way. The next five keys demonstrate being different in five supportive areas of championship selling performance.

Selling champions in their selling are:

1. Different
2. Expert
3. Professional
4. Sales Smart
5. Customer Serving
6. Big Thinking

1. *Selling champions are different and sell differently.* Champions are different inside.[3] They have a vision, mission, and passion that is untouched by most average and good salespeople. They know without question that they have a way to help the customer in a major way, and they have the self discipline and persistence to do whatever they need to do to convince the customer and to deliver the value about which they are so passionate.

Champions sell differently. Most insurance salespeople sell "insurance." The good ones sell "security and peace of mind"—a major benefit of insurance. But Joe Gandolfo sold "tax shelters." Joe sold something entirely different from either. It just happened to include insurance as a fulfilling ingredient. (Joe's strategies are discussed in some detail later in the book.) Keith Dillon sold entirely differently from his peers and competitors by giving seminars and being a consultant.

One way many champions sell differently is by performing creative marketing (Part F). An example is industry-specific marketing described in Chapter 21. One industry that Joe focused on marketing to was automobile dealerships.

Another way champions sell differently is by providing extraordinary value to customers (Part B). They may do this by "grasping" critical issues (Chapter 5), or by finding/offering specific added value (Chapter 7). Most champions sell strategically; most non-champions don't. Cultivating strategic relationships (Chapter 14) and leveraging their selling (Chapter 15) are two ways they sell strategically and differently.

2. *Selling champions develop expertise* in one or more business-related technologies that serve customers in special ways. This is the second key.

Usually, developing expertise requires that they focus their efforts. They focus into a high potential area or toward selected markets or industries. Joe developed specialized expertise in finding and evaluating tax shelters and in financial planning. Keith Dillon developed specialized expertise in real estate mortgage financing.

A sanitary maintenance sales champion (Chapter 5) developed specialized expertise in floor care. The IBM salesperson discussed in Chapter 21 developed expertise in serving the offices of physicians. The Reynolds Metals engineer in Chapter 22 was expert in alumina technology.

Specific expertise also is needed to provide specific added value (Chapter 7), pull-through marketing assistance (Chapter 23), or new business marketing assistance (Chapter 25). It is needed for sales consulting (Chapter 18), and usually in commitment to a concept/philosophy (Chapter 16).

3. *Champions are professional.* They dress neatly, and act as if they have self confidence, which they do. They adjust their selling manner to the cus-

---

3. They seem to be "wired" differently inside. The good news is that non-champions can rewire themselves by understanding where the "wires" should go and then forcing themselves to do what they should do when they should do it. Chapter 1, but also chapters such as 5, 7, 10, and 16, explain both the motivation and the method for doing so.

tomer. They dress and behave differently when calling on a working machine shop owner than when calling on a corporation president on the top floor of a high-rise building. They follow up and pay attention to details so customers are served effectively. They plan. They are organized.

Professionalism is inherent in being effective in team selling (Chapter 19) and in territory/account planning (Chapter 9). It is required to be effective in frontline marketing (Chapter 27) and facilitated problem solving and planning (Chapter 6).

4. *Champions sell smart.* In large part they sell smart through selling strategically and through developing close and long term relationships. Through carefully selecting where to focus, and with whom to develop relationships, they sell for the long term. They invest time and effort in getting to know high potential companies and key people in those companies. They become expert at finding problems and opportunities to solve, and at solving those problems and helping with those opportunities.

"Major account competitive selling" (Chapter 13) and "positioning, differentiating and focusing as in strategic marketing" (Chapter 12) contain examples of selling smart through strategic selling. Chapter 3 deals specifically with selling smart through building partnering relationships.

5. *Champions are customer serving.* They focus on customers, and their situations, wants and needs, rather than just on their own need to make sales. They develop working partnerships with customers. They deserve through their motives, behavior, and expertise to be treated as partners. They become considered as "on the customer's team." They forgo sales when those sales don't benefit the customer. They work within their own organizations to nudge and lead others to do their parts to serve customers effectively.

The customer support marketing philosophy (Chapter 20) is probably the ultimate in being customer serving. Frontline marketing (Chapter 27), facilitating problem solving and planning (Chapter 6), and finding problems/opportunities to solve (Chapter 8) all come from being customer serving.

6. *Selling champions think big.* They are continually alert to and respond to large opportunities. Examples are government contracts and partnerships with large units of Fortune 500 corporations. They invest some time and effort "on the come." They develop long term relationships. They obtain education, expertise, and celebrity status that supports their later being given large contracts or large selling arrangements. As an example, Joe Gandolfo went back to school to obtain a degree in finance. He gave free presentations on financial planning and tax shelters to industry organizations. He wrote books on effective salesmanship to position himself as a celebrity.

It takes big thinking for a salesperson to be involved in new business marketing (Chapter 24) and new business marketing assistance (Chapter

25). By facilitating problem solving and planning for upper management (Chapter 6), the salesperson thinks bigger than by just calling on the buyer or product/service user. By combining entrepreneurial attitudes and skills (Chapter 4), major account competitive selling (Chapter 13), and commitment to a concept/philosophy (Chapter 16), the salesperson can envision going after very large industry or account potentials.

These are just some examples of how the 27 strategies and skills discussed in this book support the "six keys to championship selling." By selecting a few of these strategies and skills for concentration in your selling, you practice applying the six keys. You sell more like the champions sell. You get more of the results that champions get.

Implementing the appropriate few of these 27 selling strategies and skills will help you in your selling to be different, expert, professional, sales smart, customer serving, and big thinking. It will help you to sell more like a champion. It will help you to *sell something "entirely" different, or in an "entirely" different way, or in a "far" better way than do other salespeople, by which you will provide "extraordinary" value to "high potential" customer segments.* You will be following in the selling performance footsteps of the country's most successful salespeople. As a result, you should take giant steps toward achieving their kind of championship selling results.

COMMENCEMENT

A final comment. Becoming a selling champion can be hard work. This is great news to you. Over 95 percent of your peers and competitors won't make the effort to read this book. And if they do they won't work at improving those few critical areas that can double, triple, or "zintuple" their performance. When you make that effort, the world can be your oyster.

So, whether you are a salesperson, consultant, or leader, get out your pen and paper, tape recorder, or laptop. As you read, record usable ideas that occur to you. And look for that one approach that might make you (or your people) a sales champion.

PART A

CHAMPIONS

HAVE PERSONAL POWER

1

Personal Presence, Power, and Passion

Who you are on the inside. How you affect and impress others. Your ability to get things done. How strongly you feel about the benefits and values of what you sell, and how you demonstrate those feelings.

ILLUSTRATION AND RATING—1A[1]

Champions have great personal presence, power, and passion (PPP). This is an area where they frequently are better than, but not different from, good salespeople. Almost all "good" salespeople have some personal presence, power, and passion. But champions usually have "far" more than most other salespeople, even good salespeople.

Personal presence is who you are on the inside and is demonstrated by how you carry yourself and how you speak.

Personal power is your ability to get things done; to make positive things happen for your customers and your company. It results in the ability to influence others to your way of thinking.

Passion is your strong belief in your company, product, service, and self, to the point that you believe the prospect is "absolutely out of their mind" not to do business with you.

1. The first or "A" part of each chapter defines and illustrates that strategy or skill, in this case PPP. It tells you enough about it for you to determine whether or not it should be high on your list of priorities. If you determine it to be high, then perhaps you will want to read the second or "B" part of the chapter right away. The second part usually is more detailed and involved. It explains how to implement the strategy or skill and become more knowledgeable and skilled in this area. However, if you determine the chapter to be of lower priority to you, then perhaps you will want to move on to part A of the next chapter, and read the rest of this chapter at a later time.

Be honest. How strongly do you feel about the value of what you sell? Is it "head-and-shoulders" above that of the competition in your mind? Can you prove it? You should be able to. This book shows you how to make it be that good, and prove it.

PPP is so important that a person almost can't be a good salesperson without it. For instance, Gellerman's research, reported in a recent Harvard Business Review article, indicated that the focus during a sales call depends on how seriously the customer takes the salesperson. With PPP the salesperson and the sales call objective will be taken seriously.

Almost any salesperson with lots of PPP will be a good salesperson. He or she will "passionately" direct the focus of the sales call to matters that are important, and the customer will respond positively. There is a reason for this. It is extremely difficult to be passionate about a product or service that does not have meaningful value. And if it has meaningful value, then to sell a substantial amount of it the salesperson just has to find out to whom it is valuable and present it to them with PPP.

But this book is not about good salespeople. It is about selling champions.

Selling champions have a huge amount of PPP, at least all those I have met, interviewed, or studied. And it is almost impossible to think of a salesperson being extraordinarily successful without it.

There is definitely a chicken-and-egg effect here. The more PPP salespeople have, the more they achieve great results. The better the results, the more they have PPP.

PPP may be the single most important ingredient to selling success. A recent internal study by UPS came to that conclusion.[2] But it is not exclusive. An engine needs great fuel to run at its best. But it also needs a good design, professional manufacture, good lubrication, and a solid connection to the rest of the machine. Championship salespersons have great PPP. But they must add to PPP a good product or service,[3] good selling fundamentals, and one or more of the other championship selling strategies and skills.

Dr. Peter Johnson and Nido Qubein are friends of mine. Both are highly successful business people who started with little or nothing. They also are successful business consultants, professional speakers, and selling champions. And yet they could hardly be more different. Peter is an ex-IBM executive from the northeast who now lives in Newport Beach, California. Nido came to this country as a poor boy from Lebanon, and still lives in High Point, North Carolina, where he originally started a small business. Peter bubbles with energy and force. Nido is laid back. But they have at least one thing in common—extraordinary PPP.

2. Actually the study concluded that the salesperson's passion was the key.
3. Which they have more control over than most realize. See Chapters 7, 8, 10, and 16 for starters.

When Peter and Nido first walk into a room you can sense something good is about to happen. There's a look in their eyes and a gait to their walk that says, "Relax; I'm here; all will be well for you." They first ask questions and listen. Then when they start to talk you sense their conviction, expertise, and inner excitement.

They both dress very well. They both spend time creating and thinking about how to find new value for customers. They both have helped their customers achieve great successes. They both have been paid huge sums of money. They both know that they can help their customers to be considerably more successful. This helps to further increase their presence, power, and passion.

Joe La Ferla is a highly successful salesperson and sales manager. His success came in large part because of his personal presence, power, and passion.

Joe was a pilot who was laid off by American Airlines in 1980. He took his first selling job with First Investors Corp. in 1981. He earned $124,000 in commissions his first year. He worked hard, very hard, and sold more the next year. He went back to school to get a B.B.A. in finance and insurance in 1988. He started specializing in selling IRAs to, and giving the greatest possible service to—who else?—pilots.

Joe developed an IRA concept about which he was passionate. He sold and later trained others to sell in a helpful and low-key but passionate way. His group of seven people now manages more than $100 million in pilots' money, with accounts ranging from $100,000 to more than $2 million.

If you saw a picture of Joe, you would sense his presence, power, determination, and drive that radiates from his face and stance. He looks to me like an educated Pete Rose in a business suit. Pete Rose was Mr. Enthusiasm, Mr. Determination, Mr. Passion, who got more hits than anyone else in baseball. Joe's expression demonstrates his Pete Rose type of enthusiasm, determination, and passion.

The second part of this chapter explains what Peter, Nido, Joe, and some of my other selling champion friends have, when I say they have extraordinary PPP. And it tells you how you can increase your PPP.

Thought Provokers

(1) Analyze yourself and your behavior. Videotape one of your meetings. Ask some peers for their observations. How would you describe your personal presence, power, and passion?

(2) What do you think are the keys to developing personal presence, power, and passion?

(3) How important is PPP, really? Why?

(4) What could you do to improve your PPP the most? You might need to read part of the discussion below to be ready to answer this question.

(5) Specifically, how would it help you?

(6) Is developing your PPP critically important in moving you in the direction of being a selling champion? Or are you relatively OK in this area? If it is important to you, then place it on your list for potential concentration. If you believe PPP is not a problem for you, you might consider checking that assumption with some people who know you well. Making the correct judgment can be critical to your future selling success.

Before proceeding, take the following rating exercise to estimate how important PPP is to your selling success. Note that the second or "B" item in the box below scores backwards from how "A" and "C" are scored.[4] Note also that "C" measures whether or not you can successfully improve in this area, not whether it is easy to do so. It will bring you great rewards to do something that is extraordinarily difficult and time consuming, if that is a priority area for your improved selling success.

If you get a score higher than 25, you should study the second part of this chapter with care. In fact, increased PPP may be the differentiating factor that can help you become much more of a selling champion. If you score 25 or below, it may be less important to you. Then you might decide to skip to the next chapter and come back to the more detailed material below at a later time.

CHAPTER RATING (rate A, B, and C below from 1 to 5 for this chapter's importance; then multiply)

_____ **A** = Importance or applicability to you (5 = great, 3 = moderate, 1 = poor)

_____ **B** = Your present strength or level of action (1 = great to 5 = poor) *(reverse rating)*

_____ **C** = Chances of your successful implementation or improvement (5 = great to 1 = poor)

A × B × C = your rating   (_____) × (_____) × (_____) = (_____)

If your rating is over 25, read "Implementation" now; if 25 or under, consider postponing until later.

You undoubtedly scored "A" to be 4 or 5, indicating its high importance and applicability. You may also have scored "B" and "C" high. However, if you feel that you are very strong in this area you might have scored B (your present strength and application) as a 1 or 2. If so, and especially if you don't see a way to improve substantially soon (where C = the chances of

---

4. Reading some parts of section 1B may be helpful to you in rating "A," "B," and "C."

your successful implementation or improvement), the score of A x B x C may have been 25 or below.

Implementation—1B

Personal presence, power, and passion (PPP) is critically important to all salespeople. Thus, it is critically important to you. You may want to focus on the implementation of this chapter's strategy.

Personal Presence

Personal presence is who you are on the inside. For instance, hopefully you are a knowledgeable, confident, honest, caring, results-generating person. It is represented by how you carry yourself and how you speak. By your dress, posture, and movements. It is how you feel about yourself.

You should be doing the prospect or customer a great favor by providing them with your considerable knowledge, experience, preparation, and substantial problem seeking/problem solving skills. And you should feel that way. Positive personal presence is supported by your believing this. You are appreciative for business received. But you don't act like customers are doing you a favor to see you or give you business. You do adjust your behavior, dress, and personality to customers to make them feel comfortable with you and respectful of you. But you maintain an air of confidence and self-respect.

Charisma is defined as a special magnetic charm or appeal. Extraordinary personal presence gives selling champions a special magnetic charm and appeal.

They smile. They look confident, but not smug or overbearing. Most dress professionally and stylishly, yet appropriately. They are friendly and cordial. They ask sensible questions. They listen. They are gracious. They have an inner energy and enthusiasm.

They seem to be about important matters. They care and are concerned about you and your welfare. They are knowledgeable and competent. They seem to be of high character (and of course they should be). You sense that they want to help you and that they can help you. You enjoy being around them. You are proud to do business with them. You are proud to introduce them to your friends and business associates. They have personal presence.

Your positive personal presence will be enhanced if you have a customer support marketing philosophy such as described in Chapter 20. It will be enhanced by your developing a positive market presence through employing industry-specific marketing and industry-specific self marketing as described in Chapters 21 and 22.

How do you get a more positive personal presence? Ben Franklin in his book, *The Autobiography of Ben Franklin,* described one powerful method. He made a list of 13 areas where he wanted to improve. He chose one to concentrate on for a week and then another the next week and so on. However, each evening he reviewed his day and identified how he did on each of the 13, to measure his performance and reinforce each in his mind.

Study the most successful sales and business people you know. Review the above paragraphs. Think. Talk to associates. List every trait, characteristic, and action you can think of that represents positive personal presence.

Then compare yourself with the list. Get the thoughts of associates. Following Baber's Law, choose the one or few items that make the most difference for you. Work on the most important until it becomes a natural part of you. Then work on the second and then the third. Or follow Ben Franklin's method of concentrating on one item for a week, but reviewing each evening how you did that day on all the items chosen for concentration. Then repeat the next week with the next item on the list until you have covered all the items. Repeat the cycle until you are highly proficient in all the items on the list.

As you grow in personal presence you will start demonstrating "a special magnetic charm or appeal."

Personal Power

Personal power gives you the ability to make positive things happen for your customers and your company. It comes from that ability, and from the perception of others that you have that ability. When people think you can make things happen for them they give you the power to act, whether they be customers, friends, or your own upper management.

Power comes from knowledge. From knowledge of the market—its trends and its technology related to your products and services.

Power comes from knowledge of the customer or customer company— how it does business, what problems and opportunities it faces, how results are obtained, who influences whom, who needs to know what, and who can say yes and no. From knowledge of customer decision makers and influencers—what they want and need, what will make them feel good, what will make their jobs and lives easier and better. From knowledge of the product or service being sold—and the various ways it can be used to benefit the customer.

Some of this knowledge is gained through experience and study. Some by creative thinking and planning. Some through effective vvk[5] (visual, verbal, kinesthetic) listening. Some comes through gathering, recording, and analyzing commercial information.

---

5. See Chapter 2 for a definition of vvk listening.

Power comes from relationships. From relationships with people in your own company who will respond positively to your requests for help in serving the customer. From relationships with people in the customer company. Thus, they will give you a hearing and will give you the benefit of the doubt when products or services are not perfect. Power comes from being the kind of person and doing the things that generate friendship, trust, respect, and even admiration in the other person.

Power comes from attitude—the attitude that nothing can stand in your way in accomplishing your objectives. Or in helping your customers accomplish their objectives through using your products and services. This attitude gives you persistence and tenacity—with customers, with your own people, with yourself. Scientific-Atlanta has identified determination, along with goal setting and planning, to be defining characteristics of its top salespeople.

Power comes from drive—from being "hungry," from having a goal or objective that you just won't fail at. It is non-negotiable. You'll keep trying and trying until you succeed. The biographies of Elvis Presley and Madonna demonstrate this kind of drive, and the sacrifices each went through to achieve their goals.

Power comes from skill—like the skill to perform pre-call customer and market research, ask information-gathering questions, listen, take notes, analyze information and arrive at valid conclusions, set priorities, set objectives, make plans, and carry out those plans.

Power comes from self discipline—the self discipline to do what you set out to do regardless of the pain and effort required. The self discipline to accomplish effective results, and achieve the reward of those results. The reward can include the trust, respect and "fear" of other people that gives you power over them. "Fear" in this context is the fear of letting you down or disappointing you—because they like, trust, respect, and admire you so much.

Power comes from providing evidence—that what you say is true and that you can help the customer in major ways. Evidence builds your self confidence and thus your personal presence and passion. And your personal presence and passion build your power of influence. Evidence also makes your claims more believable, which makes you and your presentation more powerful.

Power comes from the energy to work hard and smart—and keep going until successful results are achieved. Energy comes from good eating, exercise, mental relaxation, and rest habits. Energy comes from a positive, proactive attitude.

Many of the following chapters deal with how to make positive things happen for your customers and your company, and how to cause others to perceive that you have that ability—that power.

Passion

I discovered early in my own selling career that enthusiasm generates sales. Many times I could see the prospect thinking, "If this fellow believes that strongly in his product or service, there must be something to it. I'll give it a try."[6]

Passion is a level above enthusiasm. Your passion influences the customer or prospect favorably. It influences your peers and upper management favorably. It causes you to act and to keep on acting when others would stop because of discouragement. Thus, passion gives you power.

When John F. Kennedy said, "Ask not what your country can do for you; ask what you can do for your country!" and when Dr. Martin Luther King, Jr., said, "I have a dream!" it was their passion that grasped the country and future generations.

Passion comes from your belief that you absolutely and in a major way can help your customers achieve their objectives, and benefit greatly as a result.

Passion comes from your belief in your company, in yourself, and in your products and services. It comes from belief in the values and solutions your products, services, and added values bring to the customer—with the resulting benefits to the customer, to your own company, and to you and those you care for.

Why would your customers be absolutely out of their minds not to do business with you? What is it that is so wonderful about your company, your products, services, and added value? What is so wonderful about you and what you personally offer your customers? How could each of these be even more wonderful? The following chapters show you how to develop or improve your answers to these questions.

We're back to the chicken and egg. Passion builds personal presence and power, which in turn build passion. These three help bring selling success. This causes you to deserve and have more personal presence, power, and passion.

PPP is important. Appendix E adds some further thoughts in the section titled, "Generating 'Electric' Personal Power." It will pay you huge dividends to find and develop your PPP.

---

6. The life of Christopher Columbus gives historical support for this conclusion. The following is a series of sentences from pages 174/175 of the book *A History of Knowledge* by Charles Van Doren. "Columbus's monomaniacal certainty that he was right about the things that were most important to him brought him much success. His certainty was such that many were interested; they believed that a man so lacking in doubts must be right. After years of negotiations, Columbus was finally permitted to make his proposal to the Spanish king and queen in 1490. They were stunned by his demands, which were extravagant, not to say scandalous. He was turned down, whereupon he left the Spanish court early in 1492, headed for France and England. Before he got far, friends at court persuaded Ferdinand and Isabella to recall him, and all his requests were met."

2

Really Listening

Paying close attention to the speaker. Making the speaker feel comfortable and important. Being purposeful and organized in your listening. Looking for, finding, and confirming the speaker's main point and underlying meaning and emotions. Listening for and recording all information that may be or become important.

ILLUSTRATION AND RATING—2A

Cecile Satterwhite of Tyler, Texas, earns more than $100,000 annually selling shoes. People drive from all over Texas to buy shoes from Cecile for well over $100 per pair. Why? In large part because she "really listens." To quote a customer, "She treats you like there's no one else in her life but you. She will give you the same undivided attention, whether you bought just one pair of black leather pumps the last time you stopped in, or so many pairs in teal, purple, and red that they had to be carried out to your car."

When champions "really listen," they have personal power. They are "far" better if not entirely different from most other salespeople.

As I am reviewing the final draft of this book, I have just finished traveling with a "good" salesperson. He did most of the fundamentals well. But he had a problem being a good listener. More than once he was telling, telling, telling prospects about his products, services, and their wonderful properties—as I observed the prospects being somewhat bored and confused. Also, more than once there was a period of silence; the salesperson couldn't stand it and jumped in inappropriately with a comment instead of waiting for the prospect to talk.

He should have been asking questions, listening, and determining the prospect's problems and what the prospect wanted to talk about. (As soon as he finally asked the prospect a question and shut up, I could visibly see the prospect get happier and more interested.) Are you guilty of this? More than half of the salespeople I have traveled with or observed are.

Rick Conrad is executive vice president/chief operations officer of Bell Atlantic Mobile. He led his sales force to increase sales by 300 percent from 1993 to 1994. Says Rick, "Your prospects will tell you what you need to do to sell them in the first few minutes—if you'll just shut up and listen. The fatal mistake is to assume you know what your customer wants. People get frustrated with salespeople when they talk too much."

Superbroker Richard Greene of Merrill Lynch in Boston is vice president of the nation's largest brokerage firm. He's its top producer year after year. He earns several million dollars annually with just three assistants. Rich pays nearly $200,000 annually in bonuses to his three assistants, out of his own pocket. He spends two thirds of his time scouting investment ideas and one third selling. His mastery of the telephone and the personal cold call is based on an ego-stroking approach supported by "really" listening. Effective listening provides valuable information and helps him build relationships with clients. Rich says this about the impact of listening:

"If you talk, you'll like me. If I talk, I'll like you. Now, this fellow is like everyone else. His kids don't listen to him. His wife doesn't listen to him—and he doesn't listen to her. When he goes to parties the person he's talking to is looking over his shoulder to see what else is going on in the room. Then, all of a sudden he goes to breakfast with me. He starts to answer a question. And he doesn't get interrupted."

He feels special. He feels different. He feels important. He feels listened to.

Jim Duncan is a top sales person for Comdisco, distributor of computers and computer leasing out of Chicago. Says Jim, "Most people don't have anyone in their lives who will really listen to them, without interrupting and without judging them."

The point was well expressed by Dr. Elton Mayo. "One friend, one person who is truly understanding, who takes the trouble to listen to us as we consider our problem, can change our whole outlook on the world."

Listening is a "stroke," a "hug." When you listen non-judgmentally and non-critically, you sell yourself as worthy of respect and affection. This frees customers to think. They like, respect, and trust you. They like, respect, and trust themselves. They relax and think. They share. They share helpfully.

By listening you not only receive valuable information. It can be a crucial element in establishing a very close personal and business relationship with the customer. Think about the personal power you will have with the client if you are the only person in his or her life who really listens to him or her.

The following anonymous letter quoted in the book, *Listening, The Forgotten Skill*, by Madelyn Burley-Allen, makes the point in a different way:

Could You Just Listen?

When I ask you to listen to me and you start giving me advice, you have not done what I asked. When I ask you to listen to me and you begin to tell me why I shouldn't feel that way, you are trampling on my feelings. When I ask you to listen to me and you feel you have to do something to solve my problem, you have failed me—strange as that may seem.

Listen! All I ask is that you *listen*, not talk or do, just hear me. Advice is cheap. Twenty cents will give you both Dear Abby and Billy Graham in the same paper.

When you do something for me that I can and need to do for myself, you contribute to my fear and inadequacy; but when you accept as a simple fact that I do feel what I feel no matter how irrational, then I can quit trying to convince you and get down to the business of understanding it.

Irrational feelings make sense when we understand what's behind them. And when that's clear, the answers are obvious and I don't need advice. Perhaps that's why prayer works sometimes for some people—because God is mute and doesn't give advice or try to fix things. God just listens and lets you work it out for yourself.

So please just listen. If you want to talk, wait a minute for your turn and I'll listen to you.

❙❙ Listening is the art of getting meaning from a situation. ❙❙

It usually is thought of in terms of a "spoken" situation. But it can be helpful to think of what we call vvk listening—visual, verbal, and kinesthetic listening. Visual listening is getting meaning from what you see; verbal from what you hear. Kinesthetic listening is getting meaning from what you feel and the feelings the speaker is projecting.

Listening is taking information from speakers while remaining nonjudgmental and empathetic. It is acknowledging them in a way that invites communication to continue. It provides limited but encouraging input to the speaker's response, carrying the conversation forward.

❙ "Really listening" builds self esteem in the speaker, customer or prospect. It builds trust. It makes the other person feel heard, understood, liked, respected, appreciated, and helped. ❙

"Really listening" retrieves and processes valuable information; and information is power. If you don't listen well you may miss selling opportunities (customer problems, needs, and opportunities), relationship-building opportunities, and specific buying signals.

A survey of 100 major companies determined that sales and management people spend approximately 70 percent of their working hours in communication activities. This 70 percent breaks out as follows: writing–9 percent; reading–16 percent; speaking–30 percent; listening–45 percent. Listening is important.

Most people are unaware of their own listening habits or barriers. They would be more aware if they had someone observe them and comment on what they saw.

Most people listen at work and home the same way as they do in sales. And how they listen (or don't listen) greatly affects their relationships with others. So there are additional benefits to learning to listen effectively in selling.

According to Dr. Carl Rogers, listening guru, "The biggest block to personal communications is one person's inability to listen intelligently, understandably, and skillfully to another person." An anonymous quotation says it. "I know you believe you understand what I said, but I'm not sure you realize that what you heard is not what I meant."

You hear what you listen for. For example, a cricket in a crowded city. Or an emotional concern or an underlying cause in a complex sales call.

Through active listening—by giving encouraging body signals and expressions, and asking confirming and leading questions—you can and should control the listening process. In the listening process, only one third of the speaker's meaning is conveyed by words. Two thirds is conveyed by body language—indicating emotional tone. So watch your body language and watch for that of the speaker.

Other aspects of effective selling affect your listening effectiveness. Examples include: your ability to develop relationships; knowledge of effective questioning and information gathering; your ability to develop rapport, gain prospect attention, and develop prospect interest; your areas of business and technical specialization and expertise; and planning for effective information gathering—including preparing a list of questions to be answered.

Thought Provokers

(1) Do you really listen? What evidence do you have to support your answer?
(2) Are you a level 1, 2, or 3 listener as defined below? Why?
(3) When you sell, do you tell, tell, tell?
(4) What listening filters, barriers, and situations give you the most trouble?
(5) What do you need to work on the most to "really listen" better?

Take the following rating exercise to estimate how important "really listening" is to your selling success. Based on the results, you can continue on with reading about its implementation, or you can move on to Chapter 3 and Section 3A and come back later to Section 2B.

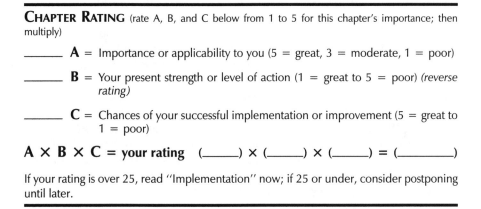

CHAPTER RATING (rate A, B, and C below from 1 to 5 for this chapter's importance; then multiply)

_____ **A** = Importance or applicability to you (5 = great, 3 = moderate, 1 = poor)

_____ **B** = Your present strength or level of action (1 = great to 5 = poor) *(reverse rating)*

_____ **C** = Chances of your successful implementation or improvement (5 = great to 1 = poor)

A × B × C = your rating   (_____) × (_____) × (_____) = (_____)

If your rating is over 25, read "Implementation" now; if 25 or under, consider postponing until later.

IMPLEMENTATION—2B

Three Levels of Listening

There are three levels to listening effectiveness.

At the first level, people pretend to pay attention, but don't really. They half-listen, being mainly concerned about themselves and what they want to say. They are easily distracted. They are blocked by a number of the "barriers to effective listening." Sometimes they talk and forget they should be listening.

At the second level, people try to listen. But they don't really work at it. They don't prepare. They hear the sounds and words, but don't actively look for the underlying meanings. They tend to be more logical listeners who are more concerned about content than feeling. They remain emotionally detached from the conversation. They don't actively participate. When they do, they often ask questions when they should remain silent. And then they make opinion statements when they should be asking subject confirmation questions or making feeling affirmation statements.

At the third—and most effective—level, people "really" listen. This level is described by the following "three keys to really listening." Applying them will move you forward in your efforts to be a selling champion.

THE THREE KEYS

1. *Make the speaker feel comfortable and important.* Be respectful. Pay strict attention, resisting and avoiding all distractions. Be and act caring and interested in both the speaker as a person and what is being said. Know and

empathize with the speaker; know and relate to her culture, prejudices, personality, and experience. Align with the speaker; support her ideas and feelings. This will develop your relationship, remove tension, and open up her mind and emotions. Mirror the speaker's behavior, but with an open style. Avoid all negative emotions and expressions. Control all your negative thoughts. Look for the positive in what the speaker is saying even if you basically disagree. Lubricate the conversation with expressions (as "Uh-huh"), non-verbals (as head nodding and an interested look), and encouragers (as "Tell me about it."). Avoid negative non-verbals such as frowning, folded arms, rigid body posture, and narrowing your eyes. Watch for inconsistent behavior—such as the speaker with a clenched fist making a friendly statement. Back off when you detect the speaker is uncomfortable with a subject; plan to come back to it at a later time.

2. *Be purposeful and organized.* Do your homework. Study both the subject and the speaker ahead of time. Have a purpose or objective for the meeting. Prepare ahead and don't forget anything you need to bring. Be problem seeking; be looking for business and personal problems and needs; but not always problem solving. Sometimes he wants an ear, not solutions. Often you can determine this only once the conversation has started. Take written notes properly and subtly; record and classify all meaningful thoughts and observations. Triple concentrate—(1) on the main point and its underlying meaning, (2) on peripheral ideas that come into your mind, and (3) on the speaker's emotions. You can think four times as fast as the speaker can speak. Use the extra thought time to think only about what is being said and what it means, not to daydream or to think about rebuttals.

3. *Look for, find and confirm the speaker's main point and underlying meaning and emotions.* Listen for the main point and its underlying meaning, not just to specific facts. Be sensitive to the speaker's feelings. Actively analyze non-verbals—such as rigid body posture, open body posture, narrowing of the eyes, relaxing of the eyes, an expression of confusion, frowning, or smiling. Then, summarize the speaker's main point, underlying meaning, and emotions. Don't interrupt; wait to ask a question until the speaker's current thoughts on a matter are fully expressed. Check the validity of your summary with either a subject confirmation question or a feeling affirmation statement. An example of a subject confirmation question is, "So what you're really looking for is a way to reduce turnover; is that correct?" An example of a feeling affirmation statement is, "You're feeling pretty upset about those late deliveries."

Listening Filters

As people listen, they "filter" what they hear through their basic nature and life's experiences. If you are not careful, this can significantly distort what you hear. As a result, what you hear may not be what the speaker said or meant.

For instance, suppose you believe that only women can be caring, not men. Then, if the speaker says, "he cared very much about our opinion," you may hear, "she cared very much." This is because you weren't listening carefully, and in your mind the second statement is the closest to one that makes any sense to you.

The following are some of the listening filters to be aware of. In each situation, one of these filters can distort what you or the other person hears and understands. Your or the other person's:

► Values
► Beliefs
► Attitudes
► Viewpoints
► Interests
► Assumptions
► Past experiences
► Prejudices
► Strong feelings
► Memories
► Images—past and future
► Expectations
► Physical environment

Barriers to Effective Listening

In addition, there a number of barriers that can lessen your listening effectiveness. Obviously, you should be aware of and remove or overcome any of the barriers that exist for you. They include:

1. External distractions (such as noise, movements, and speaker's mannerisms)
2. Internal distractions (such as preoccupation, pressure, or something else of a higher priority to you)
3. Daydreaming (and mind wandering)
4. Hard work required (such as lack of concentration, not searching for meaning, not paying physical attention, and being lazy)
5. Speaker appearance and actions (such as halo effect, equating appearance and value of message, being upset by speaker's voice level, opinions, and words)
6. Script writing (such as prejudging ideas before completed, composing reply too early, and thinking about what you will say or how you will rebut)

7. The speech/thought differential (speak 100–500 wpm; think 500–1,000 wpm or more)
8. Lack of confidence in own listening skills (you do what you are good at; self-fulfilling prophecy)
9. Listening only to echoes of your own views
10. Semantics (understanding word meanings)
11. Fatigue
12. Being self-conscious (concentrating on your own appearance; wanting to make a favorable impression)
13. Logical listening only (missing deeper meaning and emotions)
14. Not listening to non-verbal messages (no visual or kinesthetic listening)
15. Wishful hearing (hearing only what you want to hear)
16. Equating speaking, not listening, with importance
17. Paying attention only to what interests you
18. Biased listening (judging based on prejudices)
19. Faking attention
20. Interrupting
21. Emotional response (red flag—unfavorable or green flag—favorable words and phrases that affect your emotions and block your attention)
22. Illness
23. Not trusting or respecting the speaker (such as from being a stranger, or having different viewpoints)
24. Negatively pre-judging the value of the speaker's message
25. Failing to listen to the emotional content of the message
26. The message being too complicated to understand, and not asking clarifying and summarizing questions
27. Not taking appropriate notes (therefore forgetting important facts, feelings, impressions, causes, and questions to ask)
28. Taking notes in too much detail or not developing a shorthand style (so note taking either distracts the speaker or prevents you from listening)

Listening When, Where, and to Whom

To be effective in selling, you need to "really listen" *during information gathering*. This is so you can learn the prospect's situation, problems, needs, and wants before your start telling or "selling." You can relate them to your products, services, and added value. Then you can present your solutions and how they provide great benefits and value.

This may be the most frequently violated listening practice by salespeople, and was illustrated early in the chapter.

There are many other situations that require "really listening." "Really listen" when calling to make appointments. Thus, you learn what statements and questions are received well and poorly by potential prospects. And you learn the characteristics of better prospects.

"Really listen" and keep your eyes, ears, and intuition open *at all times* during a sales call or when dealing with customers, prospects, competitors, or industry influencers. You never know when something will be said that will be really valuable.

Listen to your *own technical people*, especially the creative and far-out types. They can be great sources of ideas for solving customer problems. They also can be great sources for keys to finding problems, and for added value ideas.

Listen to the *top performers* in your company and industry. Learn why they are so effective and how you might use some of what they do.

Listen to your *competitors*. You run into them out in the field and at association meetings. You never know who will say what about what. Never assume that a competitor is as smart or as clever as you. Never assume that they aren't, because they may be. But they also may slip and give you very valuable information about customers, prospects, other competitors, their own company's events and plans, or what is working for them.

Listen to *industry experts and influencers* whenever you get the chance. They have outside information and perspective that can be valuable.

Listen to *key customer contacts*, especially decision makers and influencers. For some, you may only get a few chances to hear what they have to say. For others, you may catch them in social situations where they are loose with their thoughts. In such situations you can develop relationships and learn a lot.

Listen and take notes when you read *technical materials and industry publications*. You never know when an idea or trend will be helpful. Read, think and listen about other, *related industries*. You may be able to change what you hear or read slightly and use some successful ideas employed there.

Listen to your *own top management*. Determine where they are taking the company and what they want and plan. You may be able to fit your ideas to theirs and get support for programs that will serve your customers and build your sales volume.

Listen to *customer receptionists, secretaries, and assistants*. They often have ideas to share and welcome a listening ear. Remember, most people don't have anyone in their lives who really are interested in listening to them and hearing what they have to say, without judging them.

Special Selling Situations

There are some thoughts to keep in mind when "really listening" in selling situations.

In making appointments, listen to what you say that works and what doesn't. Then do more of what works.

One way to generate leads and appointments is through legitimate *market research calls.* Make the questions short and easy to answer. Design the questions to lead to an appointment or to some action that may lead to an appointment. But don't turn the market research call into a brazen selling call. Be honest. Don't interrupt or otherwise offend the other party.

Be prepared before a sales call with a written list of problem, implication, and need-payoff questions (see Chapter 17) to use *during information gathering.* Review them before the sales call if needed. Refer to them discreetly during the call as necessary.

During the selling process the prospect or customer will sometimes say something important, but negative or sensitive, which they might *not want repeated.* If so, don't flinch or react. Be supportive. Wait until a few minutes later to make a note of it.

In handling *serious objections,* don't be anxious. Seek an in-depth understanding of the question, concern, or problem. Ask leading questions, so the prospect sells himself on the idea that the objection is not a major problem. Analyze the results so you never again face that objection unprepared and without an answer and the appropriate leading questions.

If the *prospect gets negative or testy,* change the subject for a time to something pleasant and non-threatening. Practice with peers, changing the subject to something pleasant, such as something they are proud of, or an outside interest.

When you ask a *closing* question or make a closing statement, be silent. Remain calm and serene, looking the prospect expectantly in the eye. Keep looking and not talking.

If the prospect or customer starts speaking of something seriously *personal or emotional,* then stop selling and information gathering for a time. Let the prospect talk and really listen. Give empathetic responses, such as (1) a door opener ("Would it help to talk about it?"); (2) an acknowledgment response (nodding or saying something like "I see" or "Oh"); or (3) active empathetic listening that offers empathy and acceptance and confirms understanding of the stress source ("You feel _____ because _____." An example would be, "You feel helpless because your daughter won't listen to you.")

The following is a summary of some keys to "really listening."

- ► Be purposeful: study and prepare ahead before meeting with the speaker, customer, or prospect.
- ► Know and empathize with the other person; know and relate to his culture, prejudices, personality, and experience.
- ► Listen for the main point and its underlying meaning, not just specific facts.

- Be problem seeking; be looking for business and personal problems and needs; but don't always be problem solving—sometimes the speaker just wants to be listened to.
- Be organized: take written notes properly and subtly; record and classify all meaningful thoughts and observations.
- Summarize to yourself the speaker's main point and underlying meaning, and then check whether you heard correctly by either asking a subject confirmation question or making a feeling affirmation statement.
- Don't interrupt; wait to ask a question until the speaker's current thoughts on a matter are fully expressed.
- Align with the speaker; support her ideas and feelings; this will develop your relationship, remove tension and open up her mind and emotions.
- Be respectful: pay attention, and be and act caring and interested in the speaker and what she is saying.
- Mirror the speaker's behavior, but with an open style (relaxed body and face, arms uncrossed, pleasant facial expression).
- Avoid all negative emotions and expressions; look for the positive; control and guide all negative thoughts.
- Actively analyze and respond to non-verbals—such as rigid body posture, narrowing of the eyes, sudden relaxation, or smiling or frowning.
- Concentrate on the main point and its underlying meaning, peripheral ideas that come into your mind, and the speaker's emotions.
- Control the discussion carefully with questions, but be sensitive to what the speaker wants to talk about.
- Avoid giving opinions or advice; lead them either to find their own answers or the answers you want them to find. For instance, do this by asking, "What problems does that cause?" or "How might that be solved?" or "Would xyz help?"
- Use captioning—repeating to them, perhaps in different words, a statement they made earlier. This demonstrates to them your attention and interest, and makes them feel listened to.
- Lubricate the conversation with expressions (as "Uh-huh" or "Right"), non-verbals (as head nodding and an interested look), and encouragers (as "That sounds interesting." or "What did they say?").
- Use extra thought time to think only about what is being said and what it means, not to daydream or to think about rebuttals.
- Resist and block all distractions—physical, mental, and emotional.
- When your mind wanders, tell the speaker and ask for a short repeat; this controls you and encourages the speaker.
- Be sensitive to situations where you should perform only relation-

ship-building listening; when they do occur, forget about business for the time being and discuss other appropriate matters.

► Avoid negative non-verbals such as frowning, folded arms, rigid body posture, or narrowing your eyes.

► Back off when you detect the speaker is uncomfortable with a subject; plan to come back to it at a later time.

► Watch for inconsistent behavior by the speaker—such as the speaker with a clenched fist making a friendly statement.

► People from different cultures act and listen in different ways. For instance, the Japanese often close their eyes while listening to show respect. In America, this would be disrespectful. Americans make frequent eye contact. In Japan, Korea, and Thailand it is considered rude to stare. In Saudi Arabia, one is expected to maintain strong eye contact because of the adage, "the eyes are the windows to the soul."

Put yourself in a series of listening situations. Ask some friends or peers to watch you and evaluate your listening performance, and discuss it with you regarding each of the 28 barriers and each of the 25 keys to "really listening."

3

Building Partnering Relationships

Developing friendly business and personal relationships with customers so they like you, feel comfortable with you, trust and respect you, and work with you. Therefore, they not only prefer to do business with you, but strive to work with you to develop and improve products and services that they buy or sell, or will buy or sell. They consider you to be on their business team.

ILLUSTRATION AND RATING—3A

A few years ago, I was working on a project for Monsanto Company. Monsanto had a product manager (technical support engineer) who specialized in serving the electrical and electronic industries. These industries purchased huge quantities of chemicals that were very profitable to Monsanto. Customers included companies like General Electric, Westinghouse, and Siemens. The product manager's name was Paul Benignus, and he almost was a legend in his own time.

Paul was the leader of the Monsanto customer support team. Over the years personnel from marketing, research and development, and manufacturing called on and worked with "Paul's" customers. But Paul was the long-term, solidifying force of the team.

He was highly dedicated to the welfare of his customers and they knew it. He was technically competent.

| Paul not only represented Monsanto to his customers, he represented the welfare of his customers to Monsanto Company.

He developed a very close business and personal relationship with the customers' people at all levels—both front line people and upper level managers in the plants and research facilities.

33

Customers treated Paul like one of their own (a partner in business). That came into really good stead when the PCB (polychlorobiphenyl) crisis arose.

You may be familiar with the PCB crisis. If not, then you probably are familiar with the earlier DDT crisis. DDT was a pesticide that was banned for use in this country and in most other parts of the world. This is because it entered the food chain. It worked its way up to where it entered fish, which were eaten by certain birds such as the eagle and osprey. The DDT softened the shells of the bird's eggs. As a result, some of the birds such as the bald eagle, osprey, and some other fish-eating sea birds were approaching extinction. DDT was banned. A number of years later it was determined that PCBs caused a similar problem. PCBs were produced exclusively by Monsanto Company. The government required that PCBs be quickly phased out of production and sale.

So, Monsanto faced a large dilemma. PCBs were large volume and very profitable products for the company. They were used primarily in fire retardant functional fluids for large electrical transformers, capacitors, and other products needing fire retardancy. Other competitive companies attempted to take advantage of Monsanto's problem. They introduced their products as potential replacements for the PCBs. This would have caused Monsanto great financial loss if they had been successful.

Competitors had almost no success in introducing their products, or getting the electrical companies to support their research. This is because the electrical companies were so loyal to Paul Benignus, and to Monsanto Company because of their loyalty to Paul. Thus, Monsanto had a large head start in developing replacement functional fluids. This allowed the company to retain tens of millions of profitable sales—because of the close personal (partnering) relationship of Paul Benignus with his customers.

The following is a personal anecdote illustrating why Paul had such a close personal relationship with his customers. A number of engineers and consultants, myself included, visited some of the plants and research facilities of the major electrical companies. This was in an attempt to clarify industry opportunities and needs. When we reached the first facility Paul called everyone together and said to us, "Now, don't eat more expensively or more lavishly than you would eat if you were at home." He was concerned about this because the customer companies were picking up the dinner tabs. Paul was so concerned about the welfare of his customers that he paid attention even to what we ate.

Because he had built partnering relationships, Paul had the personal power that came from those relationships. His relationship with customers was "entirely" different from that of most salespeople and vendors with their customers. Through his partnering relationships, he had a decided competitive advantage over his competitors.

1995 Champions

Partnering relationships and personal expertise were the two primary selling strengths of those chosen as the "1995 Selling All-Stars" by *Sell!ng* magazine in its March 1995 issue.

For example, John Maxwell of Oxford Health Plans developed partnering relationships with health benefits consulting firms. They control who gets the health care business of many of the nation's largest employers. The benefits consulting firms pride themselves on making researched, informed choices and never being sold to. According to them John didn't sell them. They bought from John because he had the expertise to design the best products and the communication skills to clearly explain those designs.

In 1994, John provided $125 million in managed health care programs to New York area benefits consultants. From 1992 to 1994, John's company increased major requests for proposals (RFPs) received from 15 to 120. During 1994, enrollees more than doubled. The major reason was John's expertise and partnering.

These are some of the things his customers said. "He knows his product better than any other salesperson. He's an expert at what he does." "He is straightforward and clearly explains what others have difficulty in explaining." "He develops relationships and is more responsive than most of his competitors." "He overcomes obstacles, even when they are in his own company." "John embodies the intelligence, flexibility, and sensitivity we are looking for from our medical carrier."

As another example, some subsidiary companies of Siemens provide reengineering support to their major customers. This assists partnering at the corporate level. You can provide similar partnering support at your level.[1]

How McDonald's Got Its Playground Mats

Chad Foster was a college drop-out who retired as a millionaire at age 31 to start a second profession of ministering to teenagers.

During his early twenties, Chad was a highly ranked amateur tennis player. His father taught him to meet and develop relationships with as many people as possible, especially influential people. Chad did this during his tennis days. He ended up with a list of names of many people with whom he kept in touch. It included the names of hundreds of people involved in tennis. This stood him in good stead when he went into the business of installing rubberized tennis court surfaces—containing ground-up old tires.

After adding running tracks to his business, he solved a new problem

---

1. This also is added value; see Chapter 7.

for a friend. His friend owned three McDonald's restaurants and needed a safe surface for the kids' playground area. Chad thickened his running track product, added more rubber to it, and installed it at the three restaurants. The surface worked extremely well.

Chad called on the headquarters of McDonald's for a full year attempting to sell his new product. After ten calls, he fully understood that "although McDonald's Corporation needed his product, the buyers and management people involved didn't want it." Demonstrating the drive and persistence of a champion, he didn't give up. He started again at the bottom. He made a list of more than 200 people he needed to develop relationships with to sell his concept to individual McDonald's restaurant owners. These included the major owners, construction companies, and architects.

Chad visited them all—more than once. He found out their kids' birthdays. Every year thereafter their kids received a birthday card from Chad. For the owners, he found out their anniversary with McDonald's. Every year thereafter they received an anniversary card from Chad. It probably was the only card they received on that important day. He found out what they and their kids were interested in. He hired a person to scour hundreds of newspapers and magazines looking for articles of interest to them. Every time he found one he sent it to them with a personal note.

Three years later, more than 3,000 McDonald's restaurants had Chad's playground surface. Chad had more than 200 partnering relationships and over a million dollars in the bank.

How important is it for you to develop partnering relationships with your customers? Will that give you a decided competitive advantage and help you to achieve championship results?

Thought Provokers

(1) Does it really make sense that salespeople can be considered to be partners by those they are selling to?
(2) With which types of customers (size, industry, market, and so forth) would it be easiest for you to develop partnering relationships?
(3) With which types of customers would it be most beneficial to you to develop partnering relationships? Why?
(4) If you became a partner with one or more of your customers, what would you bring to the party? What special services or capabilities would you bring? What positive character traits would you bring?
(5) Which ones of the "ways" listed below to develop partnering relationships should be most effective for you?

Take the following rating exercise to estimate how important "building partnering relationships" is to your selling success. Based on the results, you can continue on with reading about its implementation, or you can move on to Chapter 4 and Section 4A and come back later to Section 3B.

CHAPTER RATING (rate A, B, and C below from 1 to 5 for this chapter's importance; then multiply)

_____ **A** = Importance or applicability to you (5 = great, 3 = moderate, 1 = poor)

_____ **B** = Your present strength or level of action (1 = great to 5 = poor) *(reverse rating)*

_____ **C** = Chances of your successful implementation or improvement (5 = great to 1 = poor)

A × B × C = your rating   (_____) × (_____) × (_____) = (_____)

If your rating is over 25, read "Implementation" now; if 25 or under, consider postponing until later.

IMPLEMENTATION—3B

Building Partnering Relationships

The following are some ways to start building and maintaining partnering relationships:

- ► Be customer and market focused. Concentrate on learning about the customer. Learn how the customer operates in the marketplace. Learn its problems and opportunities. Learn how your services, products, and related technologies fit into the customer's operations and plans. Learn what its objectives are. Learn what is happening in its marketplace and how that affects its needs for your products and services. Learn the contribution of your products and services to its economic and market positioning. Learn where its weak spots are.
- ► Choose companies you want to partner with carefully. Make sure you can deliver what they want and they can give you the benefits you desire. Make sure your cultures fit.
- ► Be alert to changing wants and needs of partners. What was perfect last year may no longer be appropriate or desired this year.
- ► Measure the values you deliver and be prepared to communicate them to the customer. Customers may not know the great things you are doing for them.
- ► Utilize specialists in your company, as appropriate, to develop relationships with and work with those in the customer's organization who relate well with them. For instance, you might have your financial person work with the customer's financial person. But remain informed of what is going on, and lead the others to focus on

those activities (such as information gathering, problem seeking, and problem solving) that support your sales objectives and foster the partnering relationship.

- ► Be customer and market driven. Make decisions and take actions with the customer's changing objectives, wants, needs, and opportunities as primary considerations.
- ► Know your own business in detail, especially as it relates to the customer.
- ► Know the customer's business as it relates to your own.
- ► Attempt to serve as a technical or business consultant, without getting in the customer's way.
- ► Be both a problem solver and a problem seeker (see Chapter 8).
- ► Spend more time generating (learning and analyzing) information than giving information (to customers).
- ► Know the needs of your customer's customer.
- ► Help your customer to be more competitive in the marketplace.
- ► Try to think like your customers.
- ► Look at problems and situations from your customer's point of view.
- ► Be intensely service oriented.
- ► Represent your own company and products to the customer. Then represent the customer and its interests to your own company.
- ► Continually look for new and better ways to add value to your services and products that are helpful to your customer.
- ► Be an effective team worker.
- ► Be an overcommunicator, both with your customers and their people, and with your people internally as they relate to your customer.
- ► Spend proportionally more time with higher potential customers. Spend more time with innovative customers who are on the cutting edge of generating new ideas and developing new product/service needs, therefore directing your partnering time effectively.
- ► Work at developing long-term relationships with customers.
- ► Find ways to share your personal life with customers to foster personal relationships. But be sensitive to their desire or lack of desire to get "personal."
- ► Look for the "personal benefits"[2] of key customer contacts, and do what you can to support them.
- ► Really listen.
- ► Develop a confidential database of information on each prospect, so you can remember what pleases them, including birthdays and important events, where they went to school, and what they are proud of.

---

2. See Appendix B.

► Invest financial resources to solidify your relationship in areas such as taking them to ball games and other social activities that they especially enjoy, gathering information that is of interest or benefit to them, and subscribing to a paging service so they can get hold of you quickly.

People Are Different

Customers like to do business with people and companies with which they feel comfortable and compatible. Thus, it is important to understand and align yourself with each customer. Different companies have different cultures and operating styles. Different buyers have different cultural backgrounds, value systems, and personality styles. They want to be dealt with differently. So, deal with them differently.

People from different cultures and from different backgrounds feel comfortable when they are dealt with in ways that are consistent with that culture or background. Examples are the less direct Asians, the relaxed-paced Latinos, the fast-paced northeasterners, and the relationship-oriented, home-grown southerners.

Personality style selling is discussed in many books and articles.[3] It is important to deal with "Drivers," "Amiables," "Expressives," and "Analytical" personalities in different ways. For instance, being more assertive with some and more laid back with others; more businesslike with some and taking more time to develop relationships with others.

Mirroring

Neurolinguistics programming (NLP) is discussed in *Influencing with Integrity*, by Genie Labaorde, and *Unlimited Power*, by Anthony Robbins. Mirroring is one aspect of NLP. Mirroring is based on the evidence that, deep down, people feel comfortable with those that are like them, especially in subtle ways.

Suppose the prospect slouches down, is low key, speaks slowly in a high pitch voice, breathes deeply and slowly, is very serious, and has some kind of a rhythm to their movements (like swinging a pencil back and forth while they talk). To mirror that person you would change your behavior slightly in each aspect to be a bit more like that person. (For instance, you would slouch and relax a little bit more than normal.) This makes the prospect feel more comfortable with you and it builds rapport. On the other hand, if the person is just the opposite—talks very fast, etc.—to mirror them you would be more like the opposite. This includes speeding up your speak-

---

3. For instance, *Non-Manipulative Selling*, by Alessandra, Wexler and Barrera.

ing speed to be somewhat faster than normal, unless you are normally a rapid speaker.

Obviously, you make the changes in such a way that the prospect doesn't notice. Thus, suppose you are speaking to the first, slow speaking person. Suppose you normally have a stiff, military posture, and speak rapidly. You wouldn't become a slouching slow talker. If you did, the prospect would notice. Thus, he or she would feel less comfortable, not more. Instead, you would relax your shoulders a bit and speak a bit less rapidly than usual while you are with the prospect. Also, you would raise the pitch of your voice slightly, breathe a bit slower and deeper, cut out the jokes, and perhaps develop some subtle rhythm to your movements.

I have used mirroring successfully in my own selling and seen dramatic results. Anthony Robbins[4] says that he has seen it deliver near miraculous results for others.

What Attracts Everyone

Customers like to do business with people and companies they like, respect, and trust. It even helps if they admire you or feel obligated to or dependent on you. The following are some ways to earn these.

1. They like you (because):
   —You are friendly (for instance, you smile frequently).
   —You care and have concern for them.
   —You make them feel important or good about themselves.
   —They feel comfortable with you (you are like them naturally, through mirroring, or otherwise).
   —You bring them personal benefits (such as justified gifts[5] or personal recognition).
   —You participate with them in joint social activities (e.g., you take them to ball games if they like ball games).
   —You bring them joy (for example, with stories and successful experiences).
   —You really listen to them.
   —You genuinely like them.
   —You respect them.
   —You appreciate them.
   —You understand them (demonstrating your empathy, and causing you to act appropriately toward them).
2. They respect you (because):

4. In his book, *Unlimited Power.*
5. "Justified gifts" are those for which there is a meaningful business reason for the giving of them. Thus, the customer does not feel bribed, and can explain their receipt to someone else.

—You know your business.
—You know their business.
—Others have recommended you.
—You manage your time well.
—You don't waste their time.
—You solve problems for them.
—You bring them important added value.
3. They trust you (because):
—You are honest.
—You are dependable.
—Your products/services work.
—You eliminate problems for them.
4. They admire you (because):
—You are of high character.
—You have high accomplishments.
—You have a high reputation.
—You have great knowledge.
—You are dedicated to something important.
5. They feel obligated to you (because):
—You have done them a great service.
—You are holding a potential embarrassment in confidence.
—You have invested much time and effort on their behalf.
—You have done something for a friend of theirs.
—They have made a commitment to you.
—They have spoken highly of you to others.
—You have kept a difficult-to-keep promise.
6. They feel dependent on you (because):
—They see you as a valuable consultant.
—You have knowledge or expertise they consider to be valuable.
—You have helped them establish a process you are needed to maintain.
—You provide them valuable emotional support.
—You provide them valuable political support.

Review the lists. Add to them. Check yourself against them. Use them to build partnering relationships.

4

Entrepreneurial Attitudes and Skills

Using the same skills and and approaches that caused the most effective entrepreneurs (like Sam Walton of Wal-Mart, Mary Kay, Henry Ford, Ross Perot, Bill Gates, and Anita Roddick of The Body Shop) to be successful in developing and implementing sales-producing ideas and approaches—such as partnering with customers, thinking like a business owner, thinking strategically, being innovative, and making things happen.

ILLUSTRATION AND RATING—4A

Most extraordinarily successful entrepreneurs have a creative and value creation approach to business that gives them personal power and makes them and their people highly successful in selling. This chapter helps you to determine which skills, attitudes, and approaches of the most successful entrepreneurs are most applicable to you. Employing them should help you both in the selling and nonselling aspects of your work.

■| Entrepreneurs create value for their customers. |■

    Entrepreneurs aren't just successful businesspeople, consultative salespeople, or relationship developers (as positive as those characteristics are). They are creative and innovative in how they sell and how they create and deliver the value they sell.

    When you "grasp" critical issues,[1] create added value for your cus-

---

1. See Chapters 5, 7, and 10, respectively, for information on "grasping" critical issues, added value, and business cases.

tomer, and then build a business case to quantify that value, you are selling like an entrepreneur. Harold Clark, co-owner of Clark Painting Company in St. Louis, marketed creatively and created added value to address the two critical issues of his customers. These were (1) competitive price[2] and (2) assurance of satisfaction—so the key customer contacts (the persons who selected the painting contractor) wouldn't be embarrassed by a bad paint job or inconvenienced by having to do a lot of checking and follow-up work.

Harold had been a painting superintendent for a company in St. Louis. He believed there was a better way to serve customers—through hiring and motivating the best painting foremen and superintendents,[3] and providing them a higher income—and then marketing creatively based on that competent workforce. He convinced his brother, Charles, a lieutenant colonel in the U.S. Air Force, that he was right. Charles retired and handled the financial and administrative side of Harold's new commercial/industrial painting business. Harold sold the jobs and supervised the workforce. Charles found the financing. I helped them.

Within a few years, Harold had assembled the most accomplished workforce, and a group of the most effective painting foremen and superintendents, in the country. He did this by treating everyone with respect, and paying the foremen and superintendents a large percentage of the profits on each job they managed or worked on—when they came in below bid. (This in turn caused them to be creative and focused in how they got the work done.)

Because he communicated well with his competent, motivated people, Harold's company did what it said it would, when it said it would. Harold was fair on pricing. He worked closely with customers to determine their specific needs. He communicated those needs to his people. He made sure his people communicated closely with customers. He worked closely with local union officials.

He held meetings with his key people, including some frontline painters, every Saturday morning. They discussed how things were going and what could be improved. They shared ideas and made plans.

He invited the customer contacts from his larger customers to an annual technical conference in a nice vacation resort area, all expenses paid. The conferences combined meaningful technical sessions with lots of social activities.

As a result, Harold was the preferred painting contractor by more and more companies. Clark Painting wrote its bids in a way that allowed it to be low bidder, and then customers were liberal in their payments to Clark

2. Not necessarily low price, although in some cases the contract administrator couldn't admit this. This is dealt with in the paragraph above that discusses time-and-material.
3. Painters reported to foremen, who reported to superintendents, who reported to owners.

Painting for the extra time-and-material work that accompanied each project. Because of this, and because the foremen and superintendents kept performance up and costs down, customers were treated fairly and Clark Painting made a profit.

Harold's business never sold more than $20 million per year. But it was highly profitable. In ten years, he and Charles had become multimillionaires, and a number of his key people were millionaires.

Harold Clark was a successful entrepreneur who sold through developing customer relationships, and then making those key customer contacts look good through leading (rather than managing) his people to deliver a superior service.

During the 1980s much was written about the entrepreneurs of the American Business Conference. The American Business Conference is a business coalition of a hundred of America's fastest growing, most profitable midsize corporations. Part B describes what made those entrepreneurs, the leaders of those corporations, so successful.

Thought Provokers

(1) How are you most like an entrepreneur?
(2) How would it help you in your selling to exhibit more entrepreneurial characteristics?
(3) Why and how did the characteristics listed in Section 4B help Sam Walton, Mary Kay, Ross Perot, Bill Gates, Anita Roddick, Harold Clark, and others to be so successful in business marketing and selling?
(4) What is the relationship between entrepreneurship and selling success?

Take the following rating exercise to estimate how important "entrepreneurial attitudes and skills" are to your selling success. Based on the results, you can continue on with reading about its implementation, or you can move on to Chapter 5 and Section 5A and come back later to Section 4B.

CHAPTER RATING (rate A, B, and C below from 1 to 5 for this chapter's importance; then multiply)

_____ **A** = Importance or applicability to you (5 = great, 3 = moderate, 1 = poor)

_____ **B** = Your present strength or level of action (1 = great to 5 = poor) *(reverse rating)*

_____ **C** = Chances of your successful implementation or improvement (5 = great to 1 = poor)

A × B × C = your rating (_____) × (_____) × (_____) = (_____)

If your rating is over 25, read "Implementation" now; if 25 or under, consider postponing until later.

IMPLEMENTATION—4B

Entrepreneurial Characteristics

The following is a list of 25 characteristics that were culled from the material written about the American Business Conference. Each is defined or commented on as it applies to championship selling. Many of these characteristics directly support the other championship strategies and skills. Many relate to the six keys to championship selling discussed in the Introduction.

An exceptional entrepreneur:

1. *Has vision.* You should having a clear understanding of the wonderful value you have created for your customers and how you will (effectively if not creatively) communicate that value to them.

2. *Has boundless energy.* Increase your energy level. Energy gives you the personal power to work hard and put in long hours as required. It helps you to be enthusiastic, clear-thinking, and resilient even after long or hard hours.

3. *Has intellectual creativity.* Have the curiosity and innovative persistence to keep looking for different and better ways to serve customers and to sell.

4. *Has a patience quota of zero.* Be passionate. Great salespersons are patient when patience is required. But they feel so strongly about the benefits they offer that they are passionate to have the prospect or customer get on with receiving those benefits.

5. *Is antibureaucratic.* Focus your time and effort on achieving results rather than filling out forms. Tactfully nudge your peers and supervisors to do the same.

6. *Is a consummate salesperson.* Read this book from cover to cover. Then read it again carefully.

7. *Radiates self-confidence.* Be self confident. When you believe with all your heart that you have discovered ways to help the customer make a ton of money and live a better and happier life at the same time, you will be confident.

8. *Communicates a strong sense of mission.* Customers, prospects, and people in their own company can sense the passion the championship salesperson has for his or her company, products, services, and customers. They also can sense when the salesperson believes that he or she has a valuable solution for them.

9. *Is a fanatic for fundamentals.* That's what Appendix A and the final chapter of this book are all about.

10. *Is personally involved.* Work through others, but stay involved to make sure the right things are done in the right ways to serve your customers effectively.

11. *Encourages experimentation.* That's how you will prove out a new and different approach to selling. Champions sell differently.

12. *Thinks like customers.* By developing expertise in some area and applying that to help a number of customers, the champions start to walk in the customers' shoes. Continually think two thoughts: (1) how can I help this person achieve his or her personal and business objectives, and (2) what unknown or new business benefit can I provide this customer or class of customer using our products and services?

13. *Knows the customer's business as well as his or her own.* This comes from studying the customers, and their industry and technologies, related to your products and services, and from spending time helping customers to seek out and solve problems.

14. *Encourages effective communication.* Overcommunication is the watch word. Everyone wants to be communicated to and few people do it well. If something is going to be late or wrong, it is better for you to tell the customer than to have him learn it from circumstances or someone else. Your communications and leadership in your own company help prevent things from being wrong or late.

15. *Develops and motivates employee associates.* A salesperson requires the services of others in the company to serve customers effectively. The great salesperson cultivates people within the organization, knows who is competent, and nudges and leads others to serve customers with excellence.

16. *Ties incentives to company performance.* Everyone is interested in WIIFM.[4] If the incentives aren't right for you or others, then develop a plan and a justification to make them right. Build a supporting "business case."[5]

17. *Has perseverance to the point of obsession.* If you knew of a miracle that could save a friend's life or help her to be much more successful, you'd be persistent in getting her to try it. Make business friends with prospects and customers. You already have a miracle to offer them, right?[6]

18. *Takes large risks when necessary.* What do you have to lose except your job and reputation? And if you are a great salesperson you'll never be without a job or a great reputation for very long.

19. *Fixes things before they break.* If you don't make the good better before your competitor does, you may not have anything to fix. Continue to work at helping your customers improve their situation, regardless of whether it increases or decreases your own sales to them.

4. What's in it for me?
5. See Chapter 10.
6. See Chapter 1. Your "miracle" is what gives you your passion.

20. *Knows all the details of the business.* Know your business. Know the customer's business. Know the market. Know important key technologies to help the customer. Be a learner.

21. *Is a hands-on operator.* Make things happen. Use other people when you can, but stay involved.

22. *Stresses informality.* Be formal or informal, however the customer is comfortable. But above all, generate great results. Most of the successful ABC entrepreneurs in the study were informal in dealing with their own people.

23. *Has a long term outlook.* Sell for the long term. Invest in today for the benefit of tomorrow. Care about the customer and the person. Work hard and smart to help them understand the long term perspective and the wonderful benefits and values you provide over the long term.

24. *Is fiercely independent.* Team selling is becoming more important. But, champions usually are far in front of their company in being different and better. It is difficult for them to just sit back and follow company policies. They work at "creatively" following policies to generate great results. They lead teams when teams are needed to achieve these results.

25. *Is a highly motivated economic animal.* Because they believe so strongly in what they are doing and how it will benefit the customer, their company, and themselves, they are passionate. They are highly motivated. They make things happen. Be motivated. Be passionate. Make things happen.

Those are the characteristics of successful entrepreneurs. Most successful entrepreneurs are successful salespeople. Thus, many of these 25 are characteristics of entrepreneurial selling champions.

The following are some additional ideas to keep in mind when employing entrepreneurial attitudes and skills.

- ► Read books about the business lives of carefully selected, successful entrepreneurs, like *Henry Ford's Success Plan* by M. Baber.
- ► Read the book *The Winning Performance: How America's High-Growth Midsize Companies Succeed* by Clifford & Cavanagh. That book describes in more detail what many of America's most successful entrepreneurs—originators of the companies in the American Business Conference—did and how they succeeded.
- ► Read the book *Innovation and Entrepreneurship: Practices and Principles* by Peter Drucker. That book describes how to practice entrepreneurship.
- ► Learn more about entrepreneurship by associating with entrepreneurs. Learn what entrepreneurs you know do to sell effectively.

PART B

CHAMPIONS

PROVIDE CUSTOMERS GREAT VALUE

5

"Grasping"
Critical Issues

Defining issues that are critical to key customers and market segments, prioritizing them, educating yourself re: the highest priority critical issues, and developing your expertise and value relative to the high priority issues. Then positioning yourself and your organization as the person and company the customer should do business with to effectively deal with those issues.

ILLUSTRATION AND RATING—5A

Champions provide customers with great value by "grasping" critical issues.

A "critical issue" is a problem, challenge, or opportunity that the customer receives great value from solving. Your customer or competitor may or may not be acutely aware of it. That is, it may be an issue now, or you may have to create the issue in the customer's or the prospect's mind. After determining the critical issue or issues, whether for a market segment or for an individual account, determine how to solve or help with the critical issue. Then communicate effectively that you are the best to do so. Otherwise the exercise is futile. That is, you must fully "grasp" the critical issue(s).

> When you become effective at "grasping" critical issues, you provide great value to customers in the areas where they most want and need value.

Your competitors sell products and services. And they look for companies and people who need their products and services. If instead you "grasp" and sell to critical issues, you will blow your competition away.

What major purchase have you made during the past three years? Or what do you anticipate buying soon? A purchase like a new automobile or stereo system that stresses you financially? Or a twin engine jet if your financial situation allows? What were the one or very few decision factors that caused you to choose one brand over another or one seller vs. another? Those were your critical issues for that purchase.

Suppose your single critical issue was "the newest in cutting edge technology." Then it wouldn't matter what price was offered, how convenient the location, how customer service-oriented the competition was, or how nice the salespeople. You would only buy from a distributor who offered the item you considered "the newest in cutting edge technology."

On the other hand, suppose your single critical issue was "ready availability of customer oriented repair service." Then you would pay a higher price and accept a lower quality item to be assured of that service.

I was a crack shot when I was in the military and proud of it. A few years later, I was invited to go pheasant hunting. My companions brought home pheasants. I didn't hit anything all day. I was embarrassed to discover I couldn't hit a moving target. Suppose someone tried to sell me a new shotgun that evening. What would my critical issue be? The answer—how to hit a moving target. I would have gladly paid for a morning of skeet shooting lessons along with the shotgun and not thought much about the price.

Joe Gandolfo and Keith Dillon, mentioned in the Introduction, based their "different" championship selling approaches on the customer segment critical issues they identified. For Joe, it was the need of higher-income people to reduce taxes. For Keith, it was the need of real estate agents for a more effective method of helping home buyers qualify for home loans.

Mary Anderson sells air-express carrier service in competition with Federal Express and UPS. This is a mighty challenge. Let's say she is calling on XEROX. How might she compete with those two dominant, air-express "machines?"

After effective information gathering, she can determine the critical issues of XEROX. It so happens that XEROX has a special need to have repair parts delivered by 9:30 A.M. Federal Express and UPS have massive, predictable delivery "machines." They are designed to serve customers of all sizes. Their cost-efficient systems prevent them from promising delivery to anyone before 10:30 A.M.

Suppose this is a critical issue. If Mary and her company can modify their operation to deliver to XEROX by 9:30 A.M., they have a good chance of getting the business. Suppose this is the single critical issue. If Mary's company is the only one that can deliver by 9:30 A.M., they are almost assured of getting this huge chunk of business.

Thought Provokers

(1) What do you sell? Are you like the insurance salesperson who sells insurance, the one who sells peace of mind, or the one who sells tax shelters?
(2) In what industry or market segment are you an expert or celebrity?
(3) Who do you sell to? Are they mostly decision makers?
(4) Do you know their key buying concerns?
(5) Do you know their key personal concerns?
(6) Do you know their critical issues?
(7) How do you know you are right?

Take the following rating exercise to estimate how important "grasping" critical issues is to your selling success. Based on the results, you can continue on with reading about its implementation, or you can move on to Chapter 6 and Section 6A and come back later to Section 5B.

CHAPTER RATING (rate A, B, and C below from 1 to 5 for this chapter's importance; then multiply)

_____ **A** = Importance or applicability to you (5 = great, 3 = moderate, 1 = poor)

_____ **B** = Your present strength or level of action (1 = great to 5 = poor) *(reverse rating)*

_____ **C** = Chances of your successful implementation or improvement (5 = great to 1 = poor)

A × B × C = your rating   (____) × (____) × (____) = (_____)

If your rating is over 25, read "Implementation" now; if 25 or under, consider postponing until later.

IMPLEMENTATION—5B

There are five steps to "grasping" (determining and selling based on) critical issues.

1. *Define critical issues by market segment.* List the market segments (such as markets, industries, technologies, and geographical areas) into which you sell that might have different "critical issues." For each segment, find and list the potential significant customer wants and needs (problems, challenges, or opportunities) that you have the potential for fulfilling. Include both business and personal issues. These are the wants and needs from

which you believe you could obtain a substantial amount of profitable business if you fulfill one or more of them. Do this regardless of whether you presently have the capability to solve the problem or help the customer.

Repeat the process for your largest customers and prospects.

Survey and discuss needs with customers. Talk to industry experts and others who are knowledgeable outside and inside your company. Read and review industry periodicals. Hold brainstorming meetings with the most knowledgeable people in your company. List every potential critical issue.

2. *Prioritize critical issues.* Determine the most important critical issues. Concentrate your thinking on those.

Prioritize critical issues by evaluating a combination of three points. The first is potential "issue" key goal achievement (for instance, profit generation to your company). The second is relative value to the customer of solving the issue. The third is the ease of communicating your solution to decision makers and influencers. (Perhaps for some reason it would be more costly than it is worth to get your message across. Then the third point would be rated low.)

Identify high-potential critical issues (HPCI). At this point your company still may not be able to solve the issue. But it makes sense for you or your company to develop the capability if the payout is large enough.

3. *Educate yourself concerning the high-priority critical issues (HPCI).* Ask questions of knowledgeable people. Read articles and visit customers. Learn in depth about the more important issues. Learn why they are important, and what customers, competitors and others are doing and plan to do to deal with them. Learn how much these issues are costing customers now and how they might be solved. Learn everything you can about each HPCI. Then you will know how important it really is to the customer. You will get ideas on how to solve the issue. Learn what your company might be required to invest to solve it. As a result, you can make a better decision about whether or not to devote resources to solving it.

4. *Define and develop your expertise and relative "value" re: each HPCI.* Determine how to solve each high-priority critical issue. Determine which ones you or your company should solve, and which ones you should forget about. Develop solutions for those that are justified. Then professionalize your solutions. Do this by gathering supporting data, putting information on laptop computers, developing nice looking presentation charts, and taking other supportive actions. Develop justifications. Your company may have to spend capital dollars to develop solutions for chosen HPCIs. Thus, the issues may have to apply to a large number of customers and salespeople. Determine what the potential "total" $ value[1] and other value should be for customers. Develop a supporting business case. Determine how to convincingly present that to customers.

---

1. See Appendix B and Chapter 10 for $ value and business case, respectively.

This step can be taken by the company for all its salespeople, or it can be taken by the individual salesperson. An example of each follows.

A financial company provided trust services. It determined that a critical issue was the ability to provide immediate information and feedback to prospects. The trust sales consultants needed to be able to ask prospects questions and then give immediate feedback on what trust and investment services were recommended and why. The company invested more than $1 million in computer hardware, software, and data input. As a result, each trust sales consultant had available a portable laptop computer with supporting software. They could ask their prospects questions. Then they could give immediate estimated answers and prepare completed proposals within 24 hours. This resulted in many millions of additional, profitable sales.

A sanitary maintenance salesperson determined that there were two critical issues for hospitals and other major consumers of floor care chemicals and equipment. The first was assurance that the products purchased would stand up to wear and be of high quality. The second was assistance on productive floor care methods and supervision of the floor care staff. (Product price was an issue. But total cost was a critical issue, since labor costs far outweighed the costs of products used. Sometimes the salesperson had to educate the customer on the concept of total cost vs. product price.)

The salesperson took a number of steps to become a floor care expert. He spent his own money to take a week-long floor care course offered by a national floor care consulting company. He worked as a "free" floor care person with a few customers during his off hours to gain experience. He tested a large number of products from his and other suppliers to determine which were the best. He convinced his supplier to change or offer new brands in some cases. He wrote papers and gave seminars explaining his results and the best operating procedures. (This helped with his positioning—see 5 below.)

Over time he became recognized as a floor care expert. He offered his information and consulting services to those who purchased his products. Companies bought his products just to obtain his consulting services. This addressed the two critical issues. He became highly successful in selling floor care products to large accounts.

5. *Position yourself in the market segments in regard to each HPCI.* In as many ways as possible, "spread the word" that you and your company are experts at solving the chosen HPCIs. Mail flyers to customers. Write and publish articles. Give speeches. Place ads in regional and industry periodicals. Be active in local associations. Make friends with consultants, periodical editors, and leading purchase influencers (such as managers in the largest customer companies). Author a professional, explanatory pamphlet. Perhaps do this with the assistance of a professor (for technical expertise) or school teacher (for writing expertise). See Chapter 12 for more information on positioning.

The following are some additional ideas to keep in mind when "grasping" critical issues.

- ► Make a list of the key capabilities of your company and ask which ones fit critical issues for customer segments.
- ► Make a list of any special strengths or talents you have, and ask which ones fit critical issues for customer segments.
- ► Make a list of every conceivable buying issue or decision factor that your major customers and customer segments might have. Include in the lists the causes of the issues. You should come up with a large number of issues. Include major and minor needs. Then review the list for the potentially "critical" issue that no one has considered before.
- ► Think about industries that are similar to yours, and major companies that are similar to your customers in some way. Ask and answer—what do you think are their critical issues and how do those relate to the critical issues of your customers and segments?
- ► When looking for critical issues, look for the problems, and the problems of the problems—the problems caused by or causing the problems.
- ► Work hard at getting out of the box of traditional thinking. Look for issues that might be more fundamental and more important to the customer (person or company) than most people would recognize.
- ► Read the story of the hardware salesperson[2] on added value. Look for the critical issues of people and departments other than those you are calling on, which might influence the purchases of those you are calling on.
- ► Consider calling on new or different departments or people in customer companies, especially those higher up in the organization. Identify their critical issues.
- ► Companies have critical issues. Departments have critical issues. People have personal critical issues. Include all these in your thinking.

"Grasp" critical issues to provide customers great value.

---

2. Chapter 7.

6

Facilitated Problem Solving and Planning

Facilitating a meeting for customers or prospects designed to identify and solve problems, obstacles, and challenges, and to help them identify and plan for business-producing, cost-saving, and profit-producing opportunities. This positions you as a consultant and valuable planning resource, and helps to develop a professional relationship by providing customers with a valuable new service.

ILLUSTRATION AND RATING—6A

Often salespeople run into a situation where it is difficult to get an appointment with or to get serious consideration from a prospect or group of prospects. There are many reasons for this.

The prospects may be "satisfied" with or have a personal relationship with a competitive company or salesperson. They may not consider your product or service to be important enough to interrupt their busy day to consider an alternative to what they are purchasing. Based on their experience, they may not believe that salespeople representing your type of product or service bring any special value worthy of their time.

This could be a major obstacle, and opportunity, if you face a large number of such situations, or if this describes some of your largest prospects.

Would it be helpful to you to have a "tool" to help in such situations? This tool would give you something different to talk about to the prospect, and position you as a different kind and higher caliber company representative. It would impress the prospect by presenting a more professional approach than the prospect has ever seen from a salesperson. It would provide you a mechanism to gain in-depth information about the needs of key prospects. This chapter discusses such a tool, which could be of considerable value to you.

Some companies and departments participate in regular and effective strategic planning and problem solving meetings. Most don't. Most don't, even if they say they do. Even fewer hold effective problem and opportunity finding meetings. You as a salesperson can offer them a related valuable, and usually unique, service. After developing your expertise, you can promote and facilitate strategic planning and problem/opportunity meetings. Sometimes you can offer a great service to them just by suggesting that they hold such meetings and explaining how they work.

I attended a national sales meeting for a successful mid-sized corporation as a consulting observer. At the meeting were top company officers, division managers, division sales and staff marketing people, and corporate marketing people.

Near the end of the meeting I was surprised to be asked to run the final hour of the meeting. Thinking quickly, I broke the group up by divisions, assigning corporate people to divisional groups. I asked the division groups to go through a simple exercise of listing and prioritizing the problems and opportunities they were facing. Then they were to discuss how they might better deal with the most important ones. After an hour, the groups were excitedly in the middle of the process. They continued on for an additional hour instead of breaking for cocktails. It was a new process to them. They found they were learning many new things about their business.

‖ You may think it is strange that this was a new process to them. ‖
However, it is new to many managements and organizations.

Many of our company's training programs start with a problem/opportunity session. The session lists and prioritizes obstacles and challenges participants face in accomplishing the purpose of the training (such as sales, customer service, management leadership, and new business marketing). Many times people come to the training with a bad attitude. They have the attitude that "until the organization gets its act together there is little I can do to be successful."

This exercise is held in groups of four to six people. It allows each participant to bring up and discuss his or her concerns with other participants. They thereby free up their minds and feelings. This helps them to be more open to the training.

Each group makes a report of its findings to the entire class. All the obstacles and concerns are listed and prioritized. The most important then are assigned to individual groups for problem solving. The problem solving sessions use the simple-but-effective process described below. The solutions are offered back to the main group. They often are presented to upper management for consideration. Everyone feels better. Sometimes upper management receives some valuable input.

Thought Provokers

(1) Do you have a challenge "getting the time of day" from key prospects?
(2) Would you like to be positioned as a professional consultant in some of the market segments you serve?
(3) Do your best customers need this service? Why? Why not?
(4) Do you need a better mechanism to obtain in-depth knowledge about customers and prospects?

Do you need a tool to get the attention and interest of difficult prospects? Are you able to facilitate a planning meeting? Are you willing to learn how? Would it help you to be positioned more as a consultant and added value provider?

Take the following rating exercise to estimate how important offering "facilitated problem solving and planning" can be to your selling success. Based on the results, you can continue on with reading about its implementation, or you can move on to Chapter 7 and Section 7A and come back later to Section 6B.

CHAPTER RATING (rate A, B, and C below from 1 to 5 for this chapter's importance; then multiply)

_____ **A** = Importance or applicability to you (5 = great, 3 = moderate, 1 = poor)

_____ **B** = Your present strength or level of action (1 = great to 5 = poor) *(reverse rating)*

_____ **C** = Chances of your successful implementation or improvement (5 = great to 1 = poor)

A × B × C = your rating   (_____) × (_____) × (_____) = (_____)

If your rating is over 25, read "Implementation" now; if 25 or under, consider postponing until later.

IMPLEMENTATION—6B

Selling the Process

When you meet with the prospect tell him or her, "We offer a process that could be very helpful to your organization in identifying and prioritizing ways to significantly improve your operating performance. It has been extremely valuable for other clients (if it has). We offer it without charge to introduce ourselves to you in a customer-serving way."

"I will meet with a selected, small group for two hours. During this time together, we will identify extraordinarily important challenges and opportunities you are facing and develop a proven process to solve the problems or take advantage of the opportunities. We can do this overall, or we can address a particular area you already are interested in."

If the prospect asks what's in it for you to do this, you might answer, "We are a customer-serving company. This demonstrates one of many ways we provide value to our customers that is an order of magnitude above that of our competitors. Also, during this exercise I will learn many additional ways that we might assist you to improve your performance and increase your profitability. Some of our products and services might be involved in helping you do that."

Delivering the Process

Once you are in the room with the group, you announce the objective of the meeting. You may give them two minutes to think about that objective. (The objective may be to list and prioritize problems and opportunities the organization is facing related to employee morale, or productivity, or marketing effectiveness, or hiring high quality employees, or whatever you have previously identified as being important to them.)

Then have each of them tell the group everything they can think of that is a problem or opportunity in that area. Make a list on a flip chart. Have each of them choose the three (or one, five, ten, or whatever makes sense) most critical problems or opportunities from the list. Ask each in turn to tell you the three they chose as most important. Place a check by it. After everyone has participated, count the checks. There probably will be two or more with a large number of checks. Let's say there are three.

Then divide the people into three groups, with one item assigned to each group. (Note: if you have a very small group, you may choose only one and have the entire group work on that one, with or without your participation.) Explain the problem solving process below and ask each group to apply it to the item assigned. Give them time, perhaps 30 minutes for the problem solving exercise. Then have each group report their results back to the main group.

Then perhaps select the most important problem or opportunity at this point. As a group, apply the five-step planning process to it (described in the second section below).

Problem Solving Process

Identifying and prioritizing problems and opportunities is the first key step. This can be followed by problem solving. The problem solving process consists simply of answering the following six questions: What is the problem or opportunity? What are the causes? What are the fundamental causes? What are the possible solutions? What is the best solution? What is a possible implementation plan for the solution?

The second of these questions asks the participants to list the causes to the problem or opportunity. But frequently, what they list will be symptoms of the fundamental or underlying cause. So the next question asks that they dig deeper, and look for what is really wrong, or what really is providing the opportunity.

The last asks them to develop a "possible" implementation plan. In the brief time you have with them, they probably will not have the time to evaluate all implementation possibilities. So you ask them to develop a possible plan to give them good perspective on what they need to do. They can modify or further develop the plan later.

Planning Process

The following five-step planning process can be used if you or your prospect really get serious. It develops a plan of implementation for the top priority item(s) chosen. This planning process comes after determining the best solution—Step 5 of the "problem solving process." This process replaces the last (implementation) step above (Step 6).

(1) Situation summary. Answer the questions—what, who, when, where, why, and how—concerning that item. This is to give further understanding and perspective.

(2) "Baber's Law" analysis conclusion (see Introduction). Where to concentrate for most effective results. List all possible aspects related to the problem or opportunity identified. Then identify those few that if acted on should make the biggest difference.

(3) Objective(s). What is planned to be accomplished based on the analysis conclusion.

(4) Strategy(ies) (for achieving the objectives). How you plan to do it; the overall approach to achieving the objective(s).

(5) Plan(s) (for implementing the strategies). The steps to take, when to take them, and by whom.

Getting Started

At this point all this may be new and confusing to you. You can get started by experimenting. You can offer "facilitated problem solving and planning" to some smaller or less important clients and prospects. Thus, you gain some experience and familiarity with it. Through experience you determine which topics and approaches are best received. Then you may want to develop a series of "problem solving and planning" forms. These make you appear more professional and experienced. The more professional the forms look, the more you look like a legitimate consultant.

Related Tool

Another tool that may be useful to develop is a "self-assessment survey" form. This can be used separately, or in support of the above meetings. It requires that you think and plan ahead.

To create the form, start with lists. List problems, opportunities, and symptoms of problems and opportunities that prospects or customers might have. Do this overall, for major market segments, or for a major problem area that you are qualified to solve. Then develop a list of questions that identify whether or not each of these problems or opportunities exists in the prospective organization.

As an illustration, the following are two questions from Business Development Institute's "Marketing/Sales Performance Self Assessment," related to major account selling:

- ► Would your key customers say that your salespeople are valuable consultative information sources to them?
- ► Do most of your salespeople spend the highest percentage of their time and effort on high potential accounts, and do they do it in a professional, smart way?

Develop an answer sheet that indicates whether or not the prospect needs to take corrective action (perhaps using your assistance) based on the answers given.

The survey can be returned to you for scoring. Or you can make it a self-assessment by providing the scoring sheet to the prospect. Completion of the assessment indicates to you and the prospect where there are opportunities to improve. Of course, you may be able to help through providing your products and services.

Try to see and analyze the completed assessment. Then you will have a better idea of what the prospect needs and how you can help.

The following are some additional ideas to keep in mind when employing facilitated problem solving and planning.

- ► This process can be used to position you as a consultant as compared to just a salesperson.
- ► Offering it can be used as a fall-back position when you suspect you can help the prospect, but don't exactly know how. It gives you a tremendous amount of information about the prospect that you can

use to look for problems you can solve, and products and services you can sell.

► Offering it can be used as a fall-back position when the prospect "won't give you the time of day." It positions you as more than a peddler, and offers the prospect a service and value that is probably quite new and different.

► You may find that the service is so valuable that you should offer it on a fee rather than a free basis.

► You may need to develop your meeting facilitation skills. You could take a course. You could observe a few professional facilitators in action. You could practice meeting facilitation with a group in your own company, getting some feedback and improvement suggestions from your peers.

To get the time of day from difficult prospects, position yourself as a valuable resource. One way to be valuable is to provide facilitated problem solving and planning.

7

Finding and Offering Specific Added Value

Finding, providing—and selling through—products, services, and actions that are valuable to the customer (or client), and are beyond or in addition to what the customer expects, or receives, from your competition.

ILLUSTRATION AND RATING—7A

Steve was an industrial sales representative. He sold items such as hardware, nuts, and bolts to industrial accounts. His primary customer contacts were buyers in purchasing departments. His product line was considered to be a commodity. He had fierce competition and was under considerable price pressure.

Steve was an engineer and became interested in warehouse operations. During extended sales calls, and during some of his weekends, he worked with the warehouse manager of one of his accounts. Together they upgraded the account's warehouse management system. This saved the customer hundreds of thousands of dollars. His customer was impressed and appreciative. It gave all its hardware business to Steve with little concern for price, since Steve generally was price-competitive.

The president of the company and the purchasing agent referred Steve to other companies in the area. Steve helped install the cost-saving warehouse system at some of those companies. He picked up their hardware business, again with little concern about pricing. Soon Steve was calling on presidents of companies (not buyers) all over his territory. He offered the added value service of improved warehouse operations. This was accompanied of course by the purchase of his hardware line. Steve became the most successful salesperson in his company. The national Purchasing Management Association named Steve as one of its "Salespeople of the Year."

Sam was one of Square D Company's top instrumentation salespeople. He was very aggressive. But he also had good technical abilities. Over time he developed the expertise to help design, install, and maintain instrumentation systems for his clients. This was his "added value." His customers not only bought instrumentation from him. They bought instrumentation designed better to their needs, installed properly and creatively, and operating effectively, with Sam as an available and dependable consulting resource. As a result, he got referrals to other potential accounts. And he had something special to talk to them about and to offer to them.

Added value strategies and skills can be extraordinarily helpful to salespeople. They can be effective for non-selling professionals as well.

This is the case for CPAs, financial planners, bank loan officers, attorneys, and others, such as institutional managers, hotel managers, and hospital nursing administrators. Added value strategies can be used by non-selling non-professionals, such as customer service persons, secretaries, delivery drivers, bookkeepers, and receptionists. Anyone who comes into continual contact with the customer can develop and offer added value.[1] They can increase their selling and service effectiveness, and increase their support of the marketing and sales efforts of their company.

As you become successful in adding value, and selling added value, you improve your selling effectiveness. And you can help your support people to develop and provide added value as well. As a result, they will assist you and your customers. This will increase the consumption of your company's products and services. It will increase the benefits received.

There are no commodity products or services.

You are special. You should know how your products and services are special. When you add value to them, they become even more special.

You can study an industry or customer. This gives you in-depth and "gut" knowledge about how it operates and what it wants and needs. You can find and solve a need that fits with your product or service. You then can add the "need solution" to your product or service to offer something special (added value) to the customer.

The following are some miscellaneous added value examples and ideas. One or more may relate to you in some way.

A bank or financial company officer could study computers. He could then help improve his own company's processes to better serve customer needs or

---

1. Added value strategies can help with frontline marketing; see Chapter 27.

answer their questions more quickly. Or he could use that information to assist customers with their computer and systems operations. Or more simply, he could devise and offer a method to help a client in some small-but-important way with financial planning. This might be a no-charge adjunct (added value) to receiving a bank loan or money management service.

Almost any salesperson, professional, or manager could develop marketing skills and capabilities specific to a customer's industry. Then they could help customers to market their products and services more effectively.[2] The same could be done for other business skills. Example skills are purchasing, accounting, systems analysis, selling, management, leadership, market research, product/service development, research administration, problem solving, decision making, time management, warehouse administration, safety administration, and insurance cost administration.

Delivery truck drivers could provide added value by helping to unload or stock merchandise when making deliveries. They could check off items delivered against the bill of lading to help the customer's receiving clerk. They could bring items inside and stack them on shelves within the customer's facility. They could check the customer's inventory and suggest items needed for purchase or resupply. They could do many other things, such as making emergency deliveries for the customer. Anything not included in or implied by the official purchase arrangement is added value.

Moving company salespersons could provide added value to individual homeowners or corporations. They could provide the moving family with a scale drawing of their new home along with to-scale cutouts of their various pieces of furniture. This creative added value idea would help the homeowners decide where to place their furniture in the new home.

Back office accountants or clerks could record data on complaints and questions that come in to their department. Then they could develop systems to head off the complaints (remove the problems) and answer customer questions more quickly. They, as clerks, might not do this alone. They might record the data themselves. Then they might sit down with managers and peers to develop the improved systems.

The book *Value Added Selling Techniques* by Tom Reilly presents some additional helpful ideas.

Listed in Section 7B are seven different approaches to finding and offering specific added value.

2. That would be added value to customers (or clients) of the type described in Chapter 23.

Thought Provokers

(1) What organizations and salespeople in your field are offering added value now? What are they offering and how? What is it doing for them as far as increasing sales or keeping customers happy?
(2) Could they be offering even more and better added value than they are? How? Would it pay for itself in increased profitable sales?
(3) What skills or unique strengths do you have that might be incorporated in adding extra value for your customers?
(4) What is really important to your customers that they are not receiving adequately now from you, your company, or others?

Take the following rating exercise to estimate how important "finding and offering specific added value" is to your selling success. Based on the results, you can continue on with reading about its implementation, or you can move on to Chapter 8 and Section 8A and come back later to Section 7B.

CHAPTER RATING (rate A, B, and C below from 1 to 5 for this chapter's importance; then multiply)

_____ **A** = Importance or applicability to you (5 = great, 3 = moderate, 1 = poor)

_____ **B** = Your present strength or level of action (1 = great to 5 = poor) *(reverse rating)*

_____ **C** = Chances of your successful implementation or improvement (5 = great to 1 = poor)

A × B × C = your rating (_____) × (_____) × (_____) = (_____)

If your rating is over 25, read "Implementation" now; if 25 or under, consider postponing until later.

IMPLEMENTATION—7B

Seven different approaches to finding and offering specific added value are discussed below. Each of these can utilize the "Seven Steps to New Business Development" discussed in Chapter 24:

(1) Via the market route
(2) Via the product/service route
(3) Via the technology of the product/service route
(4) Via the technology of the customer route
(5) Via your business management and strength route

(6) Via the customer business route

(7) Via the changing situation route

Most of the ways and supporting examples below can be looked at either from a corporate or an individual salesperson perspective. They can generate additional sales, and support your sales effort in general. The words "product" and "service" can be used interchangeably in most cases. You as a salesperson or business owner can use the ideas and examples as a starting point for developing your own added value, even though some are large corporation examples.[3]

To use this information effectively, you must think and ponder on each of the bullets in turn, asking yourself whether and how it might apply to your situation. To do this effectively may take many hours, but these could be extraordinarily valuable hours spent. After all, we are dealing with how to become a champion.[4]

1. Via the Market Route

► Offering or adding additional services. For instance, consulting on product or service usage; or establishing a business-improvement organization related to your product or service, such as a computer software consulting or hardware repair service that supports your computer or software products.

► Developing systems to better serve present customers. Systems are groupings of equipment, procedures, and services. An airline reservation system includes computer hardware, computer software, ticket printing equipment, ticket forms, and procedures for dealing with customers.

► Developing systems to make it easier to do business with you. Such systems might include an inventory control system, or a purchasing system via computer such as employed starting in the early 1980s by American Home Products Corp., which now is common.

► Developing and providing non–product-related, extremely beneficial technologies and services. An example is Herman Miller establishing an office productivity planning unit.

► Taking a burden off customers by doing something extra for them. Servicemaster did this by managing the hospital laundries and purchasing "the right" lawn care products for hospitals at discounted prices—in addition to their normal housekeeping and maintenance services.

3. Chapter 8A lists a number of added value potentials and solutions in the section, "Potential Problems and Opportunities." Chapter 24B discusses "Seven Steps to New Business Development" that can be employed to seek out, develop, and sell added value.

4. See Appendix F. You can phone Business Development Institute without charge to obtain a clarification or to briefly discuss how to develop added value in a certain area.

► Saving money for customers by helping them do (parts of) some things for themselves. For example, provide a cleaning service, but give customers a discount for emptying their own trash; or allow customers to pump their own gas at a discount, but provide maintenance repair services.

► Acquiring new technologies that serve your customers and are related to your products. AT&T acquired construction technology to combine with its engineering of microwave towers; another example would be the sanitary maintenance supply salesperson who acquired technology in floor care.[5]

► Acquiring a corporation, unit, or capability that helps you serve your customers more effectively. AT&T acquired a construction company to supplement its engineering of microwave towers so it could offer a turn-key job.

► Bringing in outside experts to address specific customer problem areas. Examples include computerized sales management and computerized preventative maintenance systems, where consultants could help with making them more productive.

2. Via the Product/Service Route

► *Adding additional value to one of the 9 Ps of marketing:*

The 9 Ps of Marketing

(1) Product (making the product or service more valuable; such as by providing the product in different shapes or designing the service to provide faster results)
(2) Place (distribution in a more helpful or cost-efficient way)
(3) Promotion (advertising, public relations, publicity, or selling method that is more helpful to the customer)
(4) Price (pricing in a helpful way; such as renting out copiers and charging by the number of copies produced or charging for the service as value is received)
(5) Product servicing (to keep it in effective operation, such as maintaining copy machines or upgrading software)
(6) Packaging (wrapping or labeling in a more helpful way)
(7) Provider (image of the salesperson or company that helps the customer; such as making it easier for them to sell to their customer because of your positive image)
(8) Positioning (your name, logo, or reputation that helps your customer sell his products easier; such as "Intel inside!")
(9) Product support (actions taken inside your company that help the product or service do its job better for the customer)

5. See Chapter 5.

► Providing promised value through the product in an especially effective way (such as a system to assure delivery on time or early, or being packaged carefully and properly)

► Developing improved products or services to serve specific needs

► Developing auxiliary, helpful products or services (such as a lubricant for improved milling on materials purchased from your company)

3. Via the Technology of the Product/Service Route

► Providing technical product expertise, support, and services (such as consulting and training on how to use a product or service; as on how to mill a machine part, or how to use a computer program)

4. Via the Technology of the Customer Route

► Consulting and training re: the customer's manufacturing and/or operations processes (Performing R&D on improving customers' operations using your products or services. One example—if you sell carburetors, R&D on using robots for assembly of carburetors with other engine parts. Another example—acquiring expertise in banking operations to help bankers bank more effectively using your services.)

► Developing equipment and services that help the customer operate more effectively (such as developing the robots and banking services)

► Assisting with improving customer worker productivity, product quality, or other effectiveness characteristics

5. Via Your Business Management and Strength Route

► Improving your company's (non-sales) customer communications through training of your people

► Applying internal resources in support of present customers and business, such as purchasing needed employee equipment, supportive systems design, and employee training

► Developing organizational operations criteria to give better support to present customers—including your company service strategy, management systems, organizational structure, and communication policies and systems

► Identifying existing company or department business strengths that might help the customer, improving them, and using them to benefit the customer (such as financing, computer systems and technology, and providing sales training)

6. Via the Customer Business Route

► Using your specific expertise, and that within your company, to help the customer improve present systems and methods in the areas of improving sales, profitability, cash flow, and any of a number of operating conditions (such as improved lead times, backorders, and reduced risk). Chapters 23 and 25 present major examples of this.

7. Via the Changing Situation Route

Matter vs. energy, people involved, time, place, reason, method—these six aspects of the product or service can be thought about to develop customer-serving added value.[6]

Can you find a way to get your product or service to the customer quicker or *when* (time) they want it? Toyota has developed a method to allow customers to come into the showroom and choose the car they want. It rolls off the assembly line in a couple of days exactly as they requested it.

Lenscrafters was the first to grind eyeglasses for customers while they waited. What can you as an individual salesperson do to help your customers serve their customers when they want to be served? Or to help your company serve your customers when they want to be served? Or to help your customers understand a better time to be served? That provides time-based added value.

What about *where* or *how* they are to be served? What about serving or involving different *people* on your end or theirs, with resulting benefits to your customer? What about replacing physical products with consulting or information services (thereby *replacing matter with energy*), or changing the *reason* for the service?

To provide added value through the "changing situation route"—ask and answer how you can serve your customer even more effectively through that route. Perhaps you will use new technology. Perhaps you will deliver the primary product or service in a way that is more helpful to the customer.

Think about how to do this through using the six interrogative pronouns describing the product or service: its aspects of what, who, when, where, why, and how.

For each of these aspects, the customer might be better served by (you or they) changing the chosen (one of the six) aspect in one of three ways:

(1) Making it more all-encompassing (represented by the word "*any*," e.g., delivered to or by *any*body or at *any* time);

6. This section is important, but complex. It takes some concentration to understand. In this regard, refer to Appendix F, the second section, "Additional Information." Also, the serious reader might read *Future Perfect*, by Stan Davis, for further perspective.

(2) Taking the aspect to zero (represented by the word *"no,"* e.g., requiring effort by *no* one or sent to *no* place);
(3) Making the aspect infinite or all-inclusive (represented by the word *"all,"* e.g., *all* employees or *all* parts of the product).

The following are samples of questions you can ask to look for added value. One sample question is given for each of the six interrogative pronouns. Many more can be asked. For each, an answer representing each of the three ways is given. Many more questions addressing each of the six areas and each of the three ways can be asked. To find added value, ask yourself what you or your company would have to do to provide that answer. (For instance, for the first question below—what would you have to do to make your product *any*thing the customer chooses it to be? How could you provide that added value?)

These are the six sample questions with answers.

(1) What is the product made of? The following are potential answers based on each of the above three ways: *Any*thing you or they choose; *no*thing—its inherent properties come from another product; *all* things—you name it and it's made from that.
(2) Who should it benefit (or who should provide it)? Anybody; nobody; everybody.
(3) When should it be delivered? Anytime asked for; at no time—it isn't delivered, it is consumed in a different way; all the time—or continuously.
(4) Where should it be delivered (or manufactured)? Anyplace—wherever it is needed; no place (it isn't delivered; it is handled in a different way); everyplace—at every company location (for instance, maybe we have a consultant, provide a computer, or perform mini-manufacturing at every customer location).
(5) Why is it manufactured (or delivered in a certain way)? For any reason the customer develops; there is no reason—it happens automatically, caused by something else; for every reason—there are so many reasons that there is no need to ask why.
(6) How is it manufactured (or delivered, or used)? Any way you desire because of how it is designed; no way—it isn't used, it is looked at and admired; every way—there are almost countless ways it can be manufactured or used because of its special design.

Methodically think through each of the seven ways of developing added value, starting with "1. Via the Market Route." Think about how each of the supporting ideas and examples might apply to your business and customers. You almost surely will come up with some added value ideas that will help your customers and your selling success in a major way.

8

Finding Problems/ Opportunities to Solve

Looking for and finding important problems and opportunities to solve for customers and prospects, both by general observation and through a systematic approach, and supported by your having an inquiring mind combined with specific technical, industry, or customer knowledge.

ILLUSTRATION AND RATING—8A

Theodore Levitt of Harvard Business School states in his book, *The Marketing Imagination*,[1] that finding problems and opportunities to solve is more important and more difficult than solving them once they are found. My experience supports that. I'll bet yours does too. Often customers don't know what many of their own problems and opportunities are. And when they do, they often don't know how serious they are.[2] This makes your finding them even more valuable.

Have you specialized in an industry, market, or technology? Have you invested time in learning and becoming more knowledgeable in a specialized area? Have you developed expertise there? If so, you have a foundation. It will be easier for you to perform the valuable task of finding customer problems and opportunities to solve.

Nick DiBari was a salesperson and later sales manager for Comdisco, a computer equipment sales and leasing company out of Chicago. Nick earned $8 million in commissions over a five-year period during the early 1980s. He was recognized as "Salesperson of the Year" by *Sales & Marketing*

1. On page 138 of that book.
2. See Chapter 17 for the SPIN questioning method of making customers understand that their problems are much more serious and costly than they realized. Appendix B shows that most salespeople don't know how serious they are either, and what to do about it.

Management magazine. Nick had a knack for finding problems and opportunities to solve.

Before Nick called on a new company or industry, he did some telephone research. He learned what he could about that industry and about what their needs were in relationship to the types of computers, equipment, and services he represented.

His primary area of expertise was technological—the use of computers for solving business challenges. He made a list of questions that he needed answered to determine whether or not the prospect had a need for his products and services, how big the need was, and how the prospect felt about it. He then went in to visit the prospect, and did not leave the office until he had all his questions answered.

> By going through this process repeatedly Nick developed a series of questions he could select from in preparing to visit a new prospect.

Illustrations

A marketing executive requested a sales consultant client of mine to propose a sales training program for his salespeople on handling objections and closing sales. The consultant was experienced at problem finding. After asking a few questions he suggested that there may be more important problems to address in the training than the marketing executive had specified. He asked to interview a few salespeople and was given permission to do so. After the interviews he proposed a different kind of training. He got the business and was paid a higher fee than proposed by any of his competitors—because he had found more important problems and opportunities to solve.

Bank loan officers, CPAs, or financial consultants might decide to look for problems to solve in a new industry, say the construction industry. They could start by reading about the industry in general business and construction industry periodicals, looking for problems and opportunities mentioned that relate to their business. They could talk with their peers. They could interview both construction company executives and workers and ask about situations they face. They could talk to others who are knowledgeable about the industry. They could brainstorm with groups of people from the construction industry, from their own industry, or both together. They could attempt to relate what they found to their services, products, and capabilities.

In studying the industry, they might find the following problem/opportunity to solve, which I found while working with that industry. At certain times of the year (usually summer) construction companies have lots of business and need lots of working capital. Then, at other times of the year (usually winter), the money comes in and they don't need any financing.

So, the bank loan officers, CPAs, or financial consultants might develop a "business case"[3] showing how they can help construction companies deal with this situation most effectively using their services and capabilities. The business case could involve assisting them in obtaining financing at the needed times, even during difficult business conditions. They might develop a list of problem, implication, and need-payoff questions related to the identified problem and business case.[4] Whenever they called on a construction company they would then know what questions to ask to determine if the company had that problem or opportunity to solve.

A salesperson for a manufacturer of sanitary maintenance chemicals and supplies calls on both large and small regional janitor supply houses. The supply houses in turn sell germicides, floor finish, strippers, soaps, and floor maintenance machines. They sell to hospitals, office buildings, and others who do cleaning and floor maintenance.

What kinds of problems and opportunities do janitor supply houses have that the manufacturer's salesperson might look for and help to solve? The salesperson should ask and think this out. If he or she is able to find problems and opportunities successfully, and the competitors are not able to or don't try, the salesperson is going to get a lot of business.

Potential Problems and Opportunities

The following is a list of potential problems and opportunities that the salesperson for the chemical manufacturer might look for and find. Many are similar to those for other industries. Review the list and see if it gives you ideas about industries or markets you serve.

First, the smaller janitor supply houses (suppliers) may have large sales opportunities, but not the working capital to take advantage of them. (The manufacturer could help them to obtain financing to support the sale of its products by the supplier.)

Second, a smaller supplier may need to obtain a large bid bond in order to be allowed to bid on supplying the manufacturer's products for a large government (city, school district, etc.) supply contract. (It could back the supplier for the bid bond.)

It would help the supplier in selling the manufacturer's products if comparison tests had been made between competing products. These could be done by, or arranged and paid for by, the manufacturer. The resulting data would be presented in such a way as to demonstrate the superiority of one or more of the manufacturer's products. For instance, comparative floor

---

3. See Chapter 10.
4. See Chapter 17 re. developing problem, implication, and need-payoff questions.

finish tests might show that the manufacturer's floor finish has a higher gloss (shine) than that sold by competitors. Or that it lasts longer. Or it doesn't scratch as easily. Or it can be buffed back to a high shine in less time. Any of these four might be an effective differentiation selling point, depending on the wants and needs of the supplier's prospect and the skill of its salesperson.

The supplier might have the opportunity to sell a complementary line of equipment or products. The manufacturer might go into partnership with the supplier in supplying that line. Or it might help introduce the complementary line for a consulting fee. Or the manufacturer might help out just to obtain the supplier's appreciation and the resulting pull-through sales.

The supplier may be having difficulty in finding good salespeople, or in motivating the salespeople already on board.

The supplier may be having difficulty with inventory control or thievery.

The supplier might benefit from receiving training in selling, marketing, employee motivation, or basic management practices. Training could be supplied by or coordinated through the manufacturer, perhaps for a fee, or perhaps in exchange for continuing large orders.

The supplier might benefit from receiving ideas and direct assistance in effective and creative marketing, for instance, on how to effectively market janitor supply products to hospitals, nursing homes, and their industries locally (thereby moving more of the manufacturer's products).

The supplier's salespeople might benefit from receiving more comprehensive training on product features and benefits. Or on how to use the products more effectively—such as how to properly apply the floor finish to the floor. The manufacturer could put such training on videotape to be used by a number of suppliers. Or the manufacturer's salesperson could be trained to do it himself or arrange to have it done.

The supplier's salespeople might be more effective if they were supplied with better promotional literature.

The supplier might find where new or different products, with different properties or characteristics, are needed by their customers. The manufacturer could develop these new products. Or it could investigate to see how large the need is by using its nationwide contacts.

These are potential problems and opportunities related to the cleaning products supply industry. Once you develop a list related to any one industry, market, or technology, you can determine whether any of the other companies or industries you plan to call on may have the same or similar problems or opportunities. You can develop a list of questions to find out.

Thought Provokers

(1) When did you last find a problem for a customer? Did you solve it?
(2) When did you last solve a problem for a customer? Was it a big problem?

(3) What questions do you normally ask customers? Why those questions?

(4) What types of problems do your customers face? Are they like or unlike those described for the janitor supply houses?

(5) What unusual opportunity has a customer of yours found? Would it apply to other companies, industries, markets, or technologies you handle?

Take the following rating exercise to estimate how important "finding problems/opportunities to solve" is to your selling success. Based on the results, you can continue on with reading about its implementation, or you can move on to Chapter 9 and Section 9A, and come back later to Section 8B.

CHAPTER RATING (rate A, B, and C below from 1 to 5 for this chapter's importance; then multiply)

_____ **A** = Importance or applicability to you (5 = great, 3 = moderate, 1 = poor)

_____ **B** = Your present strength or level of action (1 = great to 5 = poor) *(reverse rating)*

_____ **C** = Chances of your successful implementation or improvement (5 = great to 1 = poor)

A × B × C = your rating   (_____) × (_____) × (_____) = (_____)

If your rating is over 25, read "Implementation" now; if 25 or under, consider postponing until later.

IMPLEMENTATION—8B

A Problem/Opportunity Finding Process

How do you go about finding problems and opportunities to solve? The following process is one method. It develops lists of problems and opportunities that customers and prospects might have. Studying the lists prepares you to look more effectively and deeply when you are with the customer.

1. *Specialize so you can gain in-depth knowledge and a "gut" understanding of one or more fruitful problem-finding areas.* This gives you a foundation of understanding. It feeds background knowledge into your subconscious mind. It helps ideas to pop out of your mind unexpectedly as you take the steps below and when you are with customers and prospects.

You can specialize in an industry—such as the airline industry or the warehouse distribution industry. You can specialize in a market—such as the market for plasticizer chemicals or gasoline carburetors. Or you can specialize in a technology—such as corrosion technology, metalworking, or the business use of computers.

2. *Learn to perform quick-and-dirty market research in the other two areas where you don't specialize.* Nick DiBari specialized in technology related to the business use of computers. So he developed the ability to perform quick market research in a new industry or market before making a sales call there.

3. *Meet with your peers and others who are knowledgeable about the industries, markets, or technologies (the areas) you specialize in or plan to focus on.* Meet with your key customers and others who are knowledgeable outside your company. Determine the kinds of problems and opportunities that already have been solved or observed. Think about the ones that relate to your business, products, and services. They may be faced by the prospects you plan to call on.

4. *Make a list of all the problems and opportunities that were identified in the steps above.* Separate them by market segment or by any category that makes sense to you.

5. *Make a list of problem, opportunity, and implication questions to ask that will help you identify whether the customer has each problem or opportunity listed, and how important it is.*

6. *When with the customer—listen for causes and changes.* Listen, of course, for problems, needs, and wants. Look and listen for the underlying causes or reasons for those problems, needs, and wants. They indicate underlying problems or opportunities you can address. Also, look for changes of any type—changes in key personnel, new technology being tried, new products or suppliers being offered or tried, new problems or successes of the customer's customer. Evaluating changes can lead to problems and opportunities that you can address.

You might develop a business case for the most obvious problem solutions and opportunity supports, based on your services, products, technologies, and other added value capabilities. Doing so supports problem/opportunity finding with appropriate solutions.

Before making sales calls, you can review the above lists to prepare yourself to more effectively look for and find problems and opportunities to solve.

Guidelines

In taking the above six steps, look for critical issues, those things that are really bothering or are the prime concerns of decision makers, whether or not you believe you can solve them at this time. There are problems inherent in each critical issue—and related problem questions you can ask.

In many accounts, there are people and departments that you don't normally call on. Look for problems, challenges, and opportunities that they face.

For instance, a printing supply salesperson had been calling on the marketing department of a large printing company with few positive results. She talked with others in the company looking for problems. She found a problem in operations that the marketing department was unaware of. This led to a solution for the operations department using the salesperson's products and services that reduced the number of printing passes. It significantly reduced printing costs for many jobs. As a result, the salesperson became the printing company's major supplier of her type of products and services.

Look for underlying causes, the "reasons for the problem." Once you identify a problem, look for why the problem or need exists.

For instance, a client of ours sells support services to claims adjusting departments of insurance companies. Let's say an identified problem or need is to convince physicians to speed up treatments and reduce the time, charges, and unnecessary tests spent on individual back injury patients.

An important underlying cause of the problem may be the fear of those injured that they may never get well. Therefore they feel the need for, and demand, every expensive test and treatment available to ensure the greatest chances of recovery. A competitive company may have the insurance company's business of auditing physician invoices. The championship salesperson may take this business away from the competition with an additional, creative solution to the underlying cause. Previously, neither the customer nor the competitor may have known that the underlying cause existed, or given it any serious thought.

The following are some additional ideas to keep in mind when looking both for categories of and specific problems and opportunities to solve.

- ► Immerse yourself in a selected industry, market, or technology. Attempt to form a close relationship with at least one company—preferably an innovative, leading-edge company. Spend some time on their premises dealing with and better understanding their business from the standpoint of how you might serve them.
- ► Allocate some time to talking to front line customer people, such as operating people who operate the machinery, customer service and office people who receive the customer complaints, and secretaries who overhear gossip. Seek out the source of any kind of unhappiness or negative feelings.
- ► Allocate some time for talking to industry and technical experts.
- ► Keep a problems/opportunities notebook or computer file. Record

every idea related to the selected industries, markets, or technologies for later reference.

► From time to time, review your notes looking for problems or opportunities you might solve, work on, or help with.

► Keep an open mind. Be slow to reject an idea or a potential solution. Keep your mind open to the unusual and improbable.

► Be especially alert to changes that may cause new problems or opportunities.

► Be alert to new or unusual happenings, such as a new process being tried or a new technology entering a market niche.

► Develop your questioning and listening skills. Without effective listening you may ask the right question, but fail to hear or perceive the right answer.

Problem and opportunity seeking can lead you to sales possibilities that other salespeople and companies are ignoring. Exploring them once found can lead you to new business, and sometimes to unmined gold mines of selling potential.

CHAMPIONS

PLAN AND ORGANIZE EFFECTIVELY

9

Territory/Account Planning

Identifying priorities, setting objectives, developing strategies, and making plans to effectively sell to territories, key accounts, large potential prospects, normal accounts, and account categories and people.

ILLUSTRATION AND RATING—9A

Ove Sjogren sells vacuum cleaners for Electrolux in Sweden. He is a legend in his own time. He has been the number one salesperson for Electrolux every year since 1975. Ove averages selling more than four machines a day. When most salespeople sell three machines in any one day, they consider it a great success. Ove attributes his selling success to effective planning.[1] Ove plans his sales territory. He plans his selling day. He has a plan for each sales call. Most salespeople don't.

Ove has a talent for developing systems. He was a painter before he entered sales. He watched how everyone else painted. Then, he developed a system to far outperform them. When other painters climbed up and down ladders, Ove set up scaffolding. When others washed brushes in the morning, he did it the night before. When others got by with old, outdated equipment, he bought new, more effective equipment.

His painting systems involved detailed planning. "I always knew exactly where I was going to start the next day," he says. "My colleagues said they could set their watches by my schedule."

---

1. Patrick Tylka, president of the North American Sales Group of Scientific-Atlanta, identifies the 1995 differentiating factors for his "best" salespeople to be goal setting, planning, and the determination to make or surpass those goals. This ties together Chapters 1 and 9.

> The first thing Ove did when he started selling was to watch how effective salespeople sold.

He then developed a selling system and plan to outperform them. He started with the best ideas and approaches he could find and then improved on them.

Championship salespeople plan and organize through effective territory and account planning. Most salespeople don't. This chapter discusses an approach that you should find useful. Using Ove's process, it takes the best things others are doing and improves on them. You can use it in its entirety, or you can take selected ideas from it to improve your present approach. It is nicknamed TAPP for territory/account planning process.

Ten Levels to TAPP

TAPP consists of ten levels or steps representing ten key sales effectiveness areas. It generates phenomenal payback on the time invested.

> TAPP can take weeks to complete properly, and should be continually updated. Even so, the first eight steps can be completed on a rough basis in less than a day with substantial results.

It can be done by you, or even better, by a small group including you. The planning levels or steps are:

1. Situation
2. Product/service/added value
3. Territory
4. Segment
5. Sales call process
6. Time and self management
7. Account
8. Account contacts
9. Account sales call
10. Contact sales calls

Selling champions set objectives at the territory and account level, and they are determined to achieve them. They have persistence and tenacity, based in part on their selling passion. They refuse to fail.

TAPP is a methodical approach to establishing and achieving objectives and focusing your passion.

Thought Provokers

(1) How good are you at territory and account planning?
(2) How important is this to your selling success?

(3) How could effective territory and account planning most help you to increase your sales and meet your objectives?
(4) In which of the ten steps do you do the best job?
(5) In which of the ten steps do you need to improve the most?
(6) Refer to the footnote at the beginning of this chapter. Do you have the "determination" to make your plans work?

Take the following rating exercise to estimate how important "territory/account planning" is to your selling success. Based on the results, you can continue on with reading about its implementation or you can move on to Chapter 10 and Section 10A, and come back later to Section 9B.

CHAPTER RATING (rate A, B, and C below from 1 to 5 for this chapter's importance; then multiply)

_____ **A** = Importance or applicability to you (5 = great, 3 = moderate, 1 = poor)

_____ **B** = Your present strength or level of action (1 = great to 5 = poor) *(reverse rating)*

_____ **C** = Chances of your successful implementation or improvement (5 = great to 1 = poor)

A × B × C = your rating (_____) × (_____) × (_____) = (_____)

If your rating is over 25, read "Implementation" now; if 25 or under, consider postponing until later.

IMPLEMENTATION—9B[2]

The Five-Step Planning Process for TAPP

Before discussing TAPP, let's look at a five-step repetitive planning process that can be applied at each of the ten levels of TAPP. This results in an overall look from the perspective of that level. It sets priorities, objectives, strategies, and plans for that level.

(1) **Situation Summary.** Answer the questions—what, who, when, where, why, and how concerning that step or level. This gives you further understanding and perspective.
(2) **"Baber's Law" Analysis Conclusion** (setting priorities). Where do you concentrate for most effective results? List all areas, segments,

---

2. Sections 9B and 24B are long, detail-filled, and sometimes tedious. They also are extremely important.

or action categories related to that level.[3] Then, select for emphasis those few which if acted on accomplish the largest positive results.

(3) **Objective(s).** What do you plan to accomplish based on the analysis conclusion?

(4) **Strategy(ies)** (for achieving the objective[s]). How do you plan to do it; the overall approach to achieving the objective(s)?

(5) **Plan(s)** (for implementing the strategy[ies]). What steps are taken, when are they taken, and by whom to accomplish that priority, objective, and strategy for that level?

The following is a brief discussion of each of the ten levels of TAPP.

TAPP

1. Overall Situation Analysis

Ask and answer questions such as the following:

What are the current trends and events that affect your sales effort? What does each tell you? What is the overall business situation? What are the trends for market segments you sell to or are considering selling to? Which customers and segments are doing well and poorly and why? Where is there big business potential? What are your strengths, weaknesses, vulnerabilities, problems, threats, and opportunities? What are the strengths, weaknesses, vulnerabilities, problems, and opportunities of your competition? Where have you and they done well and why? Where are you different and better than your competition? What sales objections do you often hear? How would you describe your best customers? Why are they good customers? What are each of your key customers' strengths and weaknesses in the marketplace? What problems and opportunities have you solved for them?

---

3. Baber's Law is described in the Introduction. For instance, in Step 4 you could segment by metropolitan area, industry, or account size, among others. Let's say you choose industry. Then, list all the industries that are potentials. Select the few (say, three) that have the greatest potential. Then, develop an objective, strategy, and plan for attacking those three industries. Then, continue to plan for Levels 5–10, concentrating on those three industries. Then, if you have time, continue for other industry segments. Do the same type of prioritization at the other levels. For instance, in Step 6 choose one or a few things (say, one—allocating every Saturday morning to working on important/non-urgent activities) to concentrate on to manage your time effectively. For that one then set an objective, develop a strategy, and make a plan on how to utilize your Saturday mornings. For instance, the objective could be to complete one project or make major progress on one project each week. The strategy could be to spend the first hour in creative thinking and the next three in accomplishing specific results. The plan could be for you to start at 8:00 A.M. sharp, to take a 15-minute break at 10:00, and to work until 12:00 unless a significant stopping point is reached after 11:15. You would work in your office, or somewhere else more convenient, but only if it is free of interruption.

Which customers and key prospects are leaders, early adapters, followers, and laggards?

As you answer these questions, you start developing a feeling for your overall situation. You start getting a good idea of where you stand and in what directions to consider going. You know where you need to search out more information. This is the basis for the following steps.

2. Product/Service/Added Value Planning and Strategy

Answer these questions.

Why should any customers or prospects do business with you? Why should they prefer to do business with you instead of your competitors? Why should they pay their money to you rather than keeping it in their pockets?

Answer the ten following questions concerning your major product/ service lines. If you sell a service, then replace the word "product" with the word "service" below.

(1) How do your products (or services) and lines offer something special to the marketplace and what do they offer (rather than just another quality gizmo)?

(2) How do your products or lines benefit the customer who uses them, or who uses them instead of a competitive product or line?

(3) What problems can the customer have by not using your product or not using it properly?

(4) What is the overall sales potential for each product or line?

(5) What types of accounts (segments) use the most of your products and where are your best prospects?

(6) What product support or added value—something they can really value—can you or your company offer to your customers?

(7) What specialized or technical support training would be helpful to you or your customer and how could it best be arranged?

(8) What customer questions and objections will you have to face and how can you overcome or prevent them?

(9) Where are the best sources of information on your products and their benefits, both written material and company personnel?

(10) Do you have available, clearly-written and illustrated product/service literature that "sells"?

After answering these questions, you should know what you have to sell. You know where you can provide value to the customer. You know what products and services to concentrate on selling and how to package them. You also have a good idea about where you need to work on developing more added value. You know if your company needs to make product or service improvements. If you don't need to make major improvements, you have the information to build a business case.

3. *Planning and Strategy for the Territory*

Analyze your sales territory, branch, or selling area.

There are two different approaches to estimating the total sales potential for your sales territory and to break it out by segment.

The first way is to find statistical data that estimates the total potential, and break it out by segment based on a divisor. (For instance, census or association data may list the total number of airplanes of each type in the country. You might break them out by state by the number of employees working for FBOs[4] in each state, modified by what you know about who uses what type of planes. If you know approximately how much of each of your products each type of airplane uses per year, you can calculate your total potential sales by state.)

The second way is to list all your present and potential accounts, break them out by segment, list the potential purchases for each account, and add to arrive at the total potential. (You then can compare the two results as a check.) The discussion below assumes the second approach is used.

List all known present and potential accounts. (It is particularly important to include major prospects that presently aren't customers. They could offer you more potential, perhaps with a new and different selling approach, than present customers.)

Estimate the sales and/or gross profit potential for each. Estimating profit potential is better if you can do it. On the first pass your estimates may be very rough. Then, break them out by market segment. You can segment by industry, market, end use application, added value applicability, geographical location, and other ways—whatever makes the most sense.

Add up the sales or profit potential for each segment.

Adjust the sales potential for each segment and major account by taking into account the factors in the paragraphs below. Those resulting in the highest sales or profit potential deserve your focus and attention.

The following are some considerations to be used in adjusting the potentials: relative amount of work and time required to get the business, agreeability, size of average order, present sales, their need for your key added value offerings, loyalty tendencies, creditworthiness and financial health, growth potential, account cooperativeness, sophistication of thinking and profitability (together affecting ability and willingness to pay a higher price for higher value), their fit with your strengths, and their knowledge and skills. Each may affect your ability to realize the estimated sales or profit potential.

---

4. An FBO is a "Fixed Base Operator" or airplane maintenance shop.

Each can affect the focus decision in a different way. For instance, suppose the companies in a segment have a high level of knowledge and skills. Then they can understand your more sophisticated arguments and evidence. However, they probably have less need for your consulting expertise, if that is one of your differentiating strengths or areas of added value.

In establishing potential, multiply the estimated total potential sales or profits by some factor representing the ease or difficulty in getting the business based on these factors.

Look for the few highest potential segments and key accounts. Concentrate your learning, marketing, and sales efforts on these. Sell to your entire territory. But spend more time and effort where there is greatest potential. As a result, you use your time productively.

4. Planning and Strategy for the Segment

Analyze and develop a plan for each priority segment and key potential account using the process above.

Chapters 21 and 22, industry-specific marketing and self marketing, discuss ways to gather information, find great value, and become important, recognized, and even a celebrity in an industry or market segment. The same approach can be used for any type of segment chosen.

5. Strategy and Implementation of the Sales Call Process

Determine the most effective sales call process to use to effectively sell the chosen products, services, and added value to the selected segments.

Review the material in this book on the sales call process, especially the material in the Appendix. Review notes from other training courses and books that you have found to be valuable.

Write out the best method for finding, approaching, and selling to your key prospects. Review it with knowledgeable peers to get their comments and suggestions.

For instance, should you cold call, phone for appointments, or market yourself through articles or direct mail, planning for prospects to contact you? Should you start at the top, or should you first contact and learn from a lower level, easier-to-contact, interested professional? Should you make a specific claim early in your sales presentation to generate interest, or should you gather a lot of information to learn the prospect's interest and needs before even suggesting a potential product, service, or solution? Should you use the SPIN questioning approach? If so, should you develop a list of potential problem and implication questions before making important contacts? These and many other questions are worked out at this level.

6. Time and Self Management

Develop a strategy and plan to use your time more effectively.

Keep a detailed record of your time for a typical week or longer. Make it long enough to cover all your important selling cycles. Include enough detail to be meaningful upon analysis. The following are just a few examples of time categories to be included: wasted travel time, productive travel time, time waiting at account, meeting and greeting, information gathering, proactive phone follow-up, answering calls from present customers, productive meetings, and unproductive meetings. Analyze the time record to understand where you are spending your time now. Determine how you might spend your time more effectively.

Especially look for wasted time, time that you could spend more productively. Look for where you are spending too much time dealing with small account potentials and less important matters. Separate your recorded time into four categories: urgent/important, urgent/not important, not urgent/important, and not urgent/not important.[5] If you are typical, most of your time is spent in one of the "urgent" categories. Most salespeople can increase their long-term selling results dramatically. One way is by shifting a substantial block of time to the "not urgent/important" category, and then using that time wisely.

Non-urgent/important time includes important items such as the following: planning, business reading, product knowledge development, relationship development with key customer contacts and segment influencers, Baber analysis, information gathering at key accounts, strategy development, making effective call reports and analyzing them, learning, added value development, team brainstorming, sales skill practice in key areas, organization, and communications.

See Appendix E for more on time management.

7. Planning and Strategy for the Account

Rate all present accounts and key prospects as A+, A, B, C, C− (or some similar rating) based on their purchase or profit potential. A+ accounts have a very large, realizable sales or profit potential. C− are the large number of very small customers that probably don't justify personal sales calls.

After rating for potential, upgrade or downgrade some accounts. Do this based on their present purchase level and the ease of obtaining new, profitable sales from them. For instance, if two customers have the same potential, but one presently purchases much more from you, it deserves a

---

5. *The Seven Habits of Highly Effective People*, by Steven R. Covey, contains an informative discussion of this analysis.

higher rating. If two accounts have the same potential, but one is much more difficult to work with or get business from, it deserves a lower rating.

Analyze each account and develop account objectives, penetration strategies, and plans for each. Do this first for major customers. Then do it for major account prospects. Obviously, start with A + and A accounts, then for other important accounts and prospects as time permits. These are the bases for your later sales call objectives and plans. (See 9 and 10 below.)

Develop an overall customer/prospect worksheet built around the five-step repetitive planning process presented at the beginning of this section. The situation section of the process lists, for each account, questions to be answered so you can plan and sell to the account effectively. A list of potential questions follows at the end of this section. (The worksheet also includes other information.)

Approximately 80 percent of your accounts give you only 20 percent of your sales. A somewhat different 80 percent generate only 20 percent of your gross profits. Separate the many smaller accounts into categories by their needs and how they buy. Spend some (non-urgent/important) time developing and implementing strategies to deal effectively with them in a creative, less time-consuming way, so you can reduce or eliminate personal sales calls. Perhaps these will include a combination of phone selling, regular mailings, and using lower paid associates for a major part of that effort.

Peter Drucker, the inventor of modern management, says that the mark of a good manager is knowing which projects to work on, but the mark of a great manager is knowing which projects not to work on. Correspondingly, the mark of a good salesperson is knowing which accounts to pursue. The mark of a great salesperson is knowing which accounts not to pursue, and not to spend a lot of time on.

Plan to call personally on all important customers and prospects. But spend more time and effort where the potential is largest. If, for instance, 11 accounts represent 40 percent of your business potential, then you should spend 20 percent–40 percent of your time dealing with those 11 accounts.

Calling on them doing what? These are some potential answers.

- Gathering information
- Finding their critical issues
- Determining what special added value they need
- Determining what special added value you can offer them that meets their critical issues
- Gathering data
- Calculating the $ value of the added value you offer
- Determining other reasons they should do business with you
- Finding new ways to offer added value so they want to do more business with you
- Developing a business case

- Interviewing people in the company you haven't been calling on
- Developing relationships with them; determining their wants, needs, and result wins[6]
- Determining how to leverage with them
- Reading related books and magazines and studying this account's industry and the major companies in this industry
- Becoming more expert in the account's technology, especially related to how they use and might use your products and services; perhaps working at the account (for free) for a short time period to learn their business better. Some champions have done this on their vacation.

Factors to Consider

Factors about industry and company:

- Market segment this customer/prospect falls into and resulting implications
- Special concerns (critical issues) of the industry and how you relate to them
- Critical issues of this customer or prospect
- Your current situation with this account
- Expected buyer responsiveness
- The total account purchase or profit potential
- Present, competitive suppliers
- Present supplier to this company of your type of products or services
- Other potentially competitive companies, products, or services—not now in play
- Your company's strengths and weaknesses compared to competition
- How you can be special to this account
- Sales objectives for this account
- How progress will be measured

Factors about products and services:

- What is different and better about your offerings, as compared to the competition
- Why and how your company can obviously help this account
- How you have and can out-serve present and other competitive suppliers
- Problems and needs account has or may have

6. See Appendix B, "Personal Benefits," for an explanation of result wins.

- Key problem questions to ask
- Implications of those problems and needs
- Related implication questions to ask
- Need-payoff questions to ask
- Questions related to $ value and your business case
- Your probable best offering (product/service/added value combination)
- Your offering's competitive advantages and disadvantages
- What is different and better about you (perhaps the added value you bring)
- Objections anticipated and answers to those objections
- Service watch-outs (where you have been less than perfect in developing relationships, learning customer needs, and serving customers' wants and needs)

Factors about people:

- The decision maker or focus of power
- Key decision influencers
- Who you should contact first, or next, and why
- Known personal characteristics of key persons
- Special concerns of key persons
- Key information needed about key persons
- Needed important information
- Expected preconceptions/prejudices about you, your company, your service, the competition (leading to objections or to you being favored)

Actions to Take

The following are some account actions to take or plan for, based on the above information:

- Classifying accounts by category or segment
- Identifying and classifying decision makers and decision influencers (such as their personality styles or their preference for your company)
- Judging buyer responsiveness
- Prospecting within present accounts
- Recording key information
- Establishing account objectives
- Analyzing past sales call objectives
- Judging past sales call effectiveness

8. *Planning and Strategy for Account Contacts*

Identify key contacts at each account, for instance, decision makers, decision influencers, information providers, and coaches. Develop a strategy and overall plan for working with each key account contact.[7]

In doing this, plan to identify the following business information:

- ▶ Their responsibilities
- ▶ Areas of interest
- ▶ Their influencing and decision making power
- ▶ How you can help them achieve their objectives
- ▶ Whether they are or can be coaches, users, or decision makers
- ▶ What their motives are
- ▶ How use of your products/services affects them directly and indirectly
- ▶ What their result wins and other personal benefits might be
- ▶ What benefits and $ values would appeal to them most
- ▶ What problems they face

Also, plan to develop personal information on each person—information such as the correct spelling of names and titles, who they value the opinions of, special events and people in their lives (such as birthdays and children), what has brought them great joy, what has brought them great frustration/irritation, their value system, or their personality styles.

Note: There is a purpose for each type of information. For instance, suppose you know what has brought them great joy and frustration. Then, when you are talking to them, you can link your products or services to their joys and the competitor's to their frustrations. This causes their subconscious minds to like what you offer and find fault with what the competitor offers.

Having this information is helpful to you in planning and developing strategies for the individual contact sales calls. (See 10 below.)

9. *Planning and Strategy for the Account Sales Call*

Before making on-site sales calls, complete the first part of a carefully designed call results report. An example is shown below. (Note: At first I wrote "important on-site sales calls." But if the call isn't important, you shouldn't make it at all.) Attempt to determine "known problems/needs/added value opportunities" and "call objectives" before making the call.

7. Judgment must be used, of course. You should develop a detailed strategy and plan for decision makers of individual key accounts. You probably should make a brief strategy and plan to deal with categories of smaller accounts.

Figure 3 on the next page is a call report outline that could be useful to you.

Studies show that focused sales calls tend to produce the largest orders. Unfocused calls do very poorly. Proper use of a call results report like this helps you focus your sales calls.

10. Planning and Strategy for Individual Contact Sales Calls

You won't be calling on just an account. You will be calling on individual people at the account. Ask the following questions before the call. What does that person want? What do you want? How can you get what you want by giving the other person what he or she wants?

Before arranging for the sales call, and before deciding who to call on that day, review your overall sales call objectives. Ask yourself who you should see and what you should accomplish with each person to help accomplish those objectives. This gives you focus for each individual visit. It may even cause you to change the overall sales call objective and the people you plan to see.

Figure 3. Call results report.

Report by: _____

Location: _____ No.: _____

COMPLETE BEFORE CALL

1. Account name: _____
2. Account rating (A, B, C, etc.): _____
3. Call date: _____
4. Known problems/needs/added value opportunities at this account: ___

 _____

 _____

 _____

5. Account situation—other: _____
6. Baber analysis conclusion: _____

 _____

 _____

 _____

7. Call objectives: _____
8. Call strategy: _____
9. Call plan: _____

AFTER CALL COMPLETION

10. Time spent at call: _____
11. Call results: _____
12. To do now/next (what and when): _____
13. Assistance needed, when, and from whom: _____
14. Selling strategy/skill(s) attempted/used (if any): _____
15. Selling strategy/skill use results (if any): _____
16. New information obtained at or about the account: _____
17. Support people to be sent a copy of this report: _____
18. Other comments: _____

10

Building Business Cases

Determining specifically how prospects can use your product or service and how it is financially justified for them to do so. Stating this in a supporting "business case," and using the case to build your own confidence and to select and present (make an effective sales presentation) to prospects.

ILLUSTRATION AND RATING—10A

In 1980, IBM set up 60 test sales organizations or districts around the country. IBM did this in an attempt to find the best ways to sell lower-margin and lower-serviced, mid-sized and smaller computers and associated equipment. One of the 60, primarily with inexperienced salespeople, outperformed all the rest. How?

The sales manager of that district did two things that generated very high results. First, on a weekly basis he had each of his salespeople identify their top five buying prospects (otherwise known as a "hot list"). Second, he had each describe to their peers an action plan and a "business case" for each of the top five prospects.

This focused their selling on the top prospects. It caused them to develop a plan for each prospect. The plan was supported by a "logical financial justification" (a business case) for why each prospect should buy. As a result of this process, the young salespeople and the district were highly successful.

The sales manager flew all over the country to describe to the other 59 sales districts why and how his organization had been so successful. The "business case" was the primary reason he gave for their success.

Definition

■   A "business case" is a quantification of the prospect's need.   ▊

It is in enough detail that the salesperson can clearly see that a need does exist for their product or service, that it fulfills that need, and specifically what the savings or dollar benefit would be. This supported the IBM salesperson's selection of the prospect as one of the top five for concentrated effort. It also built their confidence, enthusiasm, and PPP.[1]

To build a business case, you perform sufficient information gathering to understand the prospect's situation and needs as related to your products and services. You then determine how your solution can benefit the prospect, and in detail how it makes or saves them money, or specifically makes a measurable positive impact on their situation.

Illustrations

Suppose, for instance, you are selling "territory management" computer software for use by the prospect's sales force. Suppose during information gathering you determine that in the prospect's industry salespeople frequently quit. And they take some of their top accounts with them when they leave. Even when they don't, the records left behind are usually in a big mess. As a result, the sales manager and/or the new sales representative must spend considerable time re-prospecting the same group of companies. Also, many potential sales opportunities are lost. They are lost because of the delays in prospect and customer contacts, and the delays in selling processes already started.

This "business case" involves estimating the frequency of salespeople leaving, and estimating the number of accounts and dollars in business that would be lost in such a situation from lost accounts and lost sales opportunities because of inadequate records. Then it involves estimating the cost of the duplicate time spent by the new salesperson in having to start prospecting from scratch.

Another item is added: an estimated dollar value of the increase in efficiency and effectiveness of the salespeople who remain—resulting from using your company's territory management computer software. This is because, as a result, they are utilizing their time more effectively by using the software. (For instance, they are scheduling their time more effectively and the sales manager has a tool to watch this and make suggestions. Also, they

---

1. See Chapter 1 for PPP. The business case justifies the sale if the prospect has a certain need. In these cases, the salespeople had identified that need before developing the "hot list." In other cases, salespeople would have to ask their prospects problem questions to determine if the need exists.

are more effective at setting account and sales call objectives, in part because the sales manager has a tool to check these and follow-up as appropriate.)

The estimated cost of not purchasing is then compared with the cost of purchasing, hopefully indicating the extreme value to the customer of purchasing the software.

Once a business case has been developed for a couple of companies of a certain type, or in a certain industry, then it becomes very clear what questions need to be answered to develop a business case for related companies. Also, sometimes one business case applies to all the companies of a certain type or industry.

Almost any salesperson can profit from developing a business case.

A. L. Williams Insurance Company shook up the life insurance industry during the 1980s. It is a successful multi-level life insurance company. It obtained its success in large part by training its salespeople to develop and present a business case to each prospect. The business case explained the advantages of replacing a prospect's existing "whole life insurance policy" with the "different and better" A. L. Williams policy.

In whole life insurance, a large portion of the premium paid each year by the policy holders is invested in something like a low interest (low yield, low benefit to the policy holder) savings account. A. L. Williams converted those policies to a much less expensive term insurance policy. The savings (difference in costs of the two types of insurance) were invested in a higher payout (higher interest yield) money market account.

David, a friend of mine in Richmond, Virginia, was a top life insurance agent for Metropolitan Life Insurance Company. David successfully combated the A. L. Williams program by developing a business case of his own. It was built around an innovative insurance policy that had been developed by Metropolitan. His business case demonstrated that in many cases the A. L. Williams approach "stole" some important benefits from the policyholders. Guaranteed insurability at a later time was an example. The Metropolitan policy allowed the policy holder to retain those benefits and receive competitive financial benefits as well.

A services salesperson or professional can build a business case just as easily as a product salesperson. For instance, a business case can be built by an insurance representative, hotel salesperson, catering manager, airline salesperson calling on industrial accounts, bank loan officer, consultant, or attorney.

In building a business case, you need to make sure that you have something to sell that really is valuable to the customer. In attempting to build the case, you may find that what you are offering is not as valuable or special as you thought. Or you may already know that you have competitive problems. If so, this indicates that you need to rethink what you are offering and redevelop it. (Chapter 7 on finding and offering specific added value should be helpful in doing this.)

You may not have packaged what you sell as effectively as you can. Perhaps you need to provide added value. Perhaps you haven't identified as well as you should the many penalties the customer is paying from not using your product or service. Perhaps your product or service needs some minor, but important, modification to be of extraordinary value to a particular end user or market segment.

As a result of this rethinking, you finally will be offering (selling) a special product, service, or combination, of great value to your prospect. Around this you can build a substantial business case—and demonstrate your passion.

As an aside, the business case is very similar to a financial justification. A financial justification frequently is needed to sell an internal capital appropriation project to upper management within your own company.

Thought Provokers

(1) Can you build a business case or do you need help to do so? Who has the savvy to help you?

(2) The training that accountants and engineers receive should help them in developing business cases. Are you an accountant or an engineer? Do you know a smart one?

(3) A business case is a justification for a course of action. Can you think of ways other than in your selling that developing a business case might help you or others you deal with?

(4) Which would serve your needs better, a short, sketchy business case or a long, detailed one?

(5) Is what you sell worth buying? Why?

Take the following rating exercise to estimate how important "building business cases" is to your selling success. Based on the results, you can continue on with reading about its implementation, or you can move on to Chapter 11 and Section 11A, and come back later to Section 10B.

CHAPTER RATING (rate A, B, and C below from 1 to 5 for this chapter's importance; then multiply)

_____ **A** = Importance or applicability to you (5 = great, 3 = moderate, 1 = poor)

_____ **B** = Your present strength or level of action (1 = great to 5 = poor) *(reverse rating)*

_____ **C** = Chances of your successful implementation or improvement (5 = great to 1 = poor)

A × B × C = your rating   (_____) × (_____) × (_____) = (_____)

If your rating is over 25, read "Implementation" now; if 25 or under, consider postponing until later.

IMPLEMENTATION—10B

The following are some ideas to keep in mind when building business cases for market segments or key prospects.

- Build the business case around what the customer considers to be an important need or problem, not just around what you or your people think.
- Therefore, invest time in information gathering before building the business case.
- You may find an important problem or need with which your customer is unfamiliar. An example is reduced production costs when your prime customer contact is the marketing department. Then make sure the prime customer contact or decision maker agrees that it is indeed a problem or need. If you can't, then find another prime contact or (higher level?) decision maker.
- Tie the business case to the bottom line. Tie it to dollars earned or saved when possible, not just to benefits received. Both the computer software and the insurance business cases demonstrated the dollar savings to the client.
- Test out the business case if possible before presenting it to important prospects. Perhaps you can make calls on less important prospects and see if the business case is challenged by them. If so, discuss its validity with those prospects. Attempt to clearly understand their thinking and how to answer their questions and overcome their concerns.
- Present the business case to one or more of your sharp peers. Ask them to attempt to tear it apart, to challenge its validity.
- The business case uses an approach very similar to that of determining the $ value of a sales solution. Read Appendix B and understand the concept of $ value.

Questions to Ask

Answering the following questions can help you get started toward building a business case.

1. You sell what you are proud of. What are you proud of?
2. What does it do for the customer?
3. Why does the customer need that?
4. Under what circumstances?
5. What customer is it giving great value to now?

6. How much money does it make for that customer?
7. Specifically, how does it make money for that customer?

Answer these questions for your major offering or line of business. They may help you build sales through building and using business cases.

11

Tremendous,
Terrible Technology

Keeping up-to-date with basic technological change, especially as it relates to general business, selling, and your areas of expertise. Continually looking for opportunities to more effectively and creatively use new technologies to sell to and serve customers.

ILLUSTRATION AND RATING—11A

In the past, champions may or may not have used new technology more effectively than the average salesperson. But the future will be different. Change, and the effect of new technologies on how we do business, are on an exponential curve upward. Thus, in the future most companies and salespeople who don't quickly embrace new technologies will be left far behind. Those who figure out how to apply them first probably will be ahead.

For example, Michael Buttita, one of 700 sales reps for the United States Postal Service, handles the Sears Roebuck account. Michael, after 21 years in the Postal Service and ten of those in sales, was almost forced by his management to use a laptop computer, along with newly-developed sales automation software. After only four months using the new approach, he had doubled his sales level.

Changing Times

Most industrial corporations are significantly reducing the number of vendors they deal with. This means more upper level executives are becoming part of the buying decision. You need to be able to deal effectively with upper management. You need to bring in your upper management on major selling situations. You need to coach them to sell effectively.

The virtual (the more or less) paperless office is here. Ernst and Young is the nation's second biggest accounting firm. It is in the process of eliminating 50 percent of its total U.S. office space. It is doing this by converting most of its accountants and consultants into part-time telecommuters who literally must make reservations to use the remaining offices. How would this type of action by your customers and prospects affect your ability to reach people to sell to?

| The cost of technology keeps going down while the cost of people goes up. |

Purchases related to numbers of people will be way down in the future. Equipment buying related to upgrading technology and productivity, especially information technology, will continue to increase for a long time to come. Your customers face the challenge of raising productivity or dying. What products, services, and added values do you offer that raise productivity, especially related to producing and using information (not data, information)?

An entire, healthy-looking human corpse (dead human body) has been sliced into many thousands of thin sections. They were photographed and entered into a computer memory bank. The entire body, in three dimensional form, is available to be explored through the Internet. As a result, you can create a human body or a body part in your computer. With available software technology, you can make it age, give it diseases, or exercise its muscles, and see the results. How physicians are trained and how they operate will change entirely. Perhaps soon something similar can be done with your product, service, or system.

Many decisions about new technology are corporate decisions and out of the hands of field salespeople. Changing from mainframe computers to networked workstations and personal computers is a corporate decision. It requires a huge investment in money and time. However, purchasing a laptop computer to handle your personal communications and organization can be a personal decision, as can be how you plan your time and how you deal with voice mail. And you must deal with voice mail. Most salespeople are having great difficulty finding people to talk to on the phone these days.

Ten years from now, maybe in five years, this may be the most important chapter of this book. Because of exponential change, what it will say then probably will have little resemblance to its contents today. But its theme will be the same.

Tremendous and Terrible

Technology is "tremendous" because of the new opportunities it gives you. Technology is "terrible" because it is changing so fast. It is so difficult to anticipate. And if you miss an important application for new technology and your competitor doesn't, the results could be terrible for you.

In the early 1980s, I was doing a project with Dearborn Chemical, a second level water treatment company. Dearborn invested in computer systems technology. It developed a design program to support field sales. As a result, the field salespeople could telephone into the company's computer the prospect's situation (size and type of equipment, chemical analyses of water streams, etc.). They could determine on the spot which chemicals needed to be added and at what concentration. The system also was designed to indicate whether or not the prospect had a corrosion problem and how to treat it. Dearborn used new technology more effectively than its competitors. As a result, Dearborn's sales shot up dramatically at the expense of its major competitors. This approach was new then. It is old hat now.

An elevator maker recently equipped its sales force with laptop computer software. The salespeople produce elevator designs based on customer specifications right on the spot. The share of orders that has to go through its engineering department before reaching manufacturing dropped from 80 percent to 20 percent. This allowed the company to cut its engineering staff, reduce its costs and prices, and increase its profit.

One of our consulting associates carries a credit card size pager, small digital cellular phone, and an 800 number that calls his pager. He differentiates himself from his competition by being instantly available to clients. Regardless of where he is or when, they can reach him by calling his 800 number and keying in a special code.

Five years from now he may differentiate himself by carrying the pager and telephone in his glasses on his face. Also in his glasses may be a voice understanding computer, a microphone and speaker, and a fax and computer modem. He may be able to hear a phone call or receive a data fax translated into speech. He may ask his computer to look up data or make a series of calculations. He then would send a voice or data answer back to the client. All this without moving his hands or stopping his ongoing meeting with a second client or prospect. He will be able to do this only if he keeps up-to-date on new technological developments.

Officers of Chase Manhattan Bank can reach managers and conduct face-to-face meetings with them at offices anywhere in the world. They can do this in five seconds with a click of a computer mouse. No wonder business mail has dropped 33 percent from 1988 to 1994.

Two Points

The purpose of this chapter is to make two points: (1) effective use of new technology is becoming critically important to selling success, and (2) you should start keeping up with techno-

| logical change and thinking regularly about how you can use new technology to more effectively sell to and serve customers. |

Technology is moving so fast that whatever is on the market and being used today will be totally obsolete in a few years, perhaps next year. In fact, if it is not obvious to you that this chapter is out-of-date, you may be out-of-date. And much of what the "experts" project will be useful tomorrow will be incorrect. How changing technology pertains to effective selling is in flux. It will be a few years, if ever, before the situation settles down.

However, there are some trends and applications of technology in selling that are becoming clearer. If you keep up-to-date on technology as it pertains to sales and marketing, you will be prepared to quickly take advantage of the obvious technologies that can help you remain successful and highly competitive.

Thought Provokers

(1) What are your sources of information on new technologies?
(2) How have you used new technology to sell more effectively?
(3) Do you know what opportunities are available to you to use new technology to sell more effectively now?
(4) How might you use new technology to provide added value to customers?

Take the following rating exercise to estimate how important "tremendous, terrible technology" is to your selling success. Based on the results, you can continue on with reading about its implementation, or you can move on to Chapter 12 and Section 12A, and come back later to Section 11B.

CHAPTER RATING (rate A, B, and C below from 1 to 5 for this chapter's importance; then multiply)

_____ **A** = Importance or applicability to you (5 = great, 3 = moderate, 1 = poor)

_____ **B** = Your present strength or level of action (1 = great to 5 = poor) *(reverse rating)*

_____ **C** = Chances of your successful implementation or improvement (5 = great to 1 = poor)

A × B × C = your rating   (_____) × (_____) × (_____) = (_____)

If your rating is over 25, read "Implementation" now; if 25 or under, consider postponing until later.

IMPLEMENTATION—11B

More on Technology and Change

I am a professional speaker, in addition to being a consultant and author. Because everything else is changing so fast, so do the details regarding the topics I consult and speak on. For this reason, for years I have been looking for a way to rapidly prepare and/or modify audio tapes on various topics for my clients. One problem I have faced is that I must continually stop the tape recorder in my office studio to think about what to say next. Even with my advanced analog recorder, every time I stop to think it records an unpleasant "tick" sound on the tape. The tick must be removed expensively at a professional sound studio. Likewise, when I update a tape the same tick sounds occur.

Recently, Sony put on the market a (newer technology) digital mini-disc recorder. I purchased it because it records without putting the tick sound on the disc. This results in professional-sounding recordings to give to my clients.

This can give me a differential advantage over my competitors in two ways. First, I have a differential advantage if I provide the supporting audio discs and they don't. Second, suppose we both provide supporting audio tapes of equal value. Suppose I am aware of the new technology and they aren't. Then their tapes contain the unprofessional sounding ticks or are much more costly to produce.

CD-ROMs are read-only memory compact discs for personal computers. They hold a huge amount of data—more than in a large encyclopedia. They are a huge business today. For instance, for under $1000 you can purchase the entire D&B corporate data list for the U.S. You can obtain the data on thousands of companies according to any criteria you select (industry, location, size, etc.). Suppose in your business this is a source of valuable leads. Suppose you use the CD-ROM technology and your competitors use the old reference books. You find the prospects sooner and with much less expenditure of time and effort.

CD-ROMs are important today. But, guess what? CD-ROM technology is projected to be obsolete very soon. So much for that new technology.

Small hand-held computers, linked by phone lines to main computers, have helped FedEx and UPS keep track of packages worldwide. And the use of hand-held computers has totally changed the jobs of some drug detailers from shelf counters to marketing consultants (as explained in Chapter 25).

IBM's world has been turned upside down. There has been a rapid switch of major corporations away from emphasizing mainframe computers, where IBM is dominant. Companies are switching to networked workstations and personal computers. IBM's profitability and prospects would be better if it had anticipated that change.

But IBM is a large company. It sells lots of workstations and personal computers. One IBM salesperson outperformed the rest by utilizing available technology to implement "industry specific marketing," described in Chapter 21. IBM learned from her, and now uses that approach throughout that division.

Collaborative selling and marketing are becoming critically important in some industries. They have been aided by powerful computers, marketing databases, and improved communications systems.

Many companies have started to automate their sales systems. This provides the sales force with better management reporting. It more quickly and more easily provides management with activity tracking, sales projections, account profiles, and other required reports. It provides improved database inquiry—tools that enable quick access to information.

It eliminates wasted time looking for client names, notes, and other important information. It provides agenda management capabilities, enabling quick entry and updating of scheduled events—such as phone calls, tasks, and meetings. It supplies computerized communications—which provides the ability to send and receive information on the phone, send management reports via modems, send quotes, and communicate with the main computer. Little of this was available ten years ago. It will be much more sophisticated and valuable five years from now.

Computer Software and Hardware

Such a large number of computer-related hardware and software technologies are now available to the salesperson it is confusing.

A recent issue of *Sales & Marketing Management* magazine listed more than 600 computer software programs for sales automation. These were provided by more than 200 vendors in the following 23 categories: account/ contact management, advertising, compensation, desktop publishing, direct marketing, e-mail, field/sales reps, inquiry/order, lead tracking, mapping, market research, pricing, product management, sales and market research, sales and marketing management, sales and marketing planning, sales forecasting, sales presentations, telemarketing, time and territory management, trade show marketing, travel/entertainment, and word processing.

That's a lot of computer software to think about and try to use.

Many salespeople couldn't get by today without account contact management software such as ACT, TeleMagic, Sharkware, or FileMaker Pro. It saves them much time and effort. It wasn't available ten years ago.

Many companies have developed their own automated computerized systems. For instance, they design new products. They tell customers which products or services best fit their needs (like the Dearborn and elevator examples above). They calculate price and delivery on proposed orders. If you have this technology available and your competitor doesn't, it can give you a great advantage. The computerized system developed for the financial company trust salespersons described in Chapter 5 is an another example of this.

You are familiar with technologies used today by salespeople in large and small businesses. Most weren't available ten years ago. There are personal computers, which were available, but tens of times less powerful. There are laptop computers, which were not available. There are thousands of software programs available for use on them.

For general business use, there are numerous versions of computer software programs—for word processing, data management, spreadsheets, integrated applications, presentation, and accounting.

For desktop publishing and graphics—there is software for imaging, drawing, prepress applications, computer-aided design, graphics/publishing, utility, and visual resources.

For multimedia—there is software for 3-D modeling, animation, multimedia, special effects, desktop video, and music.

For connectivity and communications—there is computer software for communications, fax, connectivity, and network management.

For computer operations—there is software for systems enhancement, diagnostic utilities, personal organization, reference, and even entertainment and games.

There are personal computers and workstations available with more power than the largest supercomputers of the 1970s. There are sub-notebook computers, palm-sized computers, computer pen-based message pads, and electronic organizers. There are personal digital assistants. There is intelligent software, such as that used to sort your e-mail.

You don't know what will be available in five years or how valuable it will be. But you'd better stay in touch to find out before your competitor does and runs away with your business.

Then there are personal computer-related hardware items. These include laser printers; color printers; storage products, such as large external hard disc drives of many gigabytes; monitors; accelerators; scanners; specialized input devices; multimedia upgrade kits; sound cards; digital video cameras; CD-ROM drives; modems; and fax machines.

There are non–personal computer-related hardware items. They include color copy machines, answering machines, smart telephones, remote headsets, digital cellular telephones, credit card size digital pagers, and, of course, audio cassette decks for educational listening, VCRs, and flat television screens.

Added Value Example

Take the lowly VCR, for instance. Are you providing added value to your clients using the VCR or any of the other more advanced technologies?

Do some of your key customers need a better understanding about how a few of your products work and how they should be used in application? If so, you could give them a better understanding with VCR technology by doing the following.

You as a salesperson could meet with your company's technical experts and have them explain and demonstrate the product or service and its application. You could do this individually and with them in a group. You could videotape the meetings and demonstrations. You could then edit the videotapes and prepare a clear, valuable educational tool for your customers.

The company could provide this. But suppose it doesn't. And suppose some of your key customers have special needs. You could do it yourself. You could use VCR technology to provide added value to your personal customers. The equipment is readily available and moderately priced. This would differentiate you positively from your competitors.

Other, more advanced technologies might be used to accomplish this result even more effectively. In the future the same process could be used to provide CD-ROM educational tools to your customers. Or you might arrange regular video conferencing between customers and technical experts. Or you might provide key customers with desktop video conferencing tied to key technical experts in your company, such as mentioned above about Chase Manhattan. Or perhaps in five years an entirely new technology will become available through which you can provide even more valuable added value (advanced expert systems?). But you can do this only if you are aware that the new technology exists when it becomes available. Thus, it is important that you continually educate yourself on new technological developments.

New Technologies

There are numerous areas of new technology that already are in use, but soon will be expanding in application by orders of magnitude.

You might use one or more of these in your selling approach. Or you might use them, or a combination of them, to provide your accounts added value or services that are so valuable that you destroy your competition.

There is *digital interactive television*—two-way television. There are *advanced flat-panel screens*. These come in black and white or color that are similar to TV screens. They can be very large or very small.

Telecomputers are combination Touch-Tone telephones, fax machines, and computers with touch-screen inputs connected to telephone lines.

Personal communication networks are digital devices similar to cellular telephones, but smaller and less expensive. They can be used for customized data entry and transmission of voice, numbers, or graphics.

Advanced compact discs store large amounts of data, sound, text, and video in a small space. They include CD-ROM (read-only memory), CD-

ROM XA (extended architecture), CD-I (interactive), CD-R (recordable), and the Photo CD, which holds digital images.

Desktop video conferencing allows users to see and hear each other on their computer screens. With this, both computers have a built-in or attached video camera. Both data and the other person are shown on the screen at the same time.

Multimedia computers allow users to provide combinations of data, sound, and video, as (1) in an on-site sales presentation to one or a large group of people, (2) online, or (3) on advanced compact discs for later viewing.

Advanced electronic notepads are hand-held computers that can be customized by the user to a particular need. They can be used to record data, send and receive e-mail or faxes, or for other uses.

Electronic data interchange (EDI) allows companies and people to electronically and automatically link up. They can be used to share purchase, inventory, and delivery data. EDI is one of the key bases of reengineering that has become so important.

Advanced simulations are computer programs that can simulate objects or events. Virtual reality is presently the most advanced form. The U.S. intelligence services take millions of satellite photos from different angles. They digitize and input them into a huge computer. As a result, an agent can experience walking through the streets of Tehran, or almost anywhere else, by wearing a virtual reality helmet.

Digital imaging converts words, pictures, charts, and graphics into digital form in computers. They can then be sent instantly to anywhere in the world. You can now get a digitized road map fed by satellite built into your car dashboard.

Advanced expert systems are software programs that allow one or more "experts" to program how they would deal with a series of situations or problems. In theory, everyone can, in effect, take an expert with them on a sales or service call in their laptop computer.

Diamond thin films are layers of diamond molecules, only several molecules thick. They are deposited on the surface of an object giving it extraordinary properties.

Low-level satellites are changing the way people communicate. Soon everyone will have available their own light weight phone (or phone/fax/computer/modem/TV) and phone number they can take with them everywhere.

Fax-on-demand allows your customers to phone you day or night to receive any of a number of types of promotional or instructional information. They punch in what they want and it is faxed right back to them.

Rapid changes can also be expected in parallel processing computers, multisensory robotics, computer integrated manufacturing, fuzzy logic computer software, neural network computing, and object oriented software programming.

In addition, many changes are expected in the field of *biotechnology*. Order of magnitude changes are expected, and entire industries will be built up, around recombinant DNA technology, antisense gene technology, and endoscopic technology. Tiny computer- and motor-driven machines will drive around inside our bodies repairing heart muscles, cleaning out arteries, and otherwise helping us to live healthier.

Internet and Online

You are familiar with the "information superhighway" and "going online." The Internet and its associated World Wide Web is a connected network of thousands of computers.

By going through an Internet gateway company, and learning how to use the proper software, you can contact millions of people and organizations throughout the world. The data signal goes from your personal computer to your modem, and through the local phone line to the gateway's computer. The gateway's computer connects by phone lines to the other thousands of computers.

You can enter the information superhighway more easily by joining a commercial online service. Examples are CompuServe, America Online, Prodigy, GEnie, and Delphi. Microsoft has started a new and different online service, which has become a major player.

Through the online service you establish an e-mail address. This is your personal online telephone number.

You can join any of a number of online special interest groups or bulletin boards. There are more than 10,000 special interest groups. Bulletin boards are computer locations where people with a similar interest can post and share information.

You can now make voice contact, the equivalent of phone calls, online.

You now can research information about companies you plan to call on, or industry history, and trends. You can almost instantly communicate by computer with a friend, business associate, or customer anywhere in the world. You can advertise your services for sale, such as on a home page of the World Wide Web.

You can go online to a bulletin board or interest group and ask for the solution to or information about a difficult technical or sales problem. A number of knowledgeable nerds or industry experts may answer you. To show how helpful this can be, this is a quote from a recent *Time* magazine article. "He decided on his own to pose a simple question on an electronic bulletin board for aerospace engineers: 'How good is aircraft stealth technology?' A dozen engineers, scientists, and even an Air Force officer responded with data on materials used in Stealth planes, their design, and the ways radars may spot the aircraft." If this person could get what recently were government secrets online, just think what you can get that might be of use to you.

Database Marketing

Database marketing requires the fast computers and sophisticated software that recently have become available. *MaxiMarketing* (1988) and *Beyond Maxi-Marketing* (1994), by Stan Rapp and Tom Collins, discuss the importance of database marketing and how it might affect your selling and marketing.

The New Office

Through sales automation and modern computer and telecommunications technology, major divisions of companies are shutting down entire offices and having their salespeople operate from their homes. IBM and Compaq Computer are examples. During a two year period, from mid-1991 to mid-1993, Compaq doubled its sales, reduced its sales force by one third, and reduced sales costs substantially through this approach.

Anticipating this trend, a company has been set up to convert vans and minivans into mobile offices for salespeople.

The office in the back of the van includes a desk, chair, lamp, and filing cabinet. It includes a laptop computer, CD-ROM drive, printer/copier, fax/computer modem, and cellular phone and headset, all operated off the vehicle battery.

With this set-up the salesperson can maintain telecommunications (both phone and computer online) contact with home office personnel and the home office computer-server. The salesperson also has phone and online contact with customers, prospects, and online associates and advisors (through the Internet or one of the online services).

Suppose your company has set up a comprehensive customer information system (marketing database). Then any contact with any customer by any company employee is entered into the database and is available to any sales or staff person in your company.

Salespeople can send information to any customer, prospect or in-company associate online or by phone, fax, mail, or e-mail. They can print out their own letters and mailing labels for packages to be mailed from their mobile office. Or they can have the letters and labels printed and packages mailed from a central location.

If the investment is deemed worthwhile, a salesperson also can maintain computer video conferencing contact with key personnel. Who needs a permanent office location?

A salesperson could have a van office designed for herself. This shows another way to employ technology to make you more productive or effective than your competitors or peers.

You also might keep the following in mind when considering tremendous, terrible technology.

▶ If you are a novice in the areas of information and technology of the future, the following books may be of interest. The book *2020 Vision* (1991), by Stan Davis and Bill Davidson, discusses brilliantly the importance of information in the future. *Techno Trends*, by Daniel Burrus (1993), discusses 24 emerging technologies. *Paradigm Shift* (1993), by Don Tapscott and Art Caston, is a book for upper managers that discusses the promise of information technology. *Virtual Selling* (1996), by Thomas Siebel and Michael Malone, goes beyond the automated sales force to discuss how to *really* achieve effective sales automation and "total sales quality."

▶ Most business periodicals (such as *Fortune, Inc, The Wall Street Journal, Forbes, Sales and Marketing Management,* and *Home Office Computing*) run frequent articles on emerging technologies. Some have special editions on technology.

PART D

CHAMPIONS

SELL STRATEGICALLY

12

Positioning/ Differentiating/ Focusing as in Strategic Marketing

Establishing in fact (differentiation) and by perception (position-ing)—in the minds of a specific group of customers and prospects (which is focusing)—that you, your company and/or your products and services are different and better in one or more ways—ways that are important to that group.

ILLUSTRATION AND RATING—12A

One way that champions sell strategically is by positioning, differentiating, and focusing. They apply these three aspects of strategic marketing to sell-ing. Champions use them in ways that are "new, different, and better" than their peers and competitors.

In the Introduction, some of the accomplishments of Joe Gandolfo were discussed. Joe sells insurance—excellently. During the late 1970s and early 1980s, his sales were over $800 million seven years in a row. One year he sold a billion dollars of insurance. This is more than a hundred times what the average "good" salesperson sells, who might sell $3 million a year to qualify for the Million Dollar Roundtable.[1]

1. Known in the life insurance industry as MDRT.

Differentiating, Positioning, and Focusing

What does the average insurance salesperson sell? The answer may appear obvious. He sells insurance.

What does the average "good" insurance salesperson sell? Yes, he sells insurance. But that is not what he tries to get the prospect to concentrate on in making a buying decision. What he sells, or attempts to get the prospect to think about and concentrate on, is security or "peace of mind."

What did Joe Gandolfo sell? The answer—tax shelters and financial planning, something that was "new, different, and better" than what even the "good" salespeople sold. Insurance was just one vehicle Joe used to help clients accomplish their tax shelter and financial planning objectives.

Today the tax codes have changed. Tax shelters are not as valuable as they once were. But back in the 1970s they were very important. Especially for high income people who wanted to keep their taxes down. And today financial planning is a big business. But during the 1970s there were few financial planners. That demonstrates that when you apply this strategy and skill it is important to know and take into account the environment and the conditions of the times.

Joe started selling insurance the normal way. While doing this, he noticed a need. The need, especially for higher income people, was for tax shelters and financial planning.

So, while starting to offer these new benefits, Joe went back to college at night. After a few years, he obtained a degree (eventually a Ph.D.) in finance and tax planning, to add to the experience he had gained working with clients. He "differentiated" himself by developing great expertise in a new and more helpful area of customer service. Thus, he truly was qualified to help people save on taxes and plan for their financial futures. He concentrated on selling to corporation executives, physicians, and other high income people. His support staff was trained and led to provide outstanding support service. Thus, he was different from most other insurance salespeople in what he knew, how he sold, and who he sold to.

Joe also "positioned" himself in the minds of customers as a tax shelter and financial planning expert. He did this in part by "focusing" on or specializing in certain industries. Automotive dealerships is one he focused on. He marketed himself to owners in that industry, and positioned himself as a tax shelter expert. To properly position himself, he wrote articles about tax shelters and financial planning. He placed many of his articles in industry-related magazines. He gave speeches on these topics to local groups and associations. He advertised himself as the nation's number one financial planner and tax shelter expert for automotive dealerships. He did this for each selected industry on which he focused.

This gave Joe many advantages over competitive salespeople. For instance, when he phoned an automotive dealership owner and talked to a receptionist, he didn't introduce himself as an insurance salesperson. He might say, "I was the speaker on tax planning at the association meeting that your owner attended last month. I have a few ideas that might substantially reduce income taxes both for him and his dealership." Or he might say, "Your owner asked me to contact him to discuss how he can significantly reduce his income taxes." He positioned himself as someone important. He almost always was put through to the executive.

When he talked to prospects he didn't start out talking about insurance. He said something like, "Are you paying too much in taxes? Let's look at your financial situation. Let's see if we can find ways to help you keep more of the money you earn." That was of interest to executives and higher income people. It probably is of interest to you.

He did many positive things to be effective that the average and even many "good" salespeople do not do. He went back to school and studied related subjects. He invested time and money to prepare himself. He made early morning appointments. He figured that high income people are busy and their time is valuable, but most of them eat breakfast. He concentrated on calling on high income people, the ones that intimidate most salespeople. He found that it was easier to sell a million dollars of insurance to a millionaire than $30,000 of insurance to the average person.

He was very assertive because he believed in the service he was offering. When he phoned, suppose the secretary said, "Mr. Jones doesn't talk to salespeople." He might respond with the comment, "Well, I just have to talk to the only person in the country who never talks to salespeople."

So, to become one of the wealthiest and most successful insurance salespeople of all times, Joe positioned himself. He differentiated himself. He focused.

More on Differentiating

Joel Weldon is a highly successful, highly paid professional speaker. He had a life-changing experience that may be helpful to you.

In the late 1970s, Joel was having moderate success. He was a more-than-adequate professional speaker. He was spending a lot of time and effort designing his promotional material.

Each year he attended the annual convention of the National Speakers Association. One year a speaker he was listening to said something that changed his life. It had to do with getting so good that you didn't *need* promotional materials. Your listeners would promote you through word of mouth. Joel was so motivated that he got up, left the convention in the middle, went home, and immediately revised his approach to speaking. He focused on ways he could differentiate from others and be an even better speaker based on his unique talents and experience.

From that day on he spent much more time on making sure he was getting better than he did on promoting himself and his speaking topics. His audiences responded. Almost entirely through word-of-mouth Joel zoomed to the top of the speaking profession. To this day he remains one of the most successful, most highly regarded speakers in the business. One of Joel's favorite expressions is, "Find out what everyone else is doing, and don't do it!"

More on Positioning

You may be familiar with the classic story about Avis Car Rental.

Back during the 1950s and 1960s Hertz was by far the largest rental car company. National, Avis, and a few others like Budget were all fairly small and of comparable size. One year when the sales figures for the industry came out Avis was number two in sales. It was far behind Hertz, but just slightly ahead of National. Robert Townsend, president of Avis, and his associates came up with a brainstorm. They would "position" Avis. They would advertise and get into the minds of the world that—"Avis is Number Two. We Try Harder!"

So Avis positioned itself, focusing on larger companies—such as DuPont, General Motors and General Electric. It positioned itself as the second largest rental car agency in the world, just behind Hertz—that in its struggle to become number one gave better customer service. The larger companies wanted to have at least two rental car agencies to deal with. And it didn't hurt that it gave better service. So many of them chose Avis along with Hertz. Avis grew tremendously in sales volume.

Avis continually advertised this position. It sent out supporting brochures. It talked about it in the media to continually position itself as number two in the mind of the world.

Avis also differentiated itself by working at improving its customer service. It did have certain inherent advantages. For instance, their advertisements said, "Use Avis, the lines at our counters are shorter." And they were shorter, because Hertz had so much more business at that time.

Application and Examples

So, position yourself, differentiate yourself, and focus effectively. This will create a significant strategic selling advantage for you, and therefore for your company.

It is easy to present examples of this strategy/skill. However, any example for a business or situation different from yours requires that you use your creative mind to apply that example to your business and situation. You need to understand your situation, your strengths and advantages, and your potential areas of focus. You need to understand how your situation is different from the one you are considering. Then you can decide how to position and differentiate yourself using an approach similar to what others used or might use.

When AT&T spun off the Regional Bell Operating Companies (RBOCs, such as Southern Bell) the AT&T engineering departments[2] had to work very hard to keep their core business, which was doing engineering and design for the RBOCs. But the RBOCs had their own engineering departments that attempted to do more and more engineering in-house.

‖ Let's examine how we might help an AT&T central engineer to ‖
be much more effective by positioning/differentiating/focusing.

To start with, she is automatically focused. This is because AT&T's central engineers are organized by technological area—such as grounding, analog switches, and digital switches. Let's say this engineer is working on supporting Southern Bell in the area of digital switches. That's her area of focus. That's where she develops great expertise through experience and study.

We know from our work with AT&T that many of the RBOC engineers did not have well-planned and well-documented engineering skills. (Or at least that's what some at AT&T engineering believed.) As a result, five to ten years out some RBOCs should have problems locating some (or perhaps many) of their switching station lines. Consequently, that is a differentiation and positioning opportunity for our AT&T engineer.

She could position herself as a "long term engineer." This is one who designs and plans things out so there will be few problems ten years down the line. She could do this alone. Or her engineering group, or the entire central AT&T engineering organization, could use this approach.

To promote her positioning, she could send letters and promotional flyers to various management levels within the RBOC she is servicing.[3] This is so higher level people know that there is a potential problem that she claims to solve. Each of them might become uneasy that their peers would feel they are shortsighted if they don't employ a "long term engineering" approach. The easiest way for them to do that, of course, is to contact our "long term engineer" at AT&T.

She should differentiate herself. She should build actual superior skills and capabilities, in addition to positioning herself with "perceived" superior capabilities. She could start doing this by meeting with other engineers and developing specific methods to build even better data networks and keep even better engineering records. She could find and develop expertise in using a high level engineering planning process. This would help her to more effectively deliver what she is promising in her positioning efforts.

2. These are the same AT&T engineering organizations as discussed in Chapter 27.
3. See Chapters 21 and 22 for other things she could do to position and differentiate herself.

A bank trust administrator could focus in certain industries. One, for instance, could be automotive dealerships. After studying the industry, he might determine that a common concern of the owners is that their dealerships survive after the owner dies or retires. So, the bank trust administrator could become positioned as the "corporation continuation trust administrator." He could advertise and send out promotional literature with this focus to that industry. This promotes and supports his positioning. Then he could develop creative methods to help small corporations, especially auto dealership owners, to be able to stay in operation after the owner leaves. This supports his differentiation.

The IBM computer salesperson discussed in Chapter 21 focused on selling computer systems to physicians to help them run their offices better. She positioned herself and IBM as number one in hardware, software, and expertise for physician office management. She did this through her mailings and advertisements, through publicizing the large number of systems IBM sold as compared to competing companies, and through communicating that she had great knowledge about physician office management. Writing articles and giving presentations to the local physician organizations helped.

She differentiated herself by studying the office management of physicians and learning how their offices could use computers more effectively. She also remained in contact with clients and continued to learn as she helped them work through their problems and challenges.

Those are some examples you might look at as you start to position, differentiate, and focus in a "new, different, and better" way.

Thought Provokers

(1) Can you list the positioning, the differentiation, and the focus used by some highly successful salespeople you know?
(2) How about small, successful local businesses?
(3) What position, or impression of how wonderful you are or what you are good at, would be most impressive to your customers? Which would influence them and others to want to buy from you?
(4) Suppose you had that reputation. What would you need to do to deserve it (to differentiate yourself in that area)?
(5) Where might you focus even more effectively?

Take the following rating exercise to estimate how important "positioning, differentiation and focusing" is to your selling success. Based on the results, you can continue on with reading about its implementation, or you can move on to Chapter 13 and Section 13A, and come back later to Section 12B.

CHAPTER RATING (rate A, B, and C below from 1 to 5 for this chapter's importance; then multiply)

_____ **A** = Importance or applicability to you (5 = great, 3 = moderate, 1 = poor)

_____ **B** = Your present strength or level of action (1 = great to 5 = poor) *(reverse rating)*

_____ **C** = Chances of your successful implementation or improvement (5 = great to 1 = poor)

A × B × C = your rating (_____) × (_____) × (_____) = (_____)

If your rating is over 25, read "Implementation" now; if 25 or under, consider postponing until later.

IMPLEMENTATION—12B

The following are 28 ideas to keep in mind when employing the approach of positioning/differentiating/focusing as in strategic marketing. Some of these are discussed in more detail in the book *Positioning,* by Ries and Trout.

(1) Opportunities often don't look like an opportunity but "an angle," such as a lighter beer, a more classy car, a more classy taxi or bus ride, or a cheap hamburger.

(2) You can't predict the future. Instead, react to it, or try to create a new future.

(3) Consider marketing for the opposite point of view, as in marketing gourmet foods when the trend is toward dietary meals.

(4) You need a reason for your business that is compatible with the customer's reality.

(5) Try to fill a void in the marketplace from the point of view of the customer's reality.

(6) Choose something that is not easily copied. For instance, it would be difficult for McDonald's to offer flame broiling to compete with Burger King. It would require a huge investment and a complete change in cooking technique.

(7) With every positive angle comes a negative. Promote the negative, such as having a discount store in a warehouse to support the concept of lower price based on lower costs.

(8) Convert a concept or "tactic" to a strategy through continuous application. The two-for-the-price-of-one-pizza offer could be converted to a two-for-the-price-of-one-pizza business. Make it your "reason for being."

(9) Reposition the competition, such as "drugs are for losers" or Listerine gives "medicine breath."

(10) Make one single, powerful marketing move.

(11) There often is only one place a dominant competitor is vulnerable; attack there.

(12) The name of a company or service is important when positioning in the mind. The name should support the positioning strategy (*Business Week* is a better name for a business magazine than *Fortune*).

(13) The positioning target can be more special than the market you are going after (Marlboro was targeted at the cowboy; the market was *all* cigarette smokers).

(14) Consider shifting the battlefield. Shift the audience; Pepsi targeted the youth. Shift the product; Disney developed Touchtone Pictures for adults. Shift the focus; such as from generalist to specialist. One company shifted from general merchandise to toys and renamed the company Toys 'Я' Us. Shift the distribution channels; as L'Eggs pantyhose from a flat package on a shelf to plastic eggs on a rack at the front of the store.

(15) The concepts for positioning that work best "feel" like new.

(16) The best ideas often are the most obvious; insiders often reject them as "not new."

(17) Make the concept look important.

(18) Cut your losses; pour it on your successes.

(19) Develop a unique marketing presence.

(20) Be first into "position." First in the market's mind is everything: Who was the first person to step on the moon? Who was second?

(21) Take what the market gives you.

(22) Fill a hole in the mind.

(23) Ask what is lacking to make effective what already is possible: What one small step would transform your economic results? What small change would alter the capacity of the whole of your resources?

(24) Practice nichemanship; segment.

(25) Copy-proof your tactics; find a proprietary point of difference.

(26) Fit segments, niches, and positions available to your company's or unit's competency. (Monsanto could not be successful as a consumer products company; mass retailers were successful at building "mass retailing" book stores, book store companies were not.)

(27) Identify your company's areas of greatest expertise and competency, and use those as a guide.

(28) Find the critical issues for your most significant markets and customers. Use those as a guide.

13

Major Account Competitive Selling

Designing your personal marketing plan, value delivery capabilities, and competitive selling strategies to outthink competitors and overwhelm major accounts with your ability to serve their particular needs and generate great results for them.

ILLUSTRATION AND RATING—13A

The title for this chapter could have been the title for this whole book. Champions focus on major market opportunities and major accounts. Essentially every chapter deals with issues that help you to sell effectively and competitively to major accounts.

> How do you outthink competitors and overwhelm major accounts with your ability to serve their particular needs and generate great results for them?

By effectively carrying out the objectives of the six "parts" to this book:[1]

(1) Demonstrating your personal power—thus building the major account's trust and confidence, and making them feel comfortable with you.

(2) Providing great value—where the account wants and needs great value, and communicating that effectively to the account.

(3) Planning and organizing effectively—to effectively and efficiently handle the account.

1. See the section titled "Sales Leadership and Consulting" in "How to Use This Book" for a further understanding of why this is true.

(4) Selling strategically—so you are positioning, differentiating, focusing and maneuvering where it is most effective in dealing with the account and in blocking competitive moves.

(5) Selling professionally—so you are communicating with and servicing the account effectively.

(6) Performing creative marketing—so you are positioning with, communicating to, and helping the account in the highest impact way.

The 27 chapters tell you how. For instance, industry-specific marketing and self marketing help you to be known in a favorable way to the major account and its industry. They, along with "positioning, differentiating and focusing as in strategic marketing," and cultivating strategic relationships, help you to be accepted and even admired by major account decision makers and influencers. Finding and offering specific added value, building partnering relationships, customer support marketing philosophy, and sales consulting help you to deal effectively with and provide great value to major accounts.

Similar statements can be made about most of the other strategies and skills presented. Rereading all the chapters will remind you of ideas on how to be more effective in competitive selling to major accounts.

The 27 strategies and skills apply to all types of selling. Then, what is unique about "major account competitive selling?" It is primarily how you employ team selling and how you develop and implement a "brilliant" major account strategy. These are discussed below.

Six Categories of Accounts

To employ this strategy, choose a small number of major accounts on which to concentrate your selling and servicing effort. They can fall into one of six categories:

(1) very large customers where you need to protect your present business;

(2) very large customers where you want to increase your business penetration;

(3) very large prospects where you are doing little or no business, but which are large potential customers;

(4) smaller companies that are growing rapidly and that you project could become very large customers in the future;

(5) major project proposals; and

(6) major influencers and information providers.

Those in the last category may be small customers. But they share key information readily, influence the decisions of others, and/or perform cutting edge research and development and are a major source of new, business-generating ideas.

Team Selling

Major accounts deserve and usually require the resources of a selling and servicing team. The sections below discuss how that team can be employed. Chapter 19 provides further insight on team selling.

Major Account Strategy

How to apply most of the above six steps to success should be obvious after you read the "A" sections of the 27 chapters. But Step 4, selling strategically, needs further explanation regarding major account selling. It involves developing and continually implementing a "brilliant" competitive strategy that includes the following eight elements:

(1) Gaining the account's confidence and strategically aligning with account and individual account contact objectives.
(2) Identifying and dealing with critical and other key issues that are important to the account and to key account contacts.
(3) Differentiating from competitors in a significant, positive way.
(4) Focusing the account's attention toward areas where you enjoy a competitive advantage.
(5) Gathering continuing commercial intelligence and blocking significant competitive moves.
(6) Providing an effective strategic negotiator, who may or may not be the salesperson.
(7) Providing a competent, effectively led sales team, with each member of the team trained and led to carry out preassigned responsibilities.
(8) Providing strategic follow-up, designed to ensure that the account stays positive and that what is sold is delivered.

Creating a Brilliant Strategy

Paul is a partner in a small, but highly competent, management consulting firm. His firm was introduced late to a large project proposal. It was to redesign the sales approach and organization for a very large company whose industry was undergoing deregulation. It involved changing all aspects of the selling process. This included how the salespeople would be hired, managed, rewarded, and supported. Paul's firm was competing against one of the nation's largest and most highly respected consulting firms. And the larger firm had become involved with the account much earlier.

Paul was faced with a tough situation. Paul and his company were at a huge disadvantage. I was called in to help. One of my assignments was to develop a relationship of confidence and trust with the account's project leader. Another was to gather critical commercial intelligence.

Paul is a highly effective sales negotiator. That was to his advantage. (If he hadn't been, he might have brought in another partner to handle that responsibility.) The larger company did not bring in its top partners when it made its presentation. That also was to his advantage.

Paul's was a small company. But Paul still brought in a large sales team both on information gathering and presentation visits. This strategically positioned Paul's company as a major player. Each member of the team was carefully chosen to develop a relationship and align with a specific decision influencer at the prospective account, to gather needed commercial intelligence, and to provide input to the selling team.

As a result of processing the information gathered, Paul's team developed a creative, "brilliant" proposal strategy. It changed the rules on the playing field while the game was underway.

A critical issue of the most important account decision influencer, the account's project manager, was to not appear to have made a mistake in choosing the consulting firm, for instance, by choosing a firm that couldn't get the job done, thereby wasting time and money. This was a very important project for him, and, in effect, he felt his job was hanging on the outcome.

Paul and his team designed an eight-phase proposal that addressed the critical issue and blocked competition. It focused on skills and processes where Paul's firm was strong, especially during early phases. It started out very inexpensively and became more expensive as it progressed, and as his people became more knowledgeable about and more aligned with the account and its key people.

The first two steps would be performed quickly and below cost. This was far below cost for the larger competitor because of its larger overhead. (Paul's team had to be very confident in its ability to deliver to take a chance on this strategy.)

The project was designed so each step stood on its own. The major account could stop using Paul's company at the end of any step if it chose to and change to a different consulting organization. This made the account project manager comfortable, as it reduced his risk. Paul's team had devised a very creative strategy. It was essentially impossible for the larger company to compete with it. Paul made the sale. He personally was the lead consultant. That helped to ensure that there would be effective follow-up after the sale was made.

Thought Provokers

(1) Who are your major accounts? Who are your major account potentials? Are they the same?

(2) Who are your major competitors for your major accounts?

(3) Do you know enough about them to compete effectively against them?

(4) Do you know enough about your major accounts?

(5) How are you "brilliant" in competitive selling?

Take the following rating exercise to estimate how important "major account competitive selling" is to your selling success. Based on the results, you can continue on with reading about its implementation, or you can move on to Chapter 14 and Section 14A, and come back later to Section 13B.

CHAPTER RATING (rate A, B, and C below from 1 to 5 for this chapter's importance; then multiply)

_____ **A** = Importance or applicability to you (5 = great, 3 = moderate, 1 = poor)

_____ **B** = Your present strength or level of action (1 = great to 5 = poor) *(reverse rating)*

_____ **C** = Chances of your successful implementation or improvement (5 = great to 1 = poor)

A × B × C = your rating   (_____) × (_____) × (_____) = (_____)

If your rating is over 25, read "Implementation" now; if 25 or under, consider postponing until later.

IMPLEMENTATION—13B

The following sections discuss briefly how to develop and continually implement a "brilliant" competitive strategy.

(1) Gain the account's confidence and strategically align with account and individual account contact objectives. Develop a positive personal relationship[2] with all key decision makers and influencers in the account. When using a team selling strategy, specific members of your team may be selected to develop a relationship and align with specific account decision influencers, or members of their team.

To align with them means to get in step with them. It means to understand their personal and business objectives and demonstrate to them that you are in agreement with them and will support their accomplishment.

As a result, each key member of the account's organization will feel comfortable doing business with you. They might even push to do business with you as it will support their personal agendas.

---

2. Chapter 2 discusses specific ways of developing positive personal relationships.

(2) Identify and deal with critical and other key issues that are important to the account and to key account contacts. Critical issues are major concerns of the organization or key decision makers, regardless of a particular buying situation. They are discussed in Chapter 5. Key issues are those specific to a particular buying situation. Both should be identified and addressed satisfactorily by you and your sales team. They might be real issues or imagined. They might deal with real needs of the account. They might be brought up by competitors in an attempt to confuse the situation or put you on the defensive. They might be brought up by you to hint at something negative about the competition.

The following are just a few examples of potential key issues:

- The financial stability and resources of your company
- Your company's reputation for successfully completing work
- The need to have the work completed by a specified time
- The account's CEO needing to look good as a result of the purchase decision[3]
- The need to achieve specific objectives by a specified time

(3) Differentiate from competitors in a significant, positive way. There are areas where your company and your products/services are superior to your competition. There are areas where your competition is stronger.

Determine the account's wants, needs, and critical issues. Work at building up the importance in their minds of the wants and needs that you can solve more effectively than your competition. Adjust what your company offers to more closely fit their wants, needs, and critical issues as best you can. This may require that you develop some added value services.

Present and position your company and your product/service offering as being different from and better than that of the competition, as related to the account's needs and its critical issues.

(4) Focus the account's attention toward areas where you enjoy a competitive advantage. Emphasize those aspects of the account's wants, needs, critical issues, and key issues where you are strong, or where you can make a case that you are strong, as compared to competition.

Ask questions, such as SPIN questions,[4] to cause the account to think about those problems and concerns that you can solve better than the competition. Don't ask questions and encourage the customer to think about areas where your competition is stronger.[5]

---

3. The need for the account's CEO to look good generally could be a critical issue. The general need makes it a critical issue. The specific need related to this particular decision makes it a key issue.

4. See Chapter 17.

5. Remember that during this process you are doing what you can to legitimately provide the customer "great value" using the processes in Chapters 5–8, thereby giving you a legitimate competitive advantage.

(5) Gather continuing commercial intelligence and block significant competitive moves. Knowledge is power. Determine what types of information (such as account objectives, personal motives and objectives of key decision influencers and decision makers, how previous decisions were made, and competitive strengths) are needed to make effective decisions and take effective actions. Determine who should be gathering each type of information and how. Make commercial intelligence assignments. Encourage everyone involved to keep their eyes open and report any new piece of information to a central gathering point.

Once you determine that your competitor has taken a particular action that might put it in a preferred position, or that might threaten your position, then decide on what blocking moves are appropriate. Particularly threatening competitive moves might cause you to bring together the entire selling team to bring everyone up-to-date and decide the action to be taken in response.

For instance, suppose the competitor brings in its CEO to meet the account's CEO. This means that decision making might be moved to a higher level. The following are some different competitive moves you could make:

► Arrange for your CEO also to meet with the account's CEO.
► Arrange for an outside expert to meet with the CEO to help him with a specific problem or challenge. This may provide you the opportunity to meet and start to develop a relationship with the account's CEO under favorable circumstances.
► Arrange for your board of directors to meet with the account's board.
► Assign a member of your team to find out what happened at the meeting and how the meeting affects your competitive situation.
► Design a strategy to make the competitor's CEO-CEO visit into a negative, such as pointing out how a company that is so frivolous with its expensive people eventually overcharges for its services.

Of course, in addition to blocking competitive moves, you also will be proactive. Consequently, your selling team may decide on one of the above actions as an offensive rather than as a defensive move.

(6) Provide an effective strategic negotiator, who may or may not be the salesperson. You as the salesperson for a major account are the prime contact for the account. You develop relationships and stay in touch with key personnel. You lead the selling team and coordinate with one or more specialists on the team (say, an engineer) who maintain contact with specialists at the account (say, their design or process engineer). You coordinate intelligence gathering.

If there are team meetings with the account, you arrange the meetings and get them started. You stay in touch with the account after the sale is made and make sure that what is agreed to gets done.

You may or may not negotiate the contract or major arrangement with the account. If you are a strong strategic negotiator, you probably will. If you are not, or if there are major problems to deal with, you may bring in an outside negotiator to deal with that specific situation.

There are two key advantages for bringing in an outside strategic negotiator.

First, there may be another salesperson or manager who is particularly skilled at negotiating contracts or handling problem situations. She may have a better chance than you of getting the business because of her particular strengths.

Second, if your company must be "tough" in dealing with the account, or it must refuse an important request by the account, it may be advisable for you to bring in someone else to deal with that situation. That person can be the "bad guy." You, as the salesperson, can remain the "good guy." During the negotiations you might even take the side of the account. After the negotiations, you will remain behind to pick up the pieces and make the relationship work. You can do this easier if you have not been forced to confront the account in a negative way.

You can learn from the visiting "strategic negotiator." Perhaps in a similar situation you will be brought in to assist another salesperson.

(7) Provide a competent, effectively led sales team, with each member of the team trained and led to carry out preassigned responsibilities. In dealing with a large account or complex situation, you might not have the expertise or time to deal with all the account contacts and situations. Your engineer may deal more effectively with their engineer, your chemist with their chemist, and your accountant with their accountant. Lower paid customer service people may deal effectively with certain clerical and other front line people at the account, thereby freeing you up to do more important things. An upper management member may be included to provide perspective, make key decisions, and develop upper level relationships at the account. Any or all of these may be on your sales team.

Each team member will have responsibilities related to gathering information and commercial intelligence, developing relationships, seeking out and solving problems, communicating positive aspects of your company to key account decision influencers, carrying out specific assignments, and attending and participating in team strategic planning meetings.

You probably will lead the team. You will bring the team together in person and over the phone (and perhaps online through computer communications) to share information, make input from their perspectives, make joint decisions, and receive assignments.

(8) Provide strategic follow-up, designed to ensure that the account stays positive and that what is sold is delivered. Continuing, repeat, and referral business comes from satisfied customers.[6] Providing strategic follow-up is a key aspect of major account competitive selling.

More on Issues, Values, and Relationships

Determine the critical issues of major accounts. Get to know the issues so well that you know them even better than your accounts. Thus, you know where their problems and opportunities lie, what their culture is, where their business is heading, and what is important to them.

Develop your value packages[7] so you and your company offer the best total value to major accounts. Encourage your company to modify product/service lines to fit major account needs, assuming it can be profit-justified. Develop your own added value capabilities to fit their needs. If possible, become important to them because of what you do for them personally, so important that they buy from your company just to obtain your services, or those you can arrange for them.

Develop close relationships with major accounts and account contacts. Call on key decision makers, decision influencers, and sources of information, using your team members as appropriate. And stay in touch with them all. Be an overcommunicator. Keep yourself informed and keep them informed. If in doubt, communicate. Get to know the key contacts as individuals so you can adjust your calls and personality to their interests and styles.

Make a conscious effort to earn their friendships. But even more important, earn their trust and respect. Keep records on them:[8] information such as their birthdays, likes, dislikes, motives, what has brought them great joy, and what has brought them great frustration/irritation. Determine their personal objectives, agendas, and potential result-wins. Align yourself with them. Make them believe they will benefit personally by working with you and giving your company business. Deliver on those beliefs.

Anticipate the major purchases and purchase decisions they will be making. Keep your eyes open. In the most important areas related to your business, become known for your expertise. Or help a back-up person in your company become recognized for her expertise.

Proactively help major accounts establish their major decision criteria in line with your company's strengths. This is because you genuinely are concerned for the account's welfare. And you have planned ahead to solve their particular problems in a way valuable to them.

Know key competitive companies. Obtain as much knowledge as possible on competitive salespeople and their sales organizations. Know their

6. See Chapter 27 for Frontline Marketing.
7. For an explanation of $ value, see Appendix B.
8. For an interesting list of personal commercial intelligence and some supporting thoughts on its value, see *Swim With the Sharks Without Being Eaten Alive* by Harvey Mackay.

strengths, weaknesses, vulnerabilities, and how they work and think. Determine how they sell, what they claim their benefits and advantages to be, and what is their supporting evidence. Keep commercial intelligence records, and keep them up-to-date.

Competitive Strategies

The following are some fundamentals to consider in creating competitive selling strategies.

- Focus decision criteria into areas where you are strong and the competitor is weak—pick the battleground.
- Disguise your battle plan so the competitor wastes its time fighting about issues that are unimportant to the account.
- Find out what the account wants and provide it.
- Find the account's and account contacts' emotional issues and position yourself positively to them, while positioning the competitor negatively.
- Stay close to the account during days leading up to the final decision to determine last minute problems and roadblocks. Be alert to a competitive counterattack so you can quickly regroup and re-counter.
- Don't be blindsided. Don't ignore non-traditional competitors that may solve the problem with a new approach proven in another industry. In the example above, Paul blindsided the larger consulting company.
- Position your company positively in relationship to the project or to the account's critical issues.
- When appropriate, position your competitor in an unfavorable way in regard to the major account or its decision criteria. For instance, Listerine, the leading mouthwash, was positioned negatively by the competitor's advertisement about "medicine breath."

14

Cultivating Strategic Relationships

Finding and developing relationships with, and the confidence of, key, influential people and institutions that can positively influence your selling success.

ILLUSTRATION AND RATING—14A

One of our projects with AT&T was to help the engineering division find and start up new businesses. One of the new businesses was cable TV engineering support.

AT&T's goal was to become the primary engineering resource for major projects in the cable TV industry. As part of the AT&T marketing/sales effort, the sales engineers in the business unit cultivated "strategic relationships" in the industry.

They contacted industry magazine editors and established communications with them. They wrote articles for technical magazines that supported the cable TV industry. They identified key industry decision makers and influencers (for instance, suppliers of major transmission equipment) and sent regular mailings to them. They manned display booths at cable TV conventions. They gave papers at some of the meetings. They identified key movers and shakers in the industry and worked at developing professional and personal relationships with them.

Engineers and managers—especially from the smaller cable TV companies—often looked outside for engineering support. For instance, they might contact a college professor or the chief engineer at one of the larger companies for advice. They often were referred to AT&T engineering, and to a particular sales engineer at AT&T, because the AT&T sales engineers had cultivated strategic relationships within the cable TV industry.

| Strategic relationships are with people and organizations that can significantly affect your selling success. |

They can give you insight. They can provide you with valuable information, contacts, or resources. They can give you referrals and testimonials. They can put in a good word for you with the right people at the right time. They can support your company or selling proposition.

Depending on your selling situation, different types of people and organizations will be of strategic importance to you.

For the IBM computer salesperson who performed industry-support marketing,[1] the editor of the newsletter for the local AMA chapter should be a strategic relationship.

In St. Louis, the top real estate salesperson in the city had formerly worked under the manager of the relocation department for Monsanto Company, the city's second largest employer. She maintained and cultivated that strategic relationship. She received many relocation referrals for Monsanto people who were changing locations.

Many bank loan officers find it profitable to be active in the local Chamber of Commerce. There they develop relationships with corporate officers who can refer them to company financial and operations executives.

A top salesperson for a major chemical products manufacturer developed strategic relationships with retired executives from some of his major customers and prospects. Through them, he received both introductions to key decision makers in their former companies, and advice on how best to approach them.

A small cleaning supply company owner became friends with the regional chief industrial engineer for the Kroger Company. The engineer was having difficulty finding good companies to clean their supermarket floors. The Kroger engineer put the supplier in the floor cleaning business and assigned his company a number of stores to clean. This developed into a profitable new business for his company.

Thought Provokers

(1) Who—if you knew them well and they liked and respected you— could help you get significantly more business?

(2) Who would be a good source of information or leads?

(3) What is it about your personality, experience, and/or knowledge that attracts people and impresses them favorably? What types of people are so impressed?

(4) Where would it be most beneficial to you to improve your personality, experience, or knowledge?

1. Discussed in Chapter 21.

(5) What might be a good formula for you to use to cultivate strategic business relationships?

Take the following rating exercise to estimate how important "cultivating strategic relationships" is to your selling success. Based on the results, you can continue on with reading about its implementation, or you can move on to Chapter 15 and Section 15A, and come back later to Section 14B.

CHAPTER RATING (rate A, B, and C below from 1 to 5 for this chapter's importance; then multiply)

_____ **A** = Importance or applicability to you (5 = great, 3 = moderate, 1 = poor)

_____ **B** = Your present strength or level of action (1 = great to 5 = poor) *(reverse rating)*

_____ **C** = Chances of your successful implementation or improvement (5 = great to 1 = poor)

A × B × C = your rating   (_____) × (_____) × (_____) = (_____)

If your rating is over 25, read "Implementation" now; if 25 or under, consider postponing until later.

IMPLEMENTATION—14B

The following are some categories of strategic relationships to consider cultivating. Which ones should you consider for implementation?

- ► Industry association executives
- ► Industry magazine editors
- ► Retired executives from major customers and prospects
- ► Club members of organizations to which key contacts belong
- ► Business friends of key contacts
- ► Potential key decision makers within your major customers
- ► Potential key decision makers in other large potential customers
- ► Non-decision making influencers in your major customers
- ► Non-decision making influencers in other large potential customers
- ► Major suppliers to your type of industry
- ► Important, non-competitive suppliers to your customers
- ► Industry luminaries
- ► Key consultants to your industry
- ► Key consultants to industries on which you are focusing
- ► Venture capitalists
- ► Key professionals in competitive companies (perhaps for collabora-

tive relationships—to reduce your costs; to help increase your credi-
bility; to get access to new technology; to allow you to accomplish
objectives you could not accomplish alone)
- Key personnel in companies that are potential sources of a support-
  ing technology
- Potential collaborators, licensees, and marketers for your services in
  foreign countries
- Business and news press
- Trade press
- Financial analysts
- Innovating and early adapting companies and people

Strategic relationships can lead you to new potential business and then
guide you to the most effective approach for obtaining that business.

15

Leveraging Your Selling

Finding ways to increase the impact on the customer of your selling approach and presentation, or to contact and influence multiple prospects or customers at the same time or in one effort, such as by making presentations at association meetings.

ILLUSTRATION AND RATING—15A

Leveraging your selling involves both increasing the impact of your selling and finding ways to influence multiple prospects or customers at the same time. You can do either or both.

Increasing Impact

There are numerous ways to increase the impact of your selling.

One of the most effective is to obtain referrals to qualified prospects, preferably from highly satisfied customers. People are more interested in meeting with you and listening to your ideas if you have been referred to them by a respected friend or business associate. After giving great service, plan at the appropriate time to ask satisfied customers for referrals, and specify the type of referrals you are seeking—a description of the type of company or person you most likely can help in a major way based on your differentiation, positioning, and focus (see Chapter 12).

Or you might increase your impact by developing and offering creative evidence, or an unusual form of evidence, that the prospect finds both interesting and believable. An example might be a videotape of happy customers showing their facilities and processes. The customers would be making positive comments about you, your company, and its products and services.

You might design an "overwhelming" business case. Describing it makes obvious to the prospect the benefits of purchasing your product or service.

You might increase your impact by finding some way, perhaps through industry-specific self marketing, to get customers to come looking for you because they have heard of you in a favorable light, or because they think of you as a celebrity in their industry. If they come looking for you, they listen to you with more intensity and are more easily persuaded to follow your suggestions, than if you are pursuing them.

■   Selling in a way is like chopping wood.   ▉

In selling, you hit the customer repeatedly with a selling message. In chopping wood, you hit the log repeatedly with an ax head. In both, if you increase the impact, you make more progress.

(Also, if you effectively strike a number of logs together at the same time you'll cut more wood. That brings us to the next section.)

Influencing Multiple Prospects or Customers

There are a number of ways to influence a number of prospects or customers at the same time. An obvious way is through presentations.

Joe, a self-employed computer software engineer, sold primarily through offering technical presentations at maintenance association meetings. There were a lot of meetings, and it supposedly was an honor to be chosen to present at the meetings. Thus, he was positioned as an expert in designing, specifying, and servicing software programs for preventative maintenance and other maintenance systems. (He *was* an expert.) Through his presentations he was, in effect, making sales presentations for his consulting services and software products to hundreds of potential maintenance management clients at one time. He obtained a list of all those attending the meetings and followed up with mailings and phone calls.

Keith Dillon is a real estate mortgage salesperson in a large city. In the early 1980s, he totally changed his strategy and style of selling. This resulted in increasing his sales by five times, and his personal income from around $50,000 per year to more than $250,000 per year.

Recently, I asked Keith if he still was selling the new way and outdistancing all competitors in his city. He said that not only was he still dominating the marketplace, but that no one in his city had picked up on what he was doing and tried to emulate it.[1]

Before the change, Keith had sold like everyone else. He personally visited residential real estate offices. He called on real estate agents (salespeople) who were at their desks or standing around shooting the bull. He asked them to place the mortgages for houses they sold with his company.

(You might note that the agents who were selling the most houses and

---

1. Thus they may have violated the first principle of "new business marketing," discussed in strategies/skills #24 and 25—being alert to and reacting to change. One way of increasing your selling success is to determine what the very successful salespeople are doing and see if you can adapt and improve on it for your selling situation.

generating the most mortgages were usually out of the office. They were showing and listing houses, and therefore frequently unavailable for effective contact with this "normal" method of selling.)

Keith took a public speaking course. During the course, he got the idea of offering a seminar on "creative financing" to real estate offices. (Large agencies have tens of offices, each with a number of real estate agents.) He had some expertise in this area and decided to learn more. He developed a seminar on creative financing and gave it to one of the local real estate offices.

The results were very positive. The people learned a lot and were impressed by Keith's knowledge and ideas. Some phoned him later to ask questions and to get clarifications of his ideas. He spent much time on the phone with them. Many of them placed their home mortgage business with him. He became a consultant to them. He was referred to and gave creative financing seminars to a number of other real estate offices in the city. In a short period, Keith had little time to do anything else but remain in his office, answer questions on the phone, and take orders for mortgage loans. He received a commission on each order taken.

Both Keith and Joe were highly successful by leveraging their selling.

Thought Provokers

(1) What can you do to get more bang for the buck—to get more sales from your time and effort expended?
(2) Who do you know who is using leveraging in their selling? What can you learn from them?
(3) Where are opportunities for you to give presentations to groups of potential customers?
(4) Can you make an interesting presentation? If so, what might you present and to whom to leverage your selling?

Take the following rating exercise to estimate how important "leveraging your selling" is to your selling success. Based on the results, you can continue on with reading about its implementation, or you can move on to Chapter 16 and Section 16A, and come back later to Section 15B.

CHAPTER RATING (rate A, B, and C below from 1 to 5 for this chapter's importance; then multiply)

_____ **A** = Importance or applicability to you (5 = great, 3 = moderate, 1 = poor)

_____ **B** = Your present strength or level of action (1 = great to 5 = poor) *(reverse rating)*

_____ **C** = Chances of your successful implementation or improvement (5 = great to 1 = poor)

A × B × C = your rating   (_____) × (_____) × (_____) = (_____)

If your rating is over 25, read "Implementation" now; if 25 or under, consider postponing until later.

IMPLEMENTATION—15B

You can leverage your selling as a tactic or as a strategy. As a tactic, it is one of many actions you take to sell effectively. As a strategy, it is the primary way you sell, as was the case for Keith Dillon above. If Keith had sold the old way, but had used presentations as a way to obtain additional prospects, or as a way to increase his "celebrity," then what he did would have been a tactic. Many of the following ideas can be used as a tactic or as a strategy.

Increasing Impact

The following are some additional ways to increase the impact of your selling: obtaining powerful referrals, selling to upper management and getting them on your side, going after "hot" critical issues, identifying and tying to key personal benefits of decision makers or powerful decision influencers, becoming a celebrity so you are very welcome at the account, becoming a recognized expert so you have the extreme respect of the decision maker, achieving a partnership status so the account trusts you, achieving the reputation of being a success generator, and generating a major success that others wish to copy.

Making Multiple Contacts

The following are some additional ways to make multiple contacts: achieving frontline marketing whereby many people in your company assist you in selling, cross-marketing whereby other organizations market and sell your products and services, hiring or utilizing multiple assistants, effectively utilizing the members of your sales team, making multiple mailings, writing books that tend to generate inquiries, writing magazine articles that tend to generate inquiries, publishing a newsletter, developing word-of-mouth communications about you and your solutions, making association presentations, advertising, establishing a proactive referral network such as Joe Girard (judged as the world's number one salesperson by the *Guinness Book of Records)* set up by providing rewards for referrals, and obtaining favorable publicity such as from a favorable article being written about you.

    The following are some ideas to keep in mind when leveraging your selling.

- ► List all the ways you can think of to increase the impact on customers (shock them, surprise them, get them excited, impress them favorably) of your selling approach or presentation. Choose the best ones for further evaluation.
- ► List all the ways you can think of to influence a number of prospects or customers at the same time. Think beyond presentations. For in-

stance, you can involve other associates in your selling. You can hire assistants to do prospecting for you. You can send out powerful letters, articles, or videotapes. Choose the best ones for further evaluation.

- ► Proactively look for ways to provide added value to customers effectively and economically.
- ► Employ team selling as appropriate (in which different members of the team bring in different strengths and knowledge).
- ► Get customers involved in the selling process (which in itself builds their interest and commitment).
- ► Sell to individuals (and their wants, needs, and result-wins as individuals) as well as to the organizations they represent.
- ► Price products in ways that customers can conveniently buy (as, for instance, leasing to provide tax benefits and lower cash flow requirements).
- ► Initiate new ideas and approaches with "innovators" or "early adapting organizations" and not with "followers" or "laggards."
- ► Make your "selling package" (brochures, supporting materials, samples, how you dress, your customer approach) professional and appropriate.

PART E

CHAMPIONS

SELL PROFESSIONALLY

16

Commitment to a Concept/Philosophy

Developing a concept or philosophy you really believe in for providing great value to customers—related to the purchase of your company's products and services—and then preparing yourself to competently discuss it with prospects, and to ensure that it and its values are delivered after it is purchased.

ILLUSTRATION AND RATING—16A

Champions sell professionally. One way is through commitment to a concept or philosophy.

Martin Shafiroff of Lehman Brothers is one of the nation's top securities salespeople. He has a highly successful concept or selling philosophy. It is "low price-to-earning stocks that are out-of-favor with the experts, but that have, by his calculations, a low down-side risk and high growth potential."

He therefore is confident of the value he offers. He is successful at phoning executives all around the country. He discusses with them his investment concept or investment philosophy, which has made money for many others, and which he strongly believes will make money for them. He has been extremely successful. He has earned commissions of more than two million dollars a year.

Joe Gandolfo's concept[1] of providing tax shelters led him to a billion dollars in sales in one year. He saves money for customers through reducing the tax take and other financial management devices. These include insurance where appropriate.

A cleaning products supply salesperson developed the concept of

---

1. Described in strategy/skill #12.

"quality products compatible with cost-saving cleaning methods." The salesperson himself researched and tested cleaning methods on his own time. He developed superior, time-saving cleaning methods compatible with his company's products.

His company could have done this for him and its other salespeople to their mutual advantage. But it didn't. So he did. That's why he outsells his peers.

> Some concepts involve large resources and must be developed by the corporation for all the salespeople to use. Others seem to require corporate effort, but don't.

Champions take a creative approach. They often accomplish an equivalent or almost equivalent result for a small fraction of the cost. They develop and perfect the concept for their own use and selling success.

Instead of talking to your clients or prospects about buying one of your products or services, talk to them about investing in your concept. Have them purchase your concept. Get them involved with your philosophy, which will benefit them in a clear way.

> Your concept, almost by definition, will be different from anything that any other salesperson or organization has offered to them. It has special advantages and customer values that have been designed into it.

It is more difficult for prospects to refuse to see you if you are offering a concept. They can say they are satisfied with a competitive product or service. It is much more difficult for them to say they aren't interested in a concept that might make them a lot of money or bring them a lot of happiness, or that has done that for others. For one reason, on the phone it is very difficult for them to clearly understand the specifics of what you are talking about. But it sounds so good. And designed properly, a concept can provide much more value to the customer than just products and services alone.

Thought Provokers

(1) What is a concept? What is a philosophy?
(2) What was so good about Martin Shafiroff's concept or philosophy?
(3) What did it do that was special for him? What did it do for others?
(4) Why is commitment so important?
(5) Should you develop just one or a number of selling concepts?

Take the following rating exercise to estimate how important "commitment to a concept or philosophy" is to your selling success. Based on the results, you can continue on with reading about its implementation, or you can move on to Chapter 17 and Section 17A, and come back later to Section 16B.

CHAPTER RATING (rate A, B, and C below from 1 to 5 for this chapter's importance; then multiply)

_____ **A** = Importance or applicability to you (5 = great, 3 = moderate, 1 = poor)

_____ **B** = Your present strength or level of action (1 = great to 5 = poor) *(reverse rating)*

_____ **C** = Chances of your successful implementation or improvement (5 = great to 1 = poor)

A × B × C = your rating   (_____) × (_____) × (_____) = (_____)

If your rating is over 25, read "Implementation" now; if 25 or under, consider postponing until later.

IMPLEMENTATION—16B

It is a little difficult to explain what a concept or philosophy is. You almost have to think about it and play with it to grasp its meaning and significance. It is an overall approach to providing great value to the customer. It incorporates your products, services, and/or added value in some combination, which serves one or more critical issues for one or more high potential customer segments. It attracts the attention and interest of the prospect because it is different, if not unique. It produces or implies a customer benefit. But it is not obvious to most people how you are going to make that benefit happen, at least to the great extent that you imply. In a way it is a system with a reason for being, a reason for why it provides such great value.

The following are some ideas to keep in mind when looking for or employing commitment to a concept or philosophy.

► List every combination of products, services, and added value you can make that provides great value to customers.
► List every critical issue of major segments, and then write in one sentence what you might offer to solve or minister to each critical issue.
► Then look for the magic. Look for the phrase or sentence that really grabs you and really provides great value to a major customer segment.
► The first word of this strategy is "commitment." Your concept must

be something you really believe in and can defend if challenged. And it will be challenged.

► Have a group of knowledgeable friends, perhaps including some customers, meet with you to challenge your concept, help you improve it, and help you strengthen your ability to defend and present it.

► Before deciding on your concept or philosophy, make a list of all possible (competitive) concepts and compare them from the customer's point of view.

► The concept is most effective when it "grabs you" and you feel so strongly about it that even though you compare it with others, there is no comparison in your mind.

► The most effective concept usually comes out of your experience in the industry and perhaps as the result of an "aha" experience. It may not be obvious to anyone other than you, at least at first. Otherwise, it would already be widely employed.

► An effective concept or philosophy can be simple and something that people have overlooked for years. This may be because it seemed so simple and obvious and they didn't quite understand how it could be made so valuable to the customer.

► Frequently your particular experience, talents, or interests are an integral part of the concept.

► One concept (or philosophy) may be more appropriate to one customer segment (for instance, industry, market, or set of customer characteristics such as age or technology base) and another concept more appropriate to another. Thus, you can use your concept to choose your area of focus. Or you can fit your concept to the area(s) of focus you have chosen.

► From the customer's point of view, you come across as more knowledgeable and more professional when you are offering a concept (which incorporates a product or service) as compared to offering just the product or service. This assumes that the concept makes some sense to them.

► Suppose, in attempting to make an initial appointment, you say that "I would like to share a concept, philosophy, or idea with the prospect that has been of considerable help to others." You imply that whether or not the prospect purchases from you its people will come out of the meeting educated in some way that might in the future benefit them.

17

Preventing Rejection and Objections

Preventing rejection, and preventing objections instead of just handling them—through marketing yourself, having a customer-serving attitude, developing customer-serving value, and employing methods like planned SPIN questioning that lead customers to satisfying and value-producing conclusions.

ILLUSTRATION AND RATING—17A

Rejection comes in many forms to most salespeople. Dealing with rejection and objections is probably considered by most to be the most distasteful and difficult aspect of selling. It is what keeps so many people from trying selling in the first place. Dealing with rejection and objections is not the favorite pastime of most selling champions. But all have developed an approach that works for them. For most, the approach is similar.

You can't prevent all rejection. It is a natural part of the selling environment. Many prospects don't need what you sell. Some really are satisfied with their present supplier. But the "I'm satisfied" put-off is more often an excuse to not talk to another salesperson than it is a legitimate feeling or belief.

| And that gives you the first clue to preventing rejection and objections. You should not be just "another salesperson." |

You should be much more, and much more valuable to the account. You should position yourself to be, and be, a different kind of animal. You must find a way to communicate to that prospect, and to most prospects—that you are in an entirely different, and better, category than any salesperson they have ever met.

How do you do that? The strategies and skills discussed in this book tell you how. And they tell you how to be effective in dealing with reluctant prospects when you do meet them. You are more valuable to the prospect, and offer much more value than any of your competitors, if you effectively implement these strategies and skills.[1] That reduces both rejection and objections substantially.

You position yourself as an important and valuable resource who understands the prospect's business.[2] That reduces rejection and objections substantially.

You deal effectively with prospects, cause them to feel comfortable with you, and persuasively lead them to do business with you if you perform the basics creatively as discussed in the Appendixes. But even more so if you effectively implement some of the other strategies and skills.[3] That also reduces rejection and objections substantially.

A Specialized Strategy and Skill

However, there is one additional strategy and skill that will be particularly valuable to you in preventing rejection and objections.

You have been told, and probably taught, that you need to effectively handle objections. And that is correct. Keep a record of the objections you receive. Spend some "not urgent/important" time[4] devising ways to answer them effectively.

As appropriate, use the feel-felt-found method of answering objections. It goes like this. "I know how you feel. Many of our best customers felt the same way until they found (and you say at this point what great thing they found about your product or service that overcomes or should be more important to the prospect than the objection)."

Many sales managers and trainers make statements like these. "Objections are your friends." "You don't know what is important to the customer until you get an objection." "Prospects aren't interested if they aren't throwing up some objections."

There is some merit to that thinking in the more traditional ways of selling. But there is no merit to that thinking in the more effective approach to selling presented in this book. You are genuinely attempting to help the customer. You spend much time and effort learning customers' needs and how to help them solve those needs. You market and position yourself effectively. There will be questions. There is no need for objections.

---

1. Especially numbers 4, 5, 6, 7, 8, 9, 10, 11, 16, 18, 19, 20, 21, 23, 25, 26, and 27.
2. Strategies and skills numbers 4, 5, 7, 9, 10, 12, 13, 14, 20, 21, and 22.
3. Strategies and skills numbers 1, 2, 3, 14, 19, 20, 21, 22, and 27.
4. See Chapter 9, Section 6.

> For years our organization has been using and training others to use a questioning method that eliminates the need for objections.

It allows prospects to be the hero. It helps them to understand their problems, the magnitude of their problems, and the importance of solving them. It is similar to a method called SPIN questioning. SPIN questioning was developed by Neil Rackham and his company while working with XEROX in the early 1980s. We find Rackham's terminology and rationale to be clear. We now use it in our own training.

One of the advantages of "planned SPIN questioning" is that it tends to prevent objections from occurring. We'll first talk about SPIN questioning. Then we'll discuss planning for its use.

Thought Provokers

(1) Is rejection a problem for you now? Why?
(2) What ideas have you already received for better dealing with rejection?
(3) What major objections do you receive?
(4) Would it be better to anticipate and handle objections early, let them come up and handle them, or prevent them from occurring?
(5) How would you prevent them from occurring?

Take the following rating exercise to estimate how important "preventing rejection and objections" is to your selling success. Based on the results, you can continue on with reading about its implementation, or you can move on to Chapter 18 and Section 18A, and come back later to Section 17B.

CHAPTER RATING (rate A, B, and C below from 1 to 5 for this chapter's importance; then multiply)

_____ **A** = Importance or applicability to you (5 = great, 3 = moderate, 1 = poor)

_____ **B** = Your present strength or level of action (1 = great to 5 = poor) *(reverse rating)*

_____ **C** = Chances of your successful implementation or improvement (5 = great to 1 = poor)

A × B × C = your rating (_____) × (_____) × (_____) = (_____)

If your rating is over 25, read "Implementation" now; if 25 or under, consider postponing until later.

IMPLEMENTATION—17B

SPIN[5] is an acronym representing four types of questions you can ask the prospect: S for situation questions, P for problem questions, I for implication questions, and N for need-payoff questions.

Situation questions are those that help to identify the prospect's situation. They are questions like, "How many people do you have?" "Who have you purchased from?" "How did they most help you?" "Could you tell me about your growth plans?" "How do you get your instruments calibrated now?"

Problem questions are those that help to identify a problem, need, or want the prospect has. They make the prospect hurt or feel uncomfortable. These are questions like, "Where is your present system less effective than you would like?" "What pressures are you receiving from your clients?" "Are you behind in processing any claims?" "Where are you less effective than you would like, and why?" "When you don't get parts in as fast as you'd like, is this a problem?"

Implications are problems of the problem. They are implications or additional negative results that flow out of or result from a problem. *Implication questions* ask which of those down-the-line concerns the prospect has. They make the prospect hurt more. These are questions like, "Does that cause you further difficulties?" "How does that affect your office rating?" "How does that make you and your manager feel?" "Does that increase your costs?" "How does slow delivery to you affect your ability to satisfy your customers?"

Need-payoff questions are those that identify benefits the prospect will receive from solving the problems and removing the implications. Supposedly the solution uses your products and services, but during questioning the prospect is not necessarily aware of that.

Need-payoff questions make the prospect feel better, or even good and happy. They are questions like, "How would solving that help you?" "What would be the effect of closing out difficult cases sooner?" "Would it be helpful to have guaranteed one-day availability of those parts?" "What would be the result if that inventory control problem were solved?"

The average salesperson uses far too many situation questions. This can cause the prospect to become irritated. And it takes time away from the more important problem, implication, and need-payoff questions.

There is a reason salespeople tend to ask many situation questions. They are easy to ask and don't threaten the prospect. Also, many salespeople don't do enough homework. Frequently, you can get most situation questions answered before you call on a decision maker. You can review the

5. For a more detailed description of SPIN questioning and related ideas, see Neil Rackham's book, *SPIN Selling*.

annual report, read newspaper clippings, and talk to one or more non-decision makers, for instance.

Field tests indicate that there is no relationship between the number and quality of situation questions asked and the percentage of sales closed.

Field tests indicate that for the lower level sale there is a direct relationship between the number and quality of problem questions asked and percentage of sales closed. The lower level sale doesn't cost too much and/or doesn't make the prospect look too bad if it makes the wrong buying decision—like office supplies or $10.00 calculators.

However, for the higher level sale there is no direct relationship between the number and quality of problem questions asked and percentage of sales closed. The higher level sale costs a lot and/or makes the prospect look bad if it makes a mistake—like an automobile, large computer system, or major consulting contract.

But there is a direct relationship for both types of sale between the number and quality of implication and need-payoff questions and percentage of sales closed. Consequently, you should concentrate on improving the number and quality of your implication and need-payoff questions. This is particularly true for higher level sales.

The following diagram of the SPIN objection prevention process demonstrates a simple example of how the average salesperson asks questions that cause objections to occur. It then demonstrates where the salesperson goes wrong, and how to prevent objections. Objections are prevented by asking implication and need-payoff questions at the right time. Thus, prospects becomes the expert. They explain to themselves, with your help, how terrible the problem is and what great benefits would be received by solving it (supposedly by using your products or services).

OBJECTION PREVENTION PROCESS

Normal Questioning Process That Encourages Objections

Salesperson asks some:

1. *Situation questions* (such as, "What types of equipment do you have?")
   The prospect answers them.
   Then the salesperson asks some:
2. *Problem questions* (such as, "Is your present system operating fast enough?")
   The prospect answers, "No, it needs to operate faster."
3. This implies the prospect has a need for a faster system. (Implied need)

4. The salesperson has a solution: the "Fast Flow" system. (Implied solution)

The salesperson offers the solution to the implied need or problem, by saying:

5. "Our Fast Flow system is twice as fast as the one you have." (Implied benefit)

The prospect asks, "What does it cost?"

The salesperson answers, "$20,000."

6. The prospect responds, "That's more than it's worth." (Objection)

The salesperson now must answer an objection because she stopped the questioning process too early. She should have asked implication and need-payoff questions. These build the importance of the problem and the benefit and value of a solution in the prospect's mind. Let's start again at the end of step 3 where the salesperson found an implied need, and through implication and need-payoff questions turn the implied need into an explicit need.

SPIN Questioning Process That Prevents Objections

Salesperson responds to the answer, "No, it needs to operate faster," with:

4. *Implication question* (such as, "How does it hurt you to operate too slowly?")

To which the prospect responds, "It causes us to double cycle the catalyst."

To which the salesperson asks another:

5. *Implication question* (such as, "What effect does that have?")

To which the prospect responds, "We have to work an extra shift twice a week."

To which the salesperson asks a:

6. *Need-payoff question* "How would it help you to eliminate the extra shifts?"

To which the prospect responds, "Our people would be more rested and happier."

To which the salesperson asks another:

7. *Need-payoff question* "How much would it save a year to eliminate those shifts?"

To which the prospect answers after some thought, "Oh, about $30,000."

To which the salesperson (if she doesn't have any more problem questions to ask, which we will assume to save time and space) responds with a question leading into the presentation. She says something like, "Suppose you could operate twice as fast, eliminate the extra shifts, making your people more rested and happier, and also save the $30,000 per year—would that be something to talk about?"

Without any objection the prospect responds, "You bet!" (Explicit need demonstrated.) An implied need (see step 3 above) is one that is implied by what the prospect says. An explicit need is one the prospect says in his own words that he has or that he would like to solve. When the prospect says he has a need he would like to solve, he is not usually going to "object" to the solution.

Note: the prospect in the above situation may still be concerned about paying the $20,000. But through implication and need-payoff questioning you have uncovered additional implications. These implications will be solved or overcome by the purchase. In addition, additional benefits (which the prospect brought up) will be received by making the purchase and getting the Fast Flow system. In this particular case the salesperson identified that there also would be annual savings of $30,000, more than the cost of the equipment. This is a payout of less than a year.

The prospects weigh in their mind the price of your product, service, or solution against the existing cost to them of the problems that will be solved and the other benefits received. Think of it as a balance beam or scale. The purchase price is on the right side of the scale. The cost of the problems solved, and the benefits received, are on the left side. They form a value balance in the prospect's mind.

Too often, prospects don't clearly understand the depth (cost) of their problems or the number and importance of the benefits you offer in your solution. They feel your price (right side) outweighs the (implied) benefits to them (left side). Therefore, they want you to reduce your price. This way

Figure 4. Value balance.

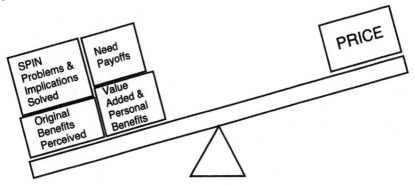

the price on the right side would weigh less than the benefits on the left side. The scale would tip to the left, and they then would feel free to buy.

You need to change their way of thinking.

Through SPIN questioning prospects tell you what their problems are. Through answering your implication questions, they tell you the many hurtful implications of those problems. And they tell you the need-payoffs to them of solving their problems with your solutions. They tell you. You don't tell them.

With your help, they pile up on the left side of the scale their many problems and their costs, hurtful implications, and beneficial need-payoffs. This makes the left side weigh much more and drop down. They see that purchasing your product or service provides them many solutions and need-payoffs and eliminates problems and implications they hadn't considered before. Thus, without your reducing your price, they see that the benefits of the purchase far outweigh your price (see Figure 4).

You can actually sketch a value balance and visually demonstrate to the prospect that the value received far outweighs the price, or the value provided by a competitor.

Planning for SPIN Questioning

Chapter 5 discusses "grasping" critical issues and Chapter 9 discusses territory/account planning. In line with both, identify the critical issues and related problems that your target customers and prospects may have. Choose ones that your products, services and added values can solve.

Then for each problem develop a problem question. Think of all the implications that could relate to each problem. For each, develop one or more implication questions. Then develop a series of need-payoff questions that relate to those problem areas. This is illustrated by the following diagram. (Note that the implication questions are directly linked to specific problem questions. The need-payoff questions are not.)

You may have a half dozen different types of prospects. Perhaps they are in a half dozen market segments, each with different critical issues. Then, for each type of prospect, develop a series of potential problems, problem questions, implications, implication questions, need-payoffs, and need-payoff questions (see Figure 5). Write the questions for each segment or type on a separate document or sheet of paper. Then before you call on a customer or prospect of that type review the list of questions.

Practice asking the questions with peers and friends. Each time you ask them a question their answer will be different. Thus, the follow-on questions you ask will be different.

For instance, on the first pass you might ask, "Does your system operate as fast as you'd like?" The answer might be, "Yes." Then you would forget that problem and move to the next problem question.

Figure 5. SPIN planning diagram.

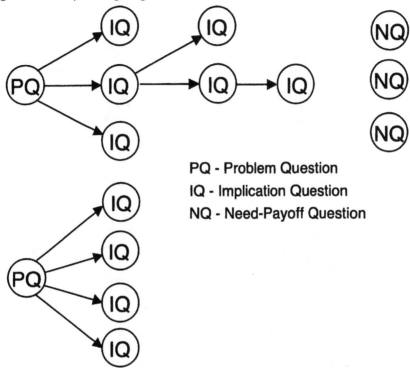

PQ - Problem Question
IQ - Implication Question
NQ - Need-Payoff Question

The next time you practice asking that question the answer might be, "No it doesn't." Then you might respond with an implication question, "How does it hurt you to operate too slow?" The response might be, "It causes us to double cycle the catalyst." To which you might respond with another implication question, "What effect does that have?"

However, the next time you ask, "How does it hurt you to operate too slow?" the response might be different. It might be, "Our operators get exasperated." Then your next question will be different from before. It might be this implication question: "How does that affect their performance?" This line of questioning is valuable, but it is entirely different from the first line. The solution (product, service, etc.) may be the same, but how you present it may be different.

Over time you will become skilled at responding to answers with implication and need-payoff questions. Then you won't need to practice or to review the sheets with questions on them.

The following are some additional ideas to keep in mind when taking action to prevent rejection and objections.

► If you really care about the welfare of your customers and prospects, they sense that. They are less likely to feel like rejecting you, avoid meeting with you, or raise a negative objection.

► If you really believe you may have something great for prospects, and if they answer your questions in a positive way, then you feel strong from within. Prospects sense that and are less likely to put you off. If they do, it has much less of a negative effect on your attitude. This is because you know that they have been harmed much more than you by the two of you not getting together.

► If you have done your homework—including identifying potential critical issues and developing problem solutions and added value—then you are doing prospects a favor by seeing them. They are not doing you a favor by seeing you.

► Concentrate on asking questions and determining what problems and concerns they have, and how it would benefit them to solve those problems and concerns. Then ask them if a certain type of solution would make sense to them. Do all this before suggesting anything they could object to. Once you have found the problems, and they have agreed that a "type of solution" would make sense, they are not in a mindset to bring up objections. Their minds are on exploring the possibilities you have presented.

► Don't tell them anything about what you have to offer until you have gotten them interested in something you might offer. There are three good ways to get them interested. The first is to make a big fat claim that the prospect can accept. The second is to make a possible big claim. An example would be, "We have found an approach to selling that has doubled the effectiveness of some sales forces and it might work for you. If after a few questions I felt it was applicable to you, would you want to pursue it?" The third method is to ask questions, such as SPIN questions, which raise the prospect's interest.

► Don't give them anything to object to. Before making your presentation, ask questions. Determine their needs and the importance of those needs. Then tailor your presentation specifically to solving those needs. Don't talk about a bunch of products and solutions that don't fit identified needs.

► Anticipate legitimate objections. Plan to handle them effectively. Deal with them early.

► Welcome all the prospect's legitimate questions and have a plan to answer them. If you know your business, and have determined solutions that may be of great value to the prospect, then answering legitimate questions should be a normal part of the discussion process.

► Encourage the prospect to do most of the talking until you are prepared to make your presentation. Even then, it is effective to make the presentation a two-way discussion, and not a one-way presentation. One way to do this is to ask clarification questions during the presentation, such as "How would this be helpful to you?" This, by the way, is a need-payoff question asked during the presentation instead of during the earlier information-gathering stage.

18

Being a Sales Consultant

Focusing on helping customers to find and solve problems and take advantage of opportunities. Developing specific, related expertise and customer relationships. Utilizing questioning and observation to uncover potential problems and opportunities; solving them, and advising on solutions and methods for obtaining solutions; following-up; and other activities related to helping customers—at all times keeping in mind how your own company's products and services can be utilized and sold.

ILLUSTRATION AND RATING—18A

A sales consultant is both a consultative salesperson and a consultant.

As a consultative salesperson, your objective is first to find a customer want, need, problem, or opportunity. It then is to determine how your products and services can solve or fulfill it. Finally, it is to convince the prospect that it should purchase those of your products or services that will solve or deal with that want, need, problem, or opportunity. You may or may not happen to have specialized knowledge or expertise.

As a consultant, your objective is to develop industry, customer, and/or technical knowledge, become an expert in some area of value to customers, and then look for and solve customer wants, needs, problems, and opportunities related to that knowledge and expertise.

As a sales consultant, you focus on utilizing your products and services in the solution. But you help solve the problem or situation regardless of whether you sell anything.

162

You thereby, in some respects, employ a customer support marketing philosophy.[1]

As a non-consultative salesperson or "pitch" salesperson, you don't do any of the above.

Many champions discussed in this book exhibited sales consulting.

Joe Gandolfo was (and is) a sales consultant on tax shelters and financial planning. Keith Dillon was a sales consultant on creative mortgage financing. A pharmacy (drug store) front end assistance example will be discussed in Chapter 25. In that example, the drug wholesaler's detailers (salespeople) were educated to have expertise in performing market research and consulting related to drug store marketing. They utilized their expertise to perform market research and then helped the pharmacy select and sell front end products.

> Any salesperson, any professional, any non-professional can study a business or market segment, and determine an area of expertise needed to solve problems in that segment.

They can develop that expertise. They can search out problems, needs, and opportunities related to that area of expertise. They can utilize their company's capabilities and their own expertise to offer solutions, preferably utilizing their company's products or services. They can persuasively communicate this to the customer to strongly encourage them to buy. When they do so, they are practicing sales consulting.

Pitch Selling

Sales consulting is the opposite approach to the old time type of "pitch" selling. In pitch selling, salespeople start with their product or service. They "pitch" it (tell their sales story in a pushy and manipulative way) to the customer. This was never professional. It is no longer effective, especially for the larger or long term sale.

Suppose a representative of our company called on your company's president, division manger, or training department. Suppose she aggressively attempted to sell them a three-day training program on Championship Selling without knowing much about your business, or attempting to determine what training you have already done, or anything about your sales training needs. That would be an example of "pitch" selling, even if our representative believed we offered a great program. But we wouldn't do that.

Also, any salesperson who pushes one particular policy or brand because it yields a higher commission is guilty of pitch selling.

1. See Chapter 20.

In opposition to this, both the consultative salesperson and sales consultant study an area, honestly determine prospects' wants and needs, encourage them to buy what is best for them, and explain why. However, if they are smart, they choose an area to study that has a good chance of bringing them profitable business, short term or long term.

Consultative Selling

Suppose a representative of our company called on you and suggested that we may be able to help you perform much more effectively in marketing, selling, or customer service effectiveness. She mentioned that we have done that successfully for a number of companies similar to yours, with a substantial measurable payout, much higher than the investment required. She might or might not have mentioned that training in Championship Selling is one approach that has been productive.

Let's say our representative requested and obtained permission to meet for an hour or so with your department manager, a couple of other key people, and one or two small groups. Then after giving a short report to your manager, she phoned a half dozen or so of your customers, or companies similar to your customers in a different part of the country. This was to get the customer's perspective as to what is needed, and perhaps how you are performing now. Then, in addition, she reviewed some magazine articles about your industry and some of your company's promotional material.

Finally, suppose our representative met with your manager and a few others to present and discuss with them her findings. She recommend either of two potential initial training programs we offer, with follow-up. Both are built on what you have already done. And both fit the needs of your organization based on the analysis performed.

The suggested program solution might have focused on Championship Selling. Or it might not, depending on what was found out during the investigation.

Let's say neither program required a large commitment by your company in time or money. But there was the expectation that if the program chosen worked out as well as expected it would be expanded, taking into account what was learned during the initial training program. Let's say from the presentation it appeared to your management that one of the suggested programs would fit your needs. It would help you obtain your overall objectives and would fit your budget. You agreed to go ahead with it. You did, and the salesperson followed up afterward to make sure your objectives were achieved. That would be an example of consultative selling.

Sales Consulting

Suppose in the above example our salesperson had no special expertise beyond what was required to determine whether our training programs can help the prospect. And suppose her entire objective was to determine whether or not there was a fit between customer needs and our company's training programs and services, and then to make a sale if and only if there were a fit. That would be "merely" consultative selling.

But suppose our salesperson had developed great expertise in determining how to improve the selling effectiveness of a sales force, regardless of whether the solution utilized our company's programs. Suppose the objective of the salesperson was to find the truth and then communicate it to the prospect, whether or not it resulted in business for our company. This is based on the philosophy that if she were able to help you, regardless of whether it brought business to her, eventually she and our company would benefit. That would make it an example of sales consulting, and it would demonstrate one thing that a sales consultant does.

Thought Provokers

(1) Does your type of business lend itself to sales consulting? For instance, sales consulting is probably more valuable in selling larger computers and training than in selling (low service, cost competitive) personal computers and siding for houses.
(2) How important is developing personal relationships to generating selling success in your business?
(3) How important is solving customer problems?
(4) What kind of expertise would be helpful in solving your customers' problems?
(5) How good a consultant are you? How good could you be?

Take the following rating exercise to estimate how important "sales consulting" is to your selling success. Based on the results, you can continue on with reading about its implementation, or you can move on to Chapter 19 and Section 19A, and come back later to Section 18B.

CHAPTER RATING (rate A, B, and C below from 1 to 5 for this chapter's importance; then multiply)

_____ **A** = Importance or applicability to you (5 = great, 3 = moderate, 1 = poor)

_____ **B** = Your present strength or level of action (1 = great to 5 = poor) *(reverse rating)*

_____ **C** = Chances of your successful implementation or improvement (5 = great to 1 = poor)

A × B × C = your rating (_____) × (_____) × (_____) = (_____)

If your rating is over 25, read "Implementation" now; if 25 or under, consider postponing until later.

IMPLEMENTATION—18B

The following are some ideas to keep in mind when employing sales consulting.

- Before investing in building your expertise, first determine what expertise to build. It should be tied to critical issues of high potential market segments when possible.[2]
- When calling on new industries, consider making a few initial calls on less important prospects. This is to learn something about the industry and its problems before calling on the more important prospects. Remember, "you only have one opportunity to make a first impression."
- Build positive relationships. People, even in this modern, enlightened age, still do business with their friends and with people with whom they feel comfortable.
- Sell yourself, your company, and your expertise as early in the relationship as possible. Do this in a non-bragging manner.
- In making a sales call, build as much trust and respect as you can before starting to ask detailed questions. This may mean delaying the asking of penetrating and threatening questions until a later visit.
- Don't ask the prospect, "Do you have any problems?" or "What are your problems?" until you know them very well, if ever. These are general problem questions. Prospects frequently say they have no problems when asked in general. Sometimes they are uncomfortable admitting to a stranger that they aren't perfect. Sometimes they think it is none of your business. Sometimes they are lying to themselves. Sometimes they have problems and opportunities and just don't know it, or don't realize how serious they are. Sometimes they have problems or opportunities and don't realize that there are solutions, so they ignore or avoid them. Sometimes they just don't want to bother to think or consider changing.
- Do ask specific problem questions when they appear appropriate.
- Start by asking general situation questions to gain an overall or background understanding. Then work your way to the more specific questions.
- Don't waste the prospect's time with unnecessary questions. You only have a limited time before the prospect gets anxious about the time spent with you.
- If you can find an area in which prospects are intensely interested,

2. See Chapter 5.

then they are much more willing to spend time with you and to answer all your questions.

- Go into each meeting with ideas as to how you can help the prospect. But be alert to other and even more pressing concerns of the prospect.
- Plan ahead and write out a list of questions you need answered before making the sales call—as best you are able.
- Plan ahead as to how the customer might respond at certain points in the meeting, and how you should respond and react to achieve the best results.
- Do not, if at all possible, allow prospects to see your list of questions. If you do, they are likely to ask for them, read them quickly, and then attempt to give you a summary answer. This is not helpful to you or to them in identifying their specific problems and opportunities.
- Be an effective and respectful listener. Ask open questions and allow the prospect to talk, at the same time directing the conversation in the direction of information you need to obtain. The prospect may reveal problems and opportunities from a general flow of comments.
- Oftentimes you need to interview more than one person to get a clear understanding of what is going on and what are the problems and needs.
- Oftentimes you need to gather information from outside the prospect or customer, as from other customers and knowledgeable industry people, to verify or clarify what you have been told.

19

Team Selling

Learning (1) the most powerful and results-generating concepts for helping customers and thereby making large sales of your products or services, and (2) which technical and other support people in your company or organization can assist you in delivering those concepts. Then leading those people individually and as a group to be effective in relationship development, information gathering, customer problem finding, problem solving, strategy development, customer presentations, and supportive problem-solving.

ILLUSTRATION AND RATING—19A

Jim Murphy was the top salesperson on the east coast for Wang Laboratories. He explained why in one of our training sessions. He concentrated on and had an effective strategy for team selling. Jim concentrated on selling to larger accounts. He brought together a number of engineering and support people to help him. This helped him sell large data processing systems and concepts. Jim organized the team, coached each member on his or her task and how to do it well, and orchestrated the team selling approach.

Team Selling Situations

There are a number of situations where team selling can be helpful. Some companies have converted completely to it for key account selling,[1] some for almost all their selling.

> There are times when a selling champion can effectively use a team. There are times when a "good" salesperson needs the support of a team.

1. Chapter 13 offers additional perspective on team selling.

For very large accounts and in complex selling situations, frequently there are more people to keep in contact with and more to do than one person can do well. Also, many of the account contacts are specialists who relate even better with people from your company with the same specialty (civil engineer, cost accountant, etc.). Your specialists can be effective at developing relationships with them and obtaining technical and specialized information and commercial intelligence.

A carefully selected team member can talk the language of the other person, such as a customer specialist or a person from a different country or culture.

If you need to be able to make high level decisions "on the spot" while meeting with the account, you may include a member of upper management on your team. If you need a considerable amount of detailed, frontline contact with the account, you may include customer service or other frontline personnel on the team.

You can bring together your group of specialists and thinkers to help you brainstorm. They can help you develop problems to solve, opportunities to exploit, and solutions to offer. They can help you put together creative strategies and plans. They also can do things you might have done, thereby freeing up your time for more important objectives and projects.

They meet separately with their counterparts in the prospective or client company, as well as with people in your own company. Then they join the team to share information, develop strategies, and plan. The specialists, or a number of them, often are included in team meetings with the prospect as well.

Some salespeople need the help of a stronger salesperson, or one with more or different expertise, to deal with higher level executives or a special selling situation. They may be effective with regular accounts, but uncomfortable with or ineffective in dealing with very large accounts, or high level company officials, or highly technical selling situations. The stronger specialist salesperson can be an advisor. Or she can become the leading salesperson or negotiator for that account or situation.

Also, some salespeople receive extra confidence and power from joint sales calls or organized back-up technical support. It helps them to be more effective overall.

> In some selling situations, even when selling to smaller accounts, it is "strategically advantageous" to bring in a team of salespeople.

Bringing in a team may advantageously position your company as being large or highly committed to the prospect's objective. This was illustrated in Chapter 13. Sometimes specialized skills and experience are needed for a particular meeting or selling situation.

Sometimes a particularly effective negotiator is needed for a highly complex or challenging situation.

In some difficult situations, it may be advisable to bring in another person to give bad news to a customer or to take a tough stand on an issue. This is so the normal salesperson can maintain a positive relationship with the customer. The normal salesperson might even take the side of the customer and argue against the position of the supplying company's team or negotiator.

Also, there may be support people in your company you depend on to provide customer support and follow-up. Or there may be powerful people you need to bring on board. You may need to convince them of the validity of your selling solution or of the importance of serving this customer with excellence. By getting them involved on your team they tend to better understand and relate to the customer, customer needs, and important aspects of your creative solution and strategy. As a result, they are more committed to helping you implement it.

Team selling can be utilized to carry cross-marketing (Chapter 26) to a higher level of "team cross-marketing." A cross-division team can strategize and sell to prospects for both divisions. A number of divisions can work together to sell the entire line of the company's products and services to a major customer in a coordinated system. For instance, General Electric organized a team of more than 50 salespeople to win an important contract with General Motors' Saturn subsidiary in 1987. The team represented eight different GE divisions.

Thought Provokers

(1) What is a team in the context of your selling?
(2) What does a selling team leader do?
(3) Which of your products, services, systems, customers, industries, and markets most lend themselves to team selling?
(4) How do you run a good meeting? What constitutes a badly-run meeting?
(5) Other than yourself, who is or should be the most important member of your selling team?

Take the following rating exercise to estimate how important "team selling" is to your selling success. Based on the results, you can continue on with reading about its implementation, or you can move on to Chapter 20 and Section 20A, and come back later to Section 19B.

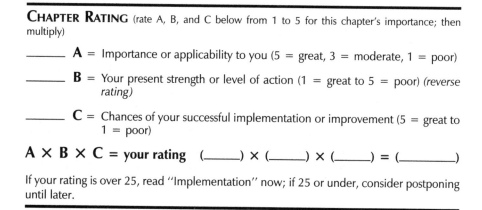

CHAPTER RATING (rate A, B, and C below from 1 to 5 for this chapter's importance; then multiply)

_____ **A** = Importance or applicability to you (5 = great, 3 = moderate, 1 = poor)

_____ **B** = Your present strength or level of action (1 = great to 5 = poor) *(reverse rating)*

_____ **C** = Chances of your successful implementation or improvement (5 = great to 1 = poor)

A × B × C = your rating (_____) × (_____) × (_____) = (_____)

If your rating is over 25, read "Implementation" now; if 25 or under, consider postponing until later.

IMPLEMENTATION—19B

To be effective in team selling, you need to understand team-related skills and concepts. You need to understand the kinds of problems, opportunities, or situations that teams fit into or help solve. How to select your team. How to develop relationships with various people in your organization who have the needed knowledge or skills to assist you. How to work with others on the team with a focus on serving the customer. How to lead a team. How to get everyone to work together where no one dominates, but where each does his or her part properly and then steps back and allows others to do their parts.

You also need to know the kinds of problems team selling can bring you and how to avoid them. For instance, team members often try to prove their worth on the team rather than just making a contribution when it needs to be made—as by talking in meetings with customers when they should be listening. Technical specialists often try to prove they are smart—for instance, by arguing with each other, or arguing with their counterparts in the account's organization, which is worse. Those not highly skilled in sales can make all the mistakes of the unskilled salesperson, such as talking about areas unimportant to the account, asking why objections are important to prospects, thereby causing them to dig in their heels, and arguing. These can be headed off by effective personnel selection, training, and leadership.

The following are some ideas to keep in mind when employing team selling.

► Team selling can increase your technical and technological competency, thus earning you more respect and trust from the prospect.

► Anticipate the types of selling challenges and account needs that fit the team selling approach. Then decide early on the internal people you would call on to make up the team for each.

► There are a number of preliminary steps you might take in preparing for team selling, and conditioning or "training" team members to sell effectively. Spend time with potential team members to get to know them better and to learn more about what they do and how they do it. Hold joint social functions to help potential team members get to know each other better and feel more comfortable with each other. Get potential team members together to discuss team selling, what each person might do, how a team functions, and what it is important for each member to do and avoid doing. You might invite selected customers to some meetings to discuss how the team might help and work most effectively with them.

► Often different persons should be selected to participate on the selling team for different accounts, because of the different needs involved.

► Every team needs leadership, but not a dictator. You are the most obvious choice for team leader. However, especially in special circumstances, there may be another person who has leadership abilities, interest, and is the most qualified to lead in that situation.

► Frequently in team situations there is an assertive member who tries to dominate or push his or her opinions more than others. And there is a very knowledgeable person who is more timid. The effective team leader skillfully holds back the assertive member and encourages the timid member.

► Consider reading a good book on leading effective meetings.

► An effective team leader plans ahead, organizes the effort, coordinates between team members and with the client, gets team members involved in decision making, cheerleads, encourages and sorts out conflicting viewpoints, keeps everyone informed, and follows up with everyone to insure proper action is taken. He or she plans ahead for and implements a policy of making decisions based on "what is right," not "who is right."

► If possible, establish a philosophy that recognizes that in certain circumstances a lower level person on the team may be the most appropriate to make a decision or take an action. This is because that person is more knowledgeable or has more expertise in the area under consideration.

► Certain members of the team may have very large strengths (perhaps technical) and very large weaknesses (perhaps in planning, paperwork, or human relations). Attempt to recognize those strengths and weaknesses, plan for them, and plan around them. An example is providing clerical assistance for the brilliant technical person who does not complete paperwork properly.

► A team may be involved in presenting and selling a product or service, and then in delivering it once it is sold. Often different people with different skills are needed for those two different tasks.

► You may face a situation where it is crucial to make important, higher level decisions while meeting with the customer, for instance, modifying a company policy. Then attempt to include on the presentation team a member with the authority to make those decisions on the spot. As best you can, anticipate those decisions and help team members prepare to deal with them properly.

► It may be important to develop a plan for measuring team results and rewarding team performance.

► It also may be important to develop a mechanism to properly measure and reward individual contributions to the team.

► Some people don't have the personality to work on a team. You should either leave these people off, or be prepared to provide them an exceptional level of motivation and leadership.

PART F

CHAMPIONS

PERFORM CREATIVE MARKETING

20

Customer Support Marketing Philosophy

A philosophy that focuses on finding and delivering ways to help customers to be more successful (in marketing, selling, manufacturing, etc.) and thereby pulling through (the purchase of) your products or services.[1]

ILLUSTRATION AND RATING—20A

A few years ago I visited Disneyland. As I was waiting for the daily Disneyland main street parade to start, I overheard a young man in costume talking to a friend about normal, young person things. Then, all of a sudden, the parade started to form. The young man literally jumped into the parade and marched off with all the enthusiasm and energy of a performer on the Broadway stage.

Disneyland is a very successful and profitable entertainment company. You probably have heard that "they don't have employees at Disneyland, they have stage performers." This demonstrates the point. This was an example of a customer support marketing philosophy in operation, which focuses on helping visitors enjoy their stay at Disneyland.

Selling champions frequently perform creative marketing, which is the subject of Part F of this book. Many of the champions we studied were creative in developing a "customer support marketing" philosophy. Paul Benignus and Joe Gandolfo are two examples.[2]

---

1. Implementing this philosophy includes some of the other strategies discussed in this book—such as "grasping" critical issues, finding/offering specific added value, pull-through marketing assistance, and frontline marketing.
2. See Chapters 3 and 12, respectively.

> Customer support marketing is a business approach that con-
> centrates on supplying customers superior, blatantly profit-gen-
> erating value through the products, services, added value, and
> solutions provided.

It emphasizes providing outstanding customer service. It develops supportive selling relationships with key customer personnel. A primary purpose of the relationships is to learn about customers' business and needs so you can serve them better. It focuses on serving the needs of customers, whether or not doing so brings immediate business to your company.

When you provide customers superior, blatantly profit-generating value, they like you. They like doing business with you. They grow to trust and admire you. They prefer to spend time with you and purchase from you.

There is no doubt that you are different from your competitors, and most other salespeople everywhere, when you effectively implement a customer support marketing philosophy.

Two Approaches

There are two different but supportive approaches to customer support marketing. The first is to do everything well, to concentrate on the fundamentals, with an emphasis on how everything you do can help the customer to be successful, both short term and long term.

The second approach is to creatively look for new and better ways to help the customer to be more successful. Both approaches can be taken at the same time, but usually one is dominant.

Aviation Service Corporation (AVSCO) is a large, Atlanta-based aircraft parts wholesale-distribution company. It became committed to a version of customer support marketing. It started a large number of small initiatives to serve customer needs better. One thing it did was to establish a direct phone line to the president that any customer could use to make a complaint or offer a suggestion. Within a year of starting on the journey, sales and profits were up substantially and AVSCO had become the talk of the industry. Long before it had completely reengineered marketing and sales, it was getting numerous verbal and written commendations from customers and suppliers alike.

A number of the championship strategies and skills in this book relate to helping and supporting the customer in specific ways.[3] The focus is on helping key customers comprehensively, in any way that relates to your experience, knowledge, and skills.

3. Thus, strategy/skill number 20 is supported by strategy/skills numbers 6, 7, 23, 25, and 27, and goes beyond them.

Company-Wide Effort

A customer support marketing (CSM) philosophy starts with identifying and focusing on key customer segments, such as industries and markets. It involves understanding the technologies and businesses of those segments. It focuses on developing products, services, and added value for serving companies in those segments. It identifies high potential customers and prospects. It treats each as a market or segment unto itself.

Customer support marketing starts with effective market and customer research. This produces a deeper understanding of customers and their needs. It continues with sales questioning to define needs, and then with discovering or developing related customer-serving products, services, or added value. It develops an understanding of clearly-spelled-out economic and personal benefits that can be provided to the customer.

> CSM is an attitude of the company's people. But it requires proper organization and support to make it work.

Fully effective customer support marketing requires that all employees of your company (or a reasonable number of them), from the president to frontline sales associates, focus on serving the customer. And they do this with the same dedication and enthusiasm as that young man at Disneyland. In a normal company, that is thought of as being silly or beyond normal job responsibilities. Customer support marketing companies are not normal. They have a genuine customer-serving attitude. They do more for the customer. They make more money. They deserve to.

Frequently, optimum customer support marketing requires reengineering of the marketing and sales functions. And it requires visible commitment from upper management. This causes realigned priorities and changes in the organization to support the new priorities. Often systems must be improved or changed. Sometimes personnel must be changed. Often some positions are added and others eliminated. Most of the time at least some marketing and sales personnel must be educated, trained, and coached to perform different responsibilities.

Sometimes you as a salesperson can provide customer support marketing. Most times you must influence others in your company to support you in this approach. Often you must "sell" them on the benefit to them and to your company to do so. You may have to "sell" upper management. A championship salesperson sells both outside and inside the company.

Thought Provokers

(1) What type of assistance do many customers, or your most important customers, need that you or your organization are qualified to provide?

(2) Is it your nature to be supportive of others, or do you have a tendency to be selfish and self-concerned?
(3) What about your company and your unit management? What do their formal and informal policies tell you?
(4) Do you believe that a customer support marketing philosophy generates sufficient dividends to justify the effort and investment required? Why or why not?

Take the following rating exercise to estimate how important a "customer support marketing philosophy" is to your selling success. Based on the results, you can continue on with reading about its implementation, or you can move on to Chapter 21 and Section 21A, and come back later to Section 20B.

CHAPTER RATING (rate A, B, and C below from 1 to 5 for this chapter's importance; then multiply)

_____ **A** = Importance or applicability to you (5 = great, 3 = moderate, 1 = poor)

_____ **B** = Your present strength or level of action (1 = great to 5 = poor) *(reverse rating)*

_____ **C** = Chances of your successful implementation or improvement (5 = great to 1 = poor)

A × B × C = your rating   (_____) × (_____) × (_____) = (_____)

If your rating is over 25, read "Implementation" now; if 25 or under, consider postponing until later.

IMPLEMENTATION—20B

What can you as a salesperson do to implement a customer support marketing philosophy?

Start by focusing on segments, industries, and customers where you can provide the greatest value and achieve the largest long term profitable sales—by supplying customers superior, blatantly profit-generating value through the products, services, added value, and solutions you provide.

You know how these customers use your products and services now. Look for ways they can use them more effectively to solve their problems and take advantage of their opportunities.

Look for added value you can develop to help them even more.

Focus your present experience and expertise on helping customers. Develop additional expertise in some additional area if appropriate, so you become a better sales consultant and help customers run their businesses better in some way.[4]

Suppose you have a strong marketing background. You might help your customers improve their marketing approach. Or you might jointly market with customers to help you both increase sales and profitability.

Suppose you once were an accomplished accountant, or have an accounting background. You may find a way to help high potential customers in the accounting area. Perhaps you could help them better account for purchases of their raw materials, or for product and service sales, in cost accounting, or in warehouse management. Or you could work within your own company to modify accounting reports to be more useful to customers.

Suppose you are an engineer. You might help customers engineer something more effectively. Or you might offer some added value (additional) engineering service(s). Or you might add some valuable-but-unusual non-engineering service(s), in addition to your normal engineering service.

Wherever your skills fit customer needs you help them, if help is needed. You also look within your company for other skills and capabilities that might help the customer to be more successful.

The help you give may have a major impact on the customer's success and profitability. Or you may help in a number of small ways. Or you may help in one small way. Through a customer support marketing philosophy you blatantly have the customer's interest in mind. You offer whatever assistance you can to help. The customer "feels" this and wants to work with you.

A good starting point is to spend some time with the selected high potential market segments and customers and research their needs, wants, and opportunities as they relate to your capabilities and those of your company. Then attempt to determine how you can help each selected customer to be more successful in any way you can. As a result, your products and services are pulled through. They are pulled through because the customer appreciates your efforts and wants to work with you more closely. They are pulled through because the customer's sales increase as a result of your having helped the customer to be more successful. This pulls through the products and services you already are selling.

---

4. See Chapter 18.

21

Industry-Specific Marketing

Specializing in one or more industries (or markets), researching it, designing added value services to fit the needs of that industry or market, committing to it for an extended time period, and using marketing approaches such as advertising, direct mail, and phone follow-up to build prospects, customers, and referrals.

ILLUSTRATION AND RATING—21A

A new IBM salesperson was selling smaller computers and associated services in a metropolitan area. She took off most of a month from her selling efforts to perform market research in her sales territory. She listed and evaluated all the types of customers, and potential customer industries and markets, that might purchase and use computers. For instance, she looked at construction companies, banks, hospitals, hotels, nursing homes, CPAs, and small businesses of many types. She finally concluded that the offices of physicians were a major potential in her territory. She decided to concentrate on those.

First, she spent a month on the market research and analysis as discussed above. Then she started focusing her efforts on selling computer systems and associated consulting services to a few physician clients.

She obtained two physician clients. She worked with them to deliver great service and understand their needs in more detail. She became a consultant to them. She got some referrals to other physicians. Over time she became active in some physicians' organizations. She wrote a paper about her computer system and how it applied to running the offices of physicians. She advertised in some of their local periodicals. She gave support to local physician-related organizations.

She sent out mailings to different categories of physicians. She followed up the mailings with telephone calls. During the next six months, she started developing a physician clientele and prospect list. At the end of eight months, her sales level was three times that of the next best salesperson in her region.

> IBM was so impressed with her results that it started a training group to institutionalize her approach of "industry-specific marketing."

Training was developed and presented to a number of IBM sales organizations across the country. It used her example as a case study teaching tool.[1]

Jim Richardson is first vice president of the biosciences group, and one of the top salespeople for CB Commercial, the largest commercial real estate company in the world. He started focusing on the biotech industry ten years ago and grew that division from 3 to 25 people. He has worked with nearly half of the 1,300 bioscience companies in the nation.

Soon after he started selling to that industry he realized its great potential. He studied the industry to determine its needs and how to best meet them. He changed to a consultative selling approach because that fit the needs and personality of the industry. As his business grew, he hired and trained people to provide a comprehensive list of expertise and services to that industry.

A bank trust division we worked with focused on serving CPAs. They made regular mailings to CPAs. They developed a newsletter that was mailed to CPAs and accounting organizations on a bimonthly basis. They developed an advisory board of CPAs that met with the bank trust division people regularly to discuss the problems and needs of CPAs. They developed a series of free seminars for CPAs on important topics, such as creative marketing, professional selling, and computer techniques.

As a result, they expanded their banking and trust business with CPAs. But much more importantly, they gained a large number of referrals for trust business.

How do you decide on a specific industry or market to focus on?

Five Criteria

Your business situation should meet five criteria for a specific industry to be chosen for focus:

(1) More than one company or business in that industry or market already use your product or service. Or they use something similar for the

---

1. Chapter 12 briefly discusses this case in light of that chapter's strategy.

same function or purpose, and are happy with it. (They may or may not be your customers or in your sales territory.) If none exist, then go out and make at least two sales.[2] Then assure yourself that the customers indeed are satisfied with their purchases.

(2) You are able to build a powerful business case for the use of your product in that industry.[3]

(3) Your product is highly competitive (in price or value received) with others that might be used for the same application. (Superior is even better.)

(4) You can clearly identify sufficient profitable sales potential to justify choosing that industry for focus.

(5) You personally are enthusiastic about selling to that industry. This implies that you are competent and have the proper tools and resources to sell successfully.

Thought Provokers

(1) Which industries or markets are your best initial candidates for industry-specific marketing?
(2) Why did you choose them?
(3) For each industry or market identified, which is your best lead product or service?
(4) How happy, really, are your customers with that product or service?

Take the following rating exercise to estimate how important "industry-specific marketing" is to your selling success. Based on the results, you can continue on with reading about its implementation, or you can move on to Chapter 22 and Section 22A, and come back later to Section 21B.

CHAPTER RATING (rate A, B, and C below from 1 to 5 for this chapter's importance; then multiply)

_____ **A** = Importance or applicability to you (5 = great, 3 = moderate, 1 = poor)

_____ **B** = Your present strength or level of action (1 = great to 5 = poor) *(reverse rating)*

_____ **C** = Chances of your successful implementation or improvement (5 = great to 1 = poor)

A × B × C = your rating   (_____) × (_____) × (_____) = (_____)

If your rating is over 25, read "Implementation" now; if 25 or under, consider postponing until later.

---

2. Whether the number is two, five, or much larger depends on the circumstances. The point is that it has been proven that this industry needs your product or service.
3. See strategy/skill number 10 for discussion of a business case.

IMPLEMENTATION—21B

The following are some steps to evaluating and implementing the strategy and skill of industry-specific marketing.

- Attempt to get agreement from your manager, if you have a manager, that your time investment in this process is worthwhile. This is so you will receive support instead of negative pressures from upper management.
- Plan your work well so you don't have to take excessive time away from direct selling activities.
- Start by listing all the potential industries, markets, and applications for your type of product or service.
- Make a list of all customers and potential customers and separate them by category or segment (industry, market, or application).
- Rate each category by both sales potential and ease of getting the business.
- Once you have selected a few potential categories for focus, write out a short description of what you would sell to each, and how it would benefit them.
- Meet with a few potential customers in each selected category and verify that they agree (1) there is a need, (2) that your product or service seems to fulfill that need, and (3) that your price seems reasonable. As part of this process, look for and ask for referrals to potential good prospects. Don't just assume that if your internal people think it is a good idea the customers will buy it.
- Sell something.
- If the above results are successful, then invest some time both in giving great service to initial customers, and in learning the business of those customers in relationship to your product or service. This is so you can build up expertise and gain recognition over time as an "expert" who is knowledgeable about and committed to this industry or market.
- Invest some time and resources in marketing activities (such as advertising, sending out promotional literature, writing articles, and giving seminars). Don't spend all your allocated time in direct selling activities.
- Do allocate a reasonable amount of time and effort to direct selling activities.
- If after a reasonable time the selling effort is unsuccessful, then reevaluate the industry, market, or services chosen for selling focus.
- On the other hand, the selling results may be much higher than, or different from, what is expected. Then reevaluate to determine if there are new or unrealized selling opportunities that need special

or different selling and marketing approaches. Perhaps these will require new or additional people.

➤ Don't scatter resources too widely. If a segment focus is working, opt in the direction of expanding on and further developing that focus, rather than choosing additional segments for focus. Do keep in mind the ultimate sales potential of the industry or market chosen.

22

Industry-Specific Self Marketing

Using "marketing practices" to make your name and credentials known and respected in a specific industry or market, with the objective of you becoming the vendor, professional, or servicer of choice, and perhaps even a "celebrity."

ILLUSTRATION AND RATING—22A

Reynolds Metals Company had a marketing/sales engineer in its alumina division. He became very involved in many areas of the alumina business.[1]

He subscribed to alumina-related magazines, such as magazines on ceramics production. He read and clipped articles related to alumina. He attended alumina association meetings whenever he could, frequently manning the company's trade show booth. He took related college courses. He met with college professors who consulted in the industry. He did some consulting himself with his customers. He contacted editors of alumina-related magazines and became known by them. He wrote some articles for their magazines. He gave some technical presentations at association meetings. He became active in the associations, serving on some committees. He was on a first name basis with the presidents of many of his customers.

▌ In a way he became an industry "celebrity." ▐

As a result of all these efforts, over time he became well known throughout the industry as an expert in alumina technology. Much business came to

---

1. Alumina is aluminum oxide, from which aluminum is refined and certain ceramics are made.

Reynolds Metals Company that might have gone to Alcoa or another competitor. This is because people sought him out as a result of his reputation within the industry. He had marketed himself to the alumina industry. He had used industry-specific self marketing.

Michael Jackson and Madonna both are extraordinarily successful entertainers, I believe for very different reasons. Michael Jackson is highly talented and creative. Madonna has average talent, but she has effectively marketed herself to the teenage market. Looking back more than ten years, Madonna was a driven but not highly successful singer. She did some personal market research and concluded there was a market for a risque, outrageous-but-vulnerable young woman singer-entertainer who would "stick it" to the older generation, otherwise known as parents. She implemented her market strategy with brilliance. The rest is money in her many pockets.

Become Jane Fonda[2]

A branch manager client was frustrated by a rather normal selling situation. A large potential prospect was not interested in seeing her. She sold healthcare services to insurance claims offices. She believed she had a superior solution to a challenge that claims office managers were facing. But that particular claims manager was "happy with the current supplier," and was not interested in seeing my client, at least for a long time.

I asked the branch manager, "What if Jane Fonda knew that the claims manager exercised regularly. Supposed she called her and asked to visit to discuss new exercise methods. How would she respond?" The answer, "Of course she would be delighted to have Jane visit!"

> My response was, "How can you become Jane Fonda?" (This was "out of the box" thinking, and the thought was totally foreign to the branch manager, until she thought about it a bit.)

In other words, how can this branch manager become a sort of celebrity? How can she become someone important in the claims adjusting industry, so that the prospect would be delighted to spend some time with her? How can she market herself so she is known in a positive way in the industry? That is a primary objective of industry-specific self marketing.

Four Criteria

The following four criteria should be met for you to choose this strategy/skill.

---

2. Dan Marino or Clint Eastwood might work better for different audiences or account segments.

First, the industry or market should be one that either considers your product or service to be important or uses large amounts of it. Therefore, you will get substantial sales if you "get your share" of the business.

Second, there must be a way that you personally can make a big difference in the customer's buying decision. You can make a big difference in non-bid situations; those in which large purchases may be involved, and they can be made on a relationship or a total value received basis. You can make a big difference when quality is important, and either your company offers great quality or you personally can influence quality. You can make a big difference when consulting and technical help is useful for the proper use of the product or service, and you can provide that.

For instance, consider cleaning products (such as germicides, floor finish, and floor maintenance machines). Their quality and supporting services are more important than just "price" to hospitals and nursing homes. However, price is more important to hotels and office buildings. Thus, hospitals and nursing homes are better prospects for industry-specific self marketing than hotels and office buildings—unless you are the low cost producer selling low price.

Third, "you make sense" in this industry or market. For instance, suppose a former car salesperson with only a high school education and no computer experience started selling computers. It wouldn't "make sense" for him to focus on marketing himself to the automotive industry to sell CAD/CAM computers and software for designing new types of robots. This wouldn't "make sense" to the customer. The salesperson wouldn't have the proper background or experience and would seem to have little special to offer. It might "make sense," however, for him to focus on marketing himself to school districts—if he has been interested in education for some time, is a past president of the local PTA, and relates well to school needs and people.

If you must choose an industry or market with which you are not intimately familiar, research it to become knowledgeable about it. Invest your time in contacting and developing relationships with customers and knowledgeable and influential prospects. Invest your time on becoming known in and valuable to that industry.

Fourth, there should be enough potential business available to justify your focusing on this specific industry or market.

Thought Provokers

(1) What personal strengths do you have that you might develop or promote to a specific industry or market?
(2) Which industry or market?
(3) How could doing so help you become a "celebrity"?
(4) Who do you know that is knowledgeable about marketing that might help you to develop a self-marketing campaign?

(5) If you were going to write a book or article, or develop a speech for a certain industry or market, what topic would you choose?

Take the following rating exercise to estimate how important "industry-specific self marketing" is to your selling success. Based on the results, you can continue on with reading about its implementation, or you can move on to Chapter 23 and Section 23A, and come back later to Section 22B.

CHAPTER RATING (rate A, B, and C below from 1 to 5 for this chapter's importance; then multiply)

_____ **A** = Importance or applicability to you (5 = great, 3 = moderate, 1 = poor)

_____ **B** = Your present strength or level of action (1 = great to 5 = poor) *(reverse rating)*

_____ **C** = Chances of your successful implementation or improvement (5 = great to 1 = poor)

A × B × C = your rating   (_____) × (_____) × (_____) = (_____)

If your rating is over 25, read "Implementation" now; if 25 or under, consider postponing until later.

IMPLEMENTATION—22B

The following are some ideas to keep in mind when employing industry-specific self marketing.

- ► Utilize the ideas from strategy/skill number 21, industry-specific marketing.
- ► Give attention to industries that seem to best fit your strengths and personality. For instance, the hospitality industry (including hotels, travel agents, and convention bureaus) is a "fun" industry dominated by "expressive," social women. The consulting engineering industry is a "serious," technical industry dominated by "analytical" men. Do you relate well with fun-loving women? How about analytical men?
- ► Concentrate as much on developing industry relationships, and on key people in the industry, as on selling products and services.
- ► Become "expert" at something that is important to that industry.
- ► Perform some original research related to that industry.
- ► Market and publicize your expertise and research results.
- ► Develop and present speeches, seminars, and papers related to your expertise and research.

► Consider writing a book or a series of articles. Or generate something of a permanent nature directed specifically toward that industry. This helps you to become a "celebrity" (very well known and respected) in that industry.

► Consider publishing a regular newsletter, built around your expertise, and filling an unfilled niche in the industry.

► Develop and implement a strategy to cultivate strategic relationships in the industry.[3]

► Become active in industry associations and organizations.

► Develop and implement a strategy to meet and become friends, over time, with as many presidents and high-level officers of your customers and larger prospects as you can.

► Develop and implement a strategy to get your name and face in front of as many industry people as you can, especially those who are decision makers and decision influencers for your type of products and services. For instance, develop a videotape on a topic of critical interest to those people, whether or not it relates to your products and services. Then subtly publicize and distribute the tape so as many as possible of the right people see it.

3. See Chapter 14.

23

Pull-Through Marketing Assistance

Understanding the business of your customers, and the marketing practices that are effective in their type of business. Then assisting customers to market more effectively with the result that they sell more of their products and services and thereby "pull through" more of your company's products and services.

In every industry some companies are much more creative and more effective in marketing than others. In some, the leader is many times as productive as the rest.

> To apply pull-through marketing assistance, you learn—for key customer industries—what the best companies do to be so creative and effective in marketing. You figure out how to improve on that.

Using this input, you help your customers in that industry to market more effectively. As a result, they sell more and appreciate you more. This helps to "pull through" more of your products and services, causing them to buy more from you.

Large companies such as airlines, electrical and chemical manufacturers, and retail chains have a marketing director or an entire marketing department. They should have considerable knowledge in marketing. If you work for one, considerable help should be available to you if you need it.

Smaller companies such as CPAs, law firms, consulting firms, and advertising and public relations firms should have one or more principals (or perhaps an outside marketing consultant) who is knowledgeable about marketing—to effectively market the firm. That person could be tapped for assistance, although it is better if you are the one who is highly knowledgeable about marketing.

To perform pull-through marketing assistance, study your customers' target industries. Determine one or more specific marketing approaches for each industry that should help your customers to sell more products and services. Devise a method to transfer this information to your customers so they can use it. Then help them test it out and prove it.

> Many professional organizations, such as consulting or engineering companies, could charge for this service.

Others such as manufacturers, banks, and large service companies could offer it without charge as an added value service.

A pleasure boat salesperson at one time owned a successful boat dealership. Marketing and sales promotion were two of his strengths. He used that background to help his customer-dealers improve their advertising and sales promotion. This helped them sell more boats—both from his company and from others. This gained him great recognition in the customer industries he sold to. It caused him to earn large commissions. He was chosen as "Salesperson of the Year" by a boat dealership association to which many of his customers belonged.

The bank trust department discussed in Chapter 21 studied effective marketing for CPA firms and helped some of them improve their marketing effectiveness.

A major soft drink syrup company trained some of its salespeople to be marketing consultants to the company's bottlers.

In most cases, bottling companies are not owned by the soft drink syrup companies. They often bottle for more than one syrup company (for example, 7-Up, Royal Crown, and Nehi). This company's salespeople were held in low regard by the bottling company owners and general managers. They didn't see any meaningful value received from them. As a result, they were slow to react to the salespeople's proddings and suggestions for expanding soft drink sales and thereby purchasing more syrup.

This changed, at least in most cases, when the syrup company's salespeople were trained to be marketing consultants.

We helped the company's marketing department study the most effective methods for marketing soft drinks, especially through supermarkets and discount chains. The marketing department developed specific marketing practices and programs the salespeople could help the bottlers use to move products. The salespeople were trained on those practices. The bottlers implemented the programs with the assistance of the company's salespeople (excuse me—marketing consultants). This moved more soft drinks. It thereby moved more of the company's soft drink syrup. And it substantially improved the image of the "marketing consultants."

Thought Provokers

(1) In what ways do your products or services influence your customer's ability to sell and market effectively?
(2) What major marketing challenges do your key customers and segments face at this time?
(3) What might they do to improve their marketing effectiveness?
(4) If you were going to offer pull-through marketing assistance, what marketing expert could help you to improve your knowledge of marketing, or team up with you to develop a highly effective marketing tool or program?

Take the following rating exercise to estimate how important "pull-through marketing assistance" is to your selling success. Based on the results, you can continue on with reading about its implementation, or you can move on to Chapter 24 and Section 24A, and come back later to Section 23B.

CHAPTER RATING (rate A, B, and C below from 1 to 5 for this chapter's importance; then multiply)

_____ **A** = Importance or applicability to you (5 = great, 3 = moderate, 1 = poor)

_____ **B** = Your present strength or level of action (1 = great to 5 = poor) *(reverse rating)*

_____ **C** = Chances of your successful implementation or improvement (5 = great to 1 = poor)

A × B × C = your rating   (_____) × (_____) × (_____) = (_____)

If your rating is over 25, read "Implementation" now; if 25 or under, consider postponing until later.

IMPLEMENTATION—23B

The following is one approach you could use to implement pull-through marketing assistance.

► Team up with a knowledgeable marketing person if you don't have sufficient marketing expertise yourself. And if you don't, read a couple of basic books[1] on marketing to give you a foundation of understanding.

- Select industries to concentrate on based on their sales potential and your suspected ability to help them with their marketing.
- Research the most successful companies in those industries to determine how they market to be so successful.
- Determine what you might recommend that could improve the marketing of the "best."
- Analyze the specific strengths, styles, and objectives of your major customers in the chosen industries. Determine what the "best" are doing that is applicable to these customers generally and specifically. Estimate how it could be improved on for use by your customers.
- At this point you have determined the best marketing approaches that are applicable to all companies in the segment. You also have determined what specifically each major customer might do to market more effectively based on its particular strengths and situation.
- List for the selected segments, or for major customers, all the major customers, industries, markets, and available market niches—as best you can based on information available. Estimate, or get selected customers to estimate, for each of these, the sales potential both for the segment and for major customers in that segment. Then estimate the probability that your customers can tap that potential, based on their strengths and the new marketing ideas you have in mind. Keep in mind the potential effects of your customers' major competitors and newly emerging technologies.
- Select a few niches or areas where you think you can help major customers increase their business through improved marketing methods.
- Check with selected customers to determine their receptivity to your marketing assistance.
- Perform research, or test with a few (smaller?) customers to prove out the best marketing approaches identified.
- Implement the best one(s).

---

1. You might start by reading: *Marketing*, by Richard L. Sandhusen, *Managing for Results*, by Peter F. Drucker, *The Marketing Imagination*, by Theodore Levitt, *The Regis Touch*, by Regis McKenna, and *The Discipline of Market Leaders*, by Treachy & Wiersema. Then look at *Guerrilla Marketing*, by Jay Conrad Levinson, *Innovation and Entrepreneurship*, by Peter F. Drucker, *Maxi-Marketing*, by Rapp & Collins, and *The Portable MBA in Marketing*, by Hiam & Schewe.

24

New Business Marketing

Using new business development skills and practices, that are within your power at your level, to find and market (sell) new services, products, market segments, or technologies.

ILLUSTRATION AND RATING—24A

Being alert to change and responding to that change is the first principle of new business marketing. That principle alone may be sufficient to allow you to develop and benefit from a new business opportunity. The following is an example.

In the late 1980s, an AT&T engineer was working in sales and support for microwave tower engineering design. The towers were primarily for the new and growing cellular telephone industry. When he was out in the field, the engineer overheard complaints from cellular company managers. They had become unhappy with the project management and tower construction that those companies provided based on AT&T's engineering design.

He thought about this. AT&T provided just the engineering design. That represented only 5 percent of the total cost (income to vendors) of microwave tower construction. He came up with the idea that AT&T might produce a turn-key microwave tower installation. AT&T would provide the design, engineering, project management, and construction of the towers. It would be responsible for the entire project and give the cellular companies only one (competent) vendor with which to deal. AT&T thus would earn 100 percent of the income from each project, or 20 times as much.

Eventually, he developed a preliminary business plan and brought it to his management. After much consideration it was approved. AT&T went into the business of turn-key microwave tower construction. The engineer became project manager and later (internal) president of the subsidiary organization.

> Within a couple of years this grew to a very profitable multi-tens of millions of dollars of business for AT&T. This was because one sales engineer was alert to change and had used just a few new business marketing principles.

As an aside, AT&T avoided the single biggest mistake in developing new business, that is, mixing the new business development effort with the traditional business once it is identified. AT&T set up a separate organization for the new business.

Two Approaches

There are two different approaches to successful new business marketing. A new business effort can be "competition-focused." In this, it tries to take existing business away from other companies through positioning and differentiation, with a focus on positioning. Or it can be "entrepreneurship-focused." In this, it tries to create new business opportunities that didn't exist before. It does this by focusing on differentiation and innovation.[1]

The successful effort by AT&T was competition-focused. Tom Mancuso in Georgia also was successful, but with an entrepreneurship-focused approach.

A number of years ago, Tom, a salesperson, was calling on a fuller's earth (absorbent clay) production plant. The plant manager complained that the plant was about to go out of business. Conditions had changed. The company just couldn't sell enough of its product.

Tom thought he could see a good business opportunity in this changed situation. Tom struck the following bargain with the plant manager. If Tom could sell out the plant, which would save the plant's business, he would receive as his commission anything he could sell the product for more than $12.00 per ton.

Tom did some market research. He realized that fuller's earth was used in cat litter as an absorbent clay. He talked to some cat magazine editors. He visited some cat litter bagging plants. He came up with a two phase new business idea. The plant would add perfume to the fuller's earth. It then would bag it as cat litter in the fuller's earth plant, rather than shipping the product to the customer's plant for bagging as was normally the practice at that time.

As a result of this idea, Tom sold out the plant at $20.00 per ton, far

---

1. Positioning and differentiation were described in Chapter 12. Innovation was touched on in Chapter 4 and is discussed in *Innovation and Entrepreneurship* by Peter Drucker.

above the amount the plant manager thought he could get. The plant received $12.00 per ton, plus the cost of the extra expenses. Tom received just under $8.00 per ton as his commission. With the commission received, Tom bought the plant. Eventually Tom purchased other plants and became a highly successful producer of fuller's earth products.

Seven Steps

New business marketing could easily be the subject for a series of books. However, the following is a seven step process that you as a salesperson can use to develop new business and new sales for your area or territory.

The Seven Steps to New Business Development

1. Opportunity Identification
2. Opportunity Preparation
3. Organizational Marketing
4. Sales Marketing (Smarketing)
5. Prospecting
6. Personal Selling
7. Servicing for Reselling

The section below expands on these seven steps and presents some mistakes to avoid. The next chapter, Chapter 25, presents additional ideas on developing and marketing new business.

Thought Provokers

(1) What changes have occurred recently in your industry or company that might indicate a new business marketing opportunity?
(2) Which applies more to your new business opportunities: being competition-focused or entrepreneurship-focused?
(3) Which is the most important of the seven steps to new business marketing listed above? Could one be missed without disastrous results?
(4) Who do you know that is most knowledgeable about or skilled in new business marketing? Would it benefit you to spend some time with that person?

Take the following rating exercise to estimate how important new business marketing is to your selling success. Based on the results, you can continue on with reading about its implementation, or you can move on to Chapter 25 and Section 25A, and come back later to Section 24B.

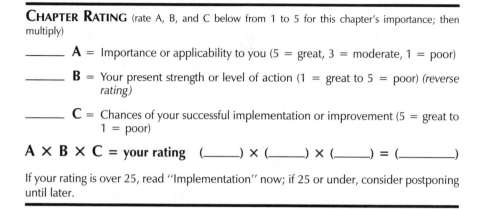

_____ **A** = Importance or applicability to you (5 = great, 3 = moderate, 1 = poor)

_____ **B** = Your present strength or level of action (1 = great to 5 = poor) *(reverse rating)*

_____ **C** = Chances of your successful implementation or improvement (5 = great to 1 = poor)

A × B × C = your rating   (_____) × (_____) × (_____) = (_____)

If your rating is over 25, read "Implementation" now; if 25 or under, consider postponing until later.

IMPLEMENTATION—24B[2]

The Seven Steps to New Business Development

The following are some checklist ideas for you to consider for accomplishing each of the seven steps. The list is comprehensive, but incomplete. Each situation requires its own thinking, planning, and action. If you sell a product instead of a service, replace the word service with the word product. Also, through this process you can develop a powerful added value service to support your product sales.

1. Opportunity Identification

► Identify all segments that you serve (such as geography, markets, or functions).
► Identify all segments you don't serve, or don't serve well, that it is logical that you could serve.
► Ask most questions, do most analyses, and take most actions for each segment individually, in addition to overall for the organization or territory.
► Look at the customers, segments, services (or product lines), and other categories where you are presently doing well or poorly and ask and answer why, and what opportunities that presents.
► Ask customers what they want and need (either in person, by phone, by survey, by focus group, or other methods).
► In addition, look for opportunities customers (or especially your

2. Sections 24B and 9B are long, detail-filled, and sometimes tedious. They also are extremely important.

major customer contacts) may not think of or even know about. (An example is the printer who was talking to the marketing department, but found a way to significantly reduce costs for the production department. This marketing department contact would never have thought of that as a problem or need to be solved.)

- Read periodicals, talk to experts, and observe the industry, looking for opportunities.
- Observe related industries and segments for what they are doing.
- Hold group brainstorming sessions.
- Hold self brainstorming sessions.
- Look at your company's existing programs, services, and products for what could be exploited or sold better.
- Look at your company's existing programs, services, and products for what could be improved to serve the market better.
- Look at your company's special strengths.
- Look at your own personal strengths.
- Look at what the most successful organizations/salespeople are doing in all industries, and ask how that could be modified to fit your circumstances.
- Think through the sources and clues to new business and new product/service opportunities listed in Chapter 25.
- Test potential opportunities in a small way with less important prospects or customers.
- Attempt to rate each opportunity by size (of sales or profit potential), importance to the marketplace, and difficulty of moving forward effectively.
- Look for a few opportunities to concentrate on that have a high potential for large results.

2. *Opportunity Preparation*

- Learn customer needs and technologies related to the opportunity, service, or product you have identified or focused on.
- Learn technologies related to effectively selling and delivering the service, product, or system to the customer.
- Make sure your company and division has in place the systems and people to deliver the service (or take advantage of the opportunity).
- Develop relationships with the appropriate people in your company so you can make improvement suggestions, get questions answered quickly, and get customer support action when requested.
- Prepare sales literature.
- Prepare presentation materials and literature.
- Look for added value, which you or your company might add or increase, to improve on the service or product, or make it more valuable or easier to use.

► Sell and test-deliver the new service or product to a few less important customers.

► Look for and check out the customer benefits and values received.

► Develop an awesome list of customer benefits and values, evidence to support your claims, and satisfied customer testimonials (by working with smaller customers first, if necessary).

► Do whatever you need to do to totally convince yourself that this new service, product, or opportunity is of extreme value to customers in the segment(s) selected. Then think through and practice a sales presentation that clearly, effectively, and dramatically communicates the values and benefits to the customer.

3. Organizational Marketing

► The purpose of marketing is to get customers to contact you asking about your new service or product, or to get them to feel favorably toward your organization and your new service so that when you contact them they are receptive.

► Obtain reference letters and improvement suggestions from the test companies discussed above.

► Start by focusing on the segments with the greatest opportunities, that is, unless you determine that you first need to focus into smaller segments. This would be either because you need to learn more, or because you don't have the resources to support the larger opportunity segment.

► After selecting segments for emphasis, prepare for advertising, direct mail, telemarketing, publicity, and other organizational communications as appropriate to support the new service or opportunity.

► Select the most effective marketing communications approach (such as direct mail supported by follow-up telemarketing), implement it, and support it effectively (in other words, if you get good leads, make sure you follow them up).

► Test different marketing approaches if necessary—in small ways or in sub-segments.

► Develop relationships with industry and market "influencers" (such as experts, magazine editors, association executives, or people of renown in leading customer companies).

► Take action to strengthen bonds with existing customers and obtain positive publicity from that relationship, such as publishing an article about how your service helped the customer, while at the same time making the customer look wise and smart.

4. Sales Marketing (Smarketing)

► Smarketing is marketing by or on behalf of a particular salesperson. It generally is done by or arranged by that individual.

- The purpose of smarketing is to get prospects or customers to contact you personally, asking about the service, or to get them to feel favorably toward either you personally or your new service or product, so when you contact them they are receptive.
- Select segments and key customers on which to focus your time and efforts. They might be selected because they have large sales or profit potential, because they should be easy to sell to, because they should be easy to partner with and learn from, because they have great influence where you want/need influence, or because they can help you sell effectively in some other way.
- Look for and implement opportunities to make you or your service well and favorably known by targeted customers and segments. For instance, develop expertise (through research, study, reading, interviewing, experimenting, and working with customers) so you are valuable to customers and/or are perceived as valuable to them. Or study a related area and write (and publish if possible) an article (perhaps with the help of a collaborator, such as a college professor). Or do direct mail and telemarketing to segments or key prospects, in addition to that done by the organization. Or get an article written about you in a key periodical. Or send a series of direct mail pieces that subtly and creatively make a favorable impression for you or your service.
- Network with customers and influencers. Join customer industry associations (regionally and/or nationally). Become active in associations. Become a resource to associations and to target markets or industries.
- Look for additional ways to leverage your selling and get known, such as giving presentations at association or customer company meetings or developing educational seminars.
- Devise and implement a strategy to develop friendly business relationships with influencers and customers. This is so they are more inclined to give you business, time, and information, and to give you referrals and names of potential prospects both in their organizations and elsewhere.
- Devise and implement a strategy to market yourself to potential prospect-generators and referral-providers, as a person and a company highly worthy of receiving referrals, so they are more likely to refer prospects to you (see Prospecting below).
- Once potential prospects are identified (see 5. below), develop and implement a program to maintain contact with potential prospects, including present and past customers, in a positive business way. For instance, send them a regular mailing with useful information, send them an irregular mailing with useful information, look for

articles and information that might be of specific interest to them, or send holiday cards.

5. Prospecting

- ► Define what a prospect looks like, as compared to a suspect. A prospect is a person or organization which has a meaningful reason to buy from you.
- ► After identifying segments and prospect types on which to focus, look for and find lists of matching potential prospects (companies, business units, or people). There are many sources of such lists both free and available for a charge: the list of largest companies in a number of categories—available in local business newspapers, Dun & Bradstreet and other financial (and information company) lists of businesses and employers, the computerized D&B list, Corporate 1000 Directory (including names, addresses and phone numbers of key persons and divisions), association directories and lists, purchased mailing lists (by SIC code, location, job function, and business area), the Yellow Pages, regional corporate directories, government industry reports, and others.
- ► Attempt to devise a strategy that identifies decision makers (and even their "superiors") in prospective companies, as compared to lower level or "just interested" people. However, "just interested" people can be gateways to people and information. They should not be ignored.
- ► If necessary, contact companies or people on the lists to determine if they indeed are prospects as you have defined prospects. For instance, do they have the potential to purchase enough of your service or product to justify being called on?
- ► Mail to and/or phone-verify prospects (companies and people on the appropriate lists who meet certain criteria)—or have it done—to make an appointment or identify general or specific interest. The mailing (or phoning) should contain a carefully designed selling message combined with a feed-back mechanism—perhaps a stamped, self-addressed card to complete and return (perhaps to receive a catalog or something else perceived by the prospect to be of value).
- ► Identify customers and non-customers who might know of a prospect fitting one of your prospect criteria. Devise a method to creatively and appropriately contact them once, or regularly, to ask for names of potential prospects. (This "method" probably includes a clear and concise description of a prospect.) If appropriate, devise a prospect reward process to encourage prospect referral.
- ► Identify customers and non-customer contacts who might give you

both a referral to a potential prospect and a positive recommendation to that referral. Contact them for positive referrals.

- Devise and implement a strategy to market yourself to potential prospect-generators and referral-providers as a person and company highly worthy of receiving referrals, so they are more likely to refer prospects to you.

6. Personal Selling

- Make an appointment with the prospect by making a "selling" phone contact, perhaps following an introductory letter. Make the letter short and powerful. Refuse to sell or give your specific "ideas" on the phone.
- Even better, make an appointment by following up on a referral.
- Carefully develop a short, powerful justification statement as to why it is extraordinarily important to the prospect that he or she spends a few face-to-face minutes with you. A potential statement might be something like, "I have some ideas that have been of major benefit to a number of organizations like yours. I need just a few minutes to share them with you. Then you can determine if they might be applicable to your situation. It'll be entirely up to you. Is that fair?" (After getting a positive response, "ask for the order"—ask for the appointment and set a specific appointment time and place. The more specific you can be in giving your justification, without giving away your "ideas," the more effective you will be.)
- Carry yourself with personal presence, power, and passion at all times, including on the phone while making the appointment. Be mature and friendly. Be appropriate. In most cases, be businesslike.
- Be professional—be prompt, be courteous, be respectful, be prepared, use clean stylish materials, be good.
- Gather as much appropriate information on the prospect as possible before you make the sales call. This impresses the prospect favorably, helps you to plan and carry out the sales call more effectively, and reduces the number of less important questions you need to ask. Thus, you are able to get to the point quicker.
- Treat each person and situation as appropriate to them and to you, but in general be businesslike and get down to business promptly. People are busy and generally don't like to waste time.
- At the first appointment, as appropriate—get the prospect's attention; generate interest in your approach or service; gather needed information through effective questioning and listening; make your presentation as focused as possible; answer questions and concerns; ask for the "right" order (see Appendix C); and leave with an understanding of the next action to be taken.

► One of the biggest mistakes in selling, and one that is made frequently, is to begin the presentation before the prospect realizes that he might have a significant problem or need, and before he is "interested" in a potential solution.

► Another major mistake is failure to ask for action, failure to ask for the order. Think about it. If you have personal presence, power, and passion, if you really believe you are helping prospects by their purchasing your service or product, then it is silly for you not to suggest that they place an order with you, thereby receiving the resulting value. If you don't believe in the value of your service or product, then "fix something," so you will believe.

► For more complex sales, make calls on, develop relationships with, sell to, and keep informed all decision makers and decision influencers.

7. Servicing for Reselling

► Follow up after the sale to make sure that what was sold was delivered properly and promptly.

► Develop relationships with key customer contacts so they want to continue to do business with you, readily share information with you, recommend you, and give you many results-generating business referrals.

► Take action to strengthen bonds with customers and obtain positive publicity from that relationship, such as publishing an article about how your service helped the customer, while at the same time making the customer look wise and smart.

► After providing service of great value, and after establishing a friendly, respectful, trusting relationship with as many key customer contacts as possible, then proactively (creatively and in most cases subtly) solicit numerous and powerful testimonials and referrals.

Mistakes to Avoid

The following are potential mistakes to avoid in employing new business marketing. If you sell a product, then replace the word "service" with the word "product."

► Not tapping the ideas of all departments and frontline people concerning company strengths and potential ideas for improved services/products and new business. Don't make the mistake of thinking that all good ideas come from the top, or from the field. Use the many eyes and ears available to you.

► Entering a business with a strategy that requires more resources than you can put together—so you develop a market for a competitor.

► Discounting new business, service, and product positioning ideas just because they appear too obvious.

► Not being market focused; ignoring unexpected successes of all kinds that don't fit in with your original goals or plans.

► Allocating resources to yesterday's winning products/services and "investments in management ego" instead of tomorrow's winners and development products and services.

► Staying with and investing in today's business technology beyond the point that obtaining benefits from new development work becomes difficult.

► Placing all product lines and businesses, including new businesses and developmental product lines, on the same financial basis, and requiring them to carry equal financial weight. (This is not an effective policy.)

► Not concentrating on working with "innovating" and "early-adapting" organizations in the development and introduction of new product/service lines and technologies.

► As market leader, "creaming" the market by charging unreasonably high prices for high-end products and allowing competitors to take the lower-priced, lower-profit business (in your selected target markets and niches). This lower-profit business eventually may become the most important part of the business. Look at what happened to XEROX and low-end copiers. XEROX gave the largest part of its business away to Sharp and others.

► Ignoring "odd ball" technologies and companies that provide solutions to seemingly less important problems, or in smaller niche markets, related to what you sell.

► Top level decision makers failing to go out personally and frequently to the marketplace and talk to customers and frontline people to get a personal "feel" of what is going on.

► Doing quantitative market research as guidance for the potential of "emerging" businesses (instead of qualitative market research and obtaining a "gut" understanding for the business area). Quantitative market research is helpful for traditional or evolving businesses, but can be quite misleading for something brand new.

► Failing to consider export opportunities and globalization of existing (and new) businesses.

► Protecting profitable or high volume products or product lines from internal competition—from different, perhaps lower-profit technologies (which then can be used against you by your competitors). Sony, for instance, makes a habit of being the company to obsolete its own best products, with cutting-edge, highly profitable new products. The mini-disc recorder is an example.

► Developing a complex, clever marketing strategy, rather than "keeping it simple."

► Trying to make too many new business development efforts at once, or to enter a large number of niches at the same time.

► Confusing innovation with high risk. Failing to keep innovative efforts simple and small, so if they fail they can be abandoned without great loss, or modified and tried in a different way.

► Failing to recognize hints that your base technology is becoming obsolete; such as disharmony and discouragement in the company laboratories, or finding out that you are doing more process R&D and less product R&D.

► Failing to examine the "limits" of your base technology (as determined by an S-curve)[3] or any technologies on which your business depends, as compared to the limits for competing technologies.

► Ignoring changes, unexpected events, or incongruities in the business or in the marketplace.

► Believing that existing industry structures and distribution channels are "the way things are supposed to be" and that they will change only slowly.

► Failing to find a way to adequately recognize and reward non-traditional, creative people who are the types who think of, develop, and push new ideas and new products and services.

---

3. This valuable concept is clearly explained in the book *Innovation*, by Richard Foster.

25

New Business Marketing Assistance

Assisting customers to find and market new services, products and businesses (related in some way to their existing services, products and technologies—and usually related to your company's products and services) with the result that they sell more and thereby "pull through" more of your company's products and services. This requires that you or an associate are knowledgeable about "new business marketing" practices.

ILLUSTRATION AND RATING—25A

This strategy builds on the prior chapter, strategy/skill number 24.

A few years ago, we worked with a national drug wholesaler (drug warehouse and distribution company) that had a problem similar to that of the soft drink syrup company discussed in Chapter 23. They solved it through educating their "salespeople" to provide "new business marketing assistance."

The salespeople for the drug wholesaler are called "detailers." Ten to twenty years ago the primary responsibility of the detailer was to come into the drug or discount store pharmacy, take an inventory of the drug merchandise on the shelves, and write out an order that would be delivered in the next couple of days. They often stocked or rearranged the shelves and evaluated shelf displays.

However, most of this service is now performed electronically by the drug or discount store personnel themselves. The shelves are scanned with a hand-held computer. The resulting data then is almost instantly sent to the drug wholesaler's warehouse computer on the phone lines.[1] Deliveries are received the next day, organized so they can promptly be placed on the shelves.

---

1. This is one example of the effects of changing technology discussed in Chapter 11.

So, the detailers are in effect out of a job. They come into the store regularly and ask if any help is needed. They "push" any specials being offered by the drug manufacturers (on which the detailers receive a bonus or a "spiff"). For a time they didn't have a definite and valuable job responsibility. Thus, they often were not highly respected by the drug or discount store managers they called on. Consequently, they had much less relationship and persuasion power than before.

We worked with this drug wholesaler to develop a program whereby the detailers were educated to perform new business marketing assistance. As a result, they did market research for their drug store customers in the neighborhoods surrounding their stores. Based on the research results, and related marketing information from headquarters, they developed recommendations for new front-end merchandising approaches (both products to be handled and promotional methods to be used). Front-end sales increased. Now, suddenly, the detailer was a very important person to the drug store. This was because successful front-end marketing was becoming more and more important to the profitable operation of drug stores.

As a result, our wholesaler became the preferred supplier in many cases. This provided additional sales for the wholesaler.

We worked with Monsanto Company in the specialty products area. The specialty chemical business unit sold upgraded organic chemicals and fluids. For instance, they sold fire resistant fluids to the aviation industry. They sold metalworking fluids, special paper and wood-treating chemicals, plasticizers, and food and fine chemicals. Some engineering specialists were trained to analyze the businesses of customers. The purpose was to find new business ideas for them that tied into, and required, specialty chemicals and specialty fluids (usually provided by Monsanto Company). As a result, Monsanto gained pull-through business.

When you find ways to provide new business marketing assistance to your market segments and customers, you stand head and shoulders above your competition in reputation and in providing something of great value to them.

Thought Provokers

(1) Are you, or can you become, qualified to offer new business marketing assistance?

(2) Is there someone else who is knowledgeable and available to help you?

(3) Which of your customers or customer industries are the best candidates to be helped?

(4) What new events or changes have occurred recently related to your

customers or their industries that might be threats to or opportunities for them?

Take the following rating exercise to estimate how important "new business marketing assistance" is to your selling success. Based on the results, you can continue on with reading about its implementation, or you can move on to Chapter 26 and Section 26A, and come back later to Section 25B.

CHAPTER RATING (rate A, B, and C below from 1 to 5 for this chapter's importance; then multiply)

_____ **A** = Importance or applicability to you (5 = great, 3 = moderate, 1 = poor)

_____ **B** = Your present strength or level of action (1 = great to 5 = poor) *(reverse rating)*

_____ **C** = Chances of your successful implementation or improvement (5 = great to 1 = poor)

A × B × C = your rating   (____) × (____) × (____) = (_____)

If your rating is over 25, read "Implementation" now; if 25 or under, consider postponing until later.

IMPLEMENTATION—25B

In implementing new business marketing assistance, review the ideas presented in Chapter 23, pull-through marketing assistance, and Chapter 24, new business marketing. Work with your customer to list and evaluate the following "sources and clues" to new business opportunities. Once you have identified a potential opportunity, then apply the marketing and business development ideas that were discussed in strategy/skill number 24.

Sources and Clues

These are some sources and clues to new business and new product/service opportunities:[2]

- ► The customer's unexpected success that it might develop into a profitable new business
- ► The unexpected success of a competitor
- ► The customer's unexpected failure that may be an opportunity in disguise

---

2. Many of these are discussed in *Innovation and Entrepreneurship* by Peter Drucker.

- The unexpected failure of a competitor
- The unexpected outside event
- Incongruities between the economic realities of an industry, which may indicate a new business opportunity
- Incongruities between reality and assumptions about it
- Incongruities between perceived and actual customer values and expectations
- Incongruities within the rhythm or logic of a process
- Process need
- Changes in industry or market structures
- Demographics
- Changes in perception
- Changes in customer values
- New knowledge
- The bright idea
- Changes in industry/customer ways of doing business
- Environmental and governmental changes
- Restraints and limitations that make the business vulnerable, impede its full effectiveness, and hold down its economic results
- Imbalances (weaknesses) of the business
- Threats—what you are afraid of, what you see as a threat to this business—and how can you use them as opportunities

26

Cross-Marketing

Cooperatively working with other internal divisions and departments (or with associated outside organizations) with the purpose of each selling and supporting the products and services of the other. Cross-marketing by you as a salesperson is more comprehensive than cross-selling, but less than corporate-wide cross-marketing (which, of course, is handled above the level of the individual salesperson or professional).

ILLUSTRATION AND RATING—26A

American Business Products, a large Atlanta corporation, performs corporate cross-marketing. Curtis 1000 is a division that sells envelopes of all types to corporations. Vanier Business Forms sells business forms and business services to large and mid-sized corporations. American Fiber Velope produces the TYVEK envelope, which is the best known super-strong mailing envelope.

Each of the divisions markets and sells the products and services of the other divisions to their customers. This gives broader marketing and sales coverage to each of the divisions. It gives each salesperson the potential for providing more customer value and obtaining larger orders and larger commissions.

> Cross-marketing at the salesperson level consists of you personally (or your department manager) contacting key people in other divisions or departments of your company—or other small companies if yours is a small company or professional firm—and arranging for you to sell and market their products and services and for them to sell and market yours.

We worked with banking organizations where we assisted the trust side and the banking side to cross-market. We arranged for the trust side to both give referrals to and sell the services of the banking side, and the banking side to give referrals to the trust side. Each side gave the other a referral fee or a pre-arranged commission, whichever was appropriate.

CPAs, attorneys, consulting organizations, and professional organizations of various types can cross-market with other organizations of their type, where each specializes in a different industry, market, or technology.

Professional organizations such as physicians, CPAs, attorneys, and consultants who specialize in specific industries, markets, or technologies frequently refer business to another organization with a different area of specialization.

We worked with a group of independent consultants that went far beyond "giving and receiving referrals," and participated in cross-marketing. Each of the consultants specialized in a different technology or industry. Each sold the businesses of others in the group along with their own business. As a result, each was building the other businesses in the group as well as their own, and earning extra commissions as well for doing so. Their customers had more resources available to them. Everyone, including the customers, benefited from cross-marketing.

Some advantages from cross-marketing include increased knowledge of sales potential, additional new business opportunities, increased sales and profits, improved customer service, increased visibility and importance to customers, increased commercial intelligence, increased spirit of teamwork, and increased cooperation with other units in the company.

Effective cross-marketing requires an attitude of teamwork and cooperation between involved units. Despite the many advantages, this frequently requires active encouragement from upper management.

TWELVE CLUES

There are 12 "clues" to cross-marketing opportunity:

1. The customers of one unit (for example, division, department, or professional firm) use or might use the products, services, or problem solutions of another unit. (For instance, bank trust, loan, and money management services serve the same customers.)

2. Two units provide different products or services, but they provide similar functions for the customer. (For instance, two McGraw-Hill divisions provide books and training programs, both of which educate.)

3. Two units perform the same or similar functions for different industries, but one has developed innovations not used by the other. (For instance, Servicemaster provides custodial and maintenance services to health care,

schools, and industrial corporations. A separate division services each. Each division may develop innovations that can be sold by the other.)

4. A unit has a unique product or service that might possibly be useful to the customers of another unit. (For instance, one AT&T engineering unit was supplying "computerized mapping" to cable companies, which could be used by other engineering units serving the Regional Bell Operating Companies, like Southwestern Bell.)

5. Through using the products or services of one unit, another unit might expand its offering to its customers in some way. (For instance, the AT&T engineering division worked with the installation division to provide a total, turn-key service for microwave towers.)

6. The technology of one unit might solve a customer problem or need of the customers of another unit. (For instance, in the 3M Company, the cleaning supplies unit provided its customers abrasives-impregnated floor polishing pads, developed and manufactured by the abrasives unit. The abrasives unit had been selling abrasives-impregnated pads to other industries in the past.)

7. Customers or prospects of one unit might purchase a different-but-related product or service provided by another unit. (For instance, at 3M Company, a computer unit prospect might not have been able to afford another batch of computers. But they might have been able to afford Kroy lettering machines, which do some of the same tasks, and were supplied by the office products unit.)

8. A condition exists where joint or team marketing covers more of the needs of the customer than one unit alone, thereby providing either a more comprehensive system or an alternative purchase. (For instance, McGraw-Hill's books supplement—or can be a less expensive alternative to—the training programs provided by the training unit.)

9. A customer in an industry in which one unit specializes also has operations in another industry where another unit (of the company) specializes. (For instance, a major account salesperson for IBM called on Philip Morris cigarette operations. But Philip Morris comprised the cigarette industry, Kraft food products, and Miller (beer) brewing operations, among others.)

10. The products, services, or technology of one unit can help get an order from, or better serve, the needs of a customer of another unit. (For instance, at Digital Equipment Corp., the mainframe unit could combine its systems offered with those of the workstation computer unit and the personal computer unit.)

11. A satisfied customer of yours has a friend in another industry served by another unit of your organization (for instance, a computer systems or software salesperson serving the hospital unit of Servicemaster,

which has a school unit and an industrial unit; or a tax attorney serving a school district, whose superintendent is close friends with a mid-sized corporation president who uses outside attorneys for litigation purposes).

12. Another unit, offering similar products and services, can better serve the needs of another part (division, district, and so on) of a customer of this unit, because of location (for instance, bank A in one city and sister bank B in another city serving a company with a branch office in the second city).

Thought Provokers

(1) If you were going to, with whom would you cross-market?
(2) What products, services, or systems do they offer that fit with yours, that you could sell easily, or that could bring great revenues or profits to your organization?
(3) What products, services, or systems does your unit offer that fit with one or more other units, that they could sell easily, or that could bring great revenues or profits to them or to the overall organization?
(4) What would be required for them to train you, or for you to train them, to be able to effectively sell the others' products or services?
(5) How would it benefit your customers?

Take the following rating exercise to estimate how important "cross-marketing" is to your selling success. Based on the results, you can continue on with reading about its implementation, or you can move on to Chapter 27 and Section 27A, and come back later to Section 26B.

CHAPTER RATING (rate A, B, and C below from 1 to 5 for this chapter's importance; then multiply)

_____ **A** = Importance or applicability to you (5 = great, 3 = moderate, 1 = poor)

_____ **B** = Your present strength or level of action (1 = great to 5 = poor) *(reverse rating)*

_____ **C** = Chances of your successful implementation or improvement (5 = great to 1 = poor)

A × B × C = your rating (_____) × (_____) × (_____) = (_____)

If your rating is over 25, read "Implementation" now; if 25 or under, consider postponing until later.

IMPLEMENTATION—26B

Ideas and Approaches

The following are some cross-marketing ideas and approaches that a salesperson or business unit can use to increase sales and market exposure:

- ► Trade shows (joint participation; allowing space for a second unit; helping the second unit to plan for the show)
- ► Joint advertising and promotion (such as media, direct mail, periodical articles, newsletters, or news releases)
- ► Cross-advertising in which one unit advertises to the industry and customers of a second, with the help of the second
- ► Market research on the needs and business opportunities in the market of one unit that might be served by the capabilities of another unit (by corporate or unit; internally or externally directed)
- ► Customer or industry seminars (joint seminars; seminars by a second unit with help from the first)
- ► Joint-mentions in articles and speeches (article or speech by a person in one unit to its industry or customer, mentioning capabilities or achievements of a sister unit, which are in some way related to the needs of this industry or customer)
- ► Joint-mentions in major sales presentations
- ► Jointly written articles by two units published in one unit's market or industry
- ► Article written by one unit for another unit's market with the assistance of the second unit
- ► Market research meetings or sales presentations by one unit to customers of a second unit, arranged by the second unit

Cross-Marketing Actions

The following are some sales actions that support cross-marketing.

- ► Sell the lines of two units, yours and another.
- ► Proactively look for cross-marketing opportunities and bring other units in on your sales calls.
- ► Look for opportunities and refer them to salespeople you know in other units.
- ► Look for opportunities and refer them to sales coordinators you don't know personally in other units.
- ► Pave the way and arrange contacts for salespeople from other divisions when requested.

► Coach people from other units, when requested, about approaching and dealing with your unit's customers.

► Solicit help and make prior arrangements to get help from people in other units to help you with the two actions immediately above.

► Keep other units informed on your sales and marketing strategies and efforts, and encourage them to participate and keep you similarly informed.

► Make arrangements to be informed on the sales and marketing strategies of other units.

► Team selling (Chapter 19) can be utilized to carry cross-marketing to a higher level of "team cross-marketing." A cross-division team can strategize and sell to prospects for both divisions. A number of divisions can work together to sell the entire line of the company's products and services to a major customer in a coordinated system. For instance, General Electric organized a team of more than 50 salespeople to win an important contract with General Motors' Saturn subsidiary in 1987. The team represented eight different GE divisions. The team made the sale.

27

Frontline Marketing

Specific approaches and skills whereby non-selling, frontline people who come into contact with customers and prospects develop a positive and proactive attitude, provide outstanding service, and at the same time take specific selling actions. These actions might include information gathering, prospecting, looking for referrals and testimonials, and being supportive of their company or institution and its products and services while in contact with customers. The salesperson, professional, or manager can assist and encourage peers and associates to "frontline market," and thereby gain frontline support for their selling efforts.

ILLUSTRATION AND RATING—27A

Frontline marketing is marketing by frontline personnel. In certain circumstances, such as for AT&T engineering in the illustration below, it can be critically important to your success as a salesperson and to the success of your corporation or business unit.[1]

This most frequently is the case when you have many frontline people in direct contact with customers, when good customer service is important to customer satisfaction, and when non-sales, frontline employees are or can be an important information source, for instance, on customer satisfaction, purchases, and business leads.

❙❙ In frontline marketing employees who have no official selling responsibility at all take actions not only to give great customer ❙❙

---

1. The beginning of the book's Introduction, about paragraph 10, talks about "getting it." Hopefully by now, if not long before, you have "gotten it." Some people might wonder why this chapter is in a book on selling. It is because under certain conditions the contents of this chapter are more important to your selling success than positioning yourself, "grasping" critical issues, getting appointments, closing sales, or anything else people normally think of as "selling."

service, but indirectly to help sell the company's products and services.

These could include accountants, customer service people, bank tellers, hospital nurses, functional specialists, delivery truck drivers, warehouse people, research and development engineers, purchasing and production employees, and operating department managers, among others.

They develop positive relationships with customers. They are supportive of the company and its products, services, and people when dealing with customers.

They may learn how to ask questions, probe, and listen effectively. They may search out opportunities for new sales, up-selling, or product/service development. They may pass this information on to a salesperson, manager, or professional. Or they may talk to customers, ask questions, probe further, and encourage the customers to purchase a product or service.

They may have the confidence to nudge the customer or suggest that the customer take action. For instance, they might suggest that the customer specify or request their company's products or services, and explain why. This is because you and your company's management did things to boost their self confidence, product knowledge, and communication skills.

You as a salesperson can train, lead, and nudge the people who support your selling efforts to take these and other frontline marketing actions.

As a result, for instance, delivery truck drivers could look for ways to add extra value. And while they are stocking or checking shelves for the customer to determine restocking needs, they could think about and suggest additional items that the customer could purchase. They could look for opportunities to speak positively about your company. They could remind the customer's employees about the extra and high level services being provided by your company. All these should positively influence sales and customer satisfaction.

When we were working with the engineering divisions of AT&T,[2] the company had just divested the Regional Bell Operating Companies (called RBOCs) part of the business—such as Southwestern Bell, Pacific Bell, and Southern Bell. By the time I was involved, the RBOCs had started doing much of their own engineering. As a result, the engineering divisions of central AT&T were thinking about looking for new business opportunities. They also were trying, with mixed success, to convince the RBOCs that they should continue to use the services of AT&T central engineering for the majority of their engineering work.

---

2. These are the same AT&T engineering organizations discussed in Chapter 12.

Through management, we worked with the thousands of AT&T frontline engineers to help them perfect their skills related to frontline marketing. As a result, they developed more positive relationships with RBOC engineers. (Before the divestiture, the central engineers had treated the RBOC engineers rather shabbily. Also, AT&T released some engineers who took jobs at the RBOCs. These made the new task even more difficult.)

The AT&T engineers were trained and coached to probe to find the engineering needs of the RBOCs. Then they determined which needs were the types that AT&T central engineering could perform much better than RBOC engineering, and reported this back to their managements (who reported the larger opportunities to the sales department). The AT&T engineers presented evidence to RBOC engineers as to why they should use the services of AT&T engineering—and why they should specify or request engineering services from AT&T.

Five FLM Topics

The following were the five frontline marketing (FLM) topics addressed in the AT&T frontline marketing training and follow-up:

1. Belief in themselves, AT&T, and the quality of their engineering services
2. Product knowledge (engineering needed by the RBOCs, how to look for it, which is best performed by AT&T central engineering, and the benefits to the RBOCs of using AT&T instead of doing it themselves)
3. Relationship development
4. Listening for sales opportunities
5. Responding to sales opportunities

As a result of the frontline engineers employing these five frontline marketing skills, it is believed that AT&T central engineering saved many tens of millions of dollars in profitable business.

Other organizations—including banks, savings associations, credit unions, hotels, and hospitals—have been successful in employing frontline marketing. It has been helpful to salespeople, managers, and consultants in large corporations. It has been helpful to owners and professionals in smaller companies. It has helped them to get their people involved in giving better service and in marketing and selling the company's products and services.

Thought Provokers

(1) Which of your frontline people have the most contact with customers and the greatest ability to positively or negatively influence customer attitudes and behavior?

(2) If they were effective in frontline marketing, you and your company would benefit. How would your frontline people benefit? What could be done to improve the benefit to them?

(3) What could be done to improve the benefit to your customers?

(4) How could some of your frontline people directly influence customer purchases? In other words, what could they do to help you sell?

Take the following rating exercise to estimate how important "frontline marketing" is to your selling success. Based on the results, you can continue on with reading about its implementation, you can go back and read about the implementation of previous strategies and skills, or you can move on to the final chapter and Appendixes—and come back later to Section 27B.

CHAPTER RATING (rate A, B, and C below from 1 to 5 for this chapter's importance; then multiply)

_____ **A** = Importance or applicability to you (5 = great, 3 = moderate, 1 = poor)

_____ **B** = Your present strength or level of action (1 = great to 5 = poor) *(reverse rating)*

_____ **C** = Chances of your successful implementation or improvement (5 = great to 1 = poor)

A × B × C = your rating (_____) × (_____) × (_____) = (_____)

If your rating is over 25, read "Implementation" now; if 25 or under, consider postponing until later.

IMPLEMENTATION—27B

FLM Process[3]

The following are some action ideas for you to keep in mind when encouraging frontline marketing.

➤ Proactively determine what are the most effective ways frontline and other support people can assist in frontline marketing.

➤ Communicate to your people what frontline marketing is, especially the aspects related to supporting selling activities.

---

3. Added value strategies can be helpful in accomplishing effective frontline marketing. See Chapter 7. *Integrated Business Leadership through Cross-Marketing* by Michael Baber addresses in detail how to accomplish frontline marketing.

- Obtain ideas from them as to how they might be more effective in delivering effective customer service and in supporting the selling effort.
- Design and implement a training program to educate and lead frontline people to frontline market in those specific areas where they can be most effective.
- Have each frontline and supervisory person, and team, complete a "T" diagram. A "T" diagram lists on the left side "ways to create and keep customers," and on the right side "ways to enrage and drive away customers." Then have them select from the two sides the few items that should yield for them the greatest positive results. Have them develop and implement action plans to put into effect the best ideas. Follow-up on the action plans.
- Consider having each team create a "T" diagram for other units with which they are closely associated. They can then review the diagram with those teams, to help them gain outside perspective. This requires a positive, supporting attitude by both teams.
- Consider having certain customers or customer groups create a "T" diagram for your company or unit.
- Consider implementing an action plan process in which every frontline person completes a (simple) weekly action plan giving their frontline marketing objectives and plans for accomplishing those objectives. Then follow-up on those action plans without fail. Provide help as needed when people are unable to accomplish their objectives.
- Develop and implement a recognition and reward program to support effective frontline marketing.

FLM Ideas and Truths

The following are some philosophical ideas and "truths" to keep in mind when implementing, or nudging your supporting associates to be active in, frontline marketing.

- The first priority of frontline people is to perform their assigned duties with excellence.
- To perform a job with excellence, one must know what the job is, how it relates to the customer and to unit objectives, and exactly what one must do to perform with excellence, including how that is measured.
- Teamwork and cooperation with others is almost always required to perform your own work with excellence.
- Even when it isn't, teamwork and cooperation helps others do their

jobs better. This helps give the customer better service, which results in more sales and profitability for your company.

► Frontline people should be proactive in looking for ways to serve the customer better and in looking for ways to help in the selling process. Being proactive means reaching out and making things happen rather than being reactive and waiting for things to happen, or for people to come to you.

► They should be "perpetually dissatisfied." There almost always is a better way to do a job or serve a customer.

► The world is changing so rapidly that an action or approach that was best five years ago almost by definition is not best today.

► You probably can be much more important to the success of your company if you proactively look for ways to do so.

► The best way to find out what customers expect and how you are doing as compared to those expectations is to ask them. Often the so-called "wisest" people in your company think they know what the customer expects and they are wrong.

► On the other hand, often customers don't realize what they or some other unit in their organization needs that you might provide. You may have to research this and then communicate the need to your customer contact.

► Most people have slack time in their jobs that could be used for finding ways to improve performance. Or, it could be used for prospecting and other indirect selling activities, if they plan their work and work their plans.

PART G

CHAMPIONS

IMPLEMENTATION

28

How You Can Sell Like a Champion

Sales champions sell something "entirely" different, or in an "entirely" different way, or in a "far" better way than do other salespeople; by which they provide "extraordinary" value to "high potential" customer segments.

So, to become a sales champion, or at least to "far outsell" your peers and competitors, "Go and do likewise." At this point, hopefully, you are convinced that accomplishing this is something you can do.

Baber's Law states that performing the few most important actions well, by itself, goes a long way toward achieving the highest level of performance.

Your first objective should be to identify the one or the few strategies or skills on which to concentrate to achieve the greatest positive results. Perhaps you did this when reading and evaluating the "A" section of Chapters 1–27. Appendix E lists additional ways, but you probably will not need them.

Your second objective should be to prepare one or more action plans. Through these you effectively implement the selected few strategies and skills, and make them a integral part of how you sell. These can be based on the "B" section of the one, or the few, chapters (strategies or skills) you select for emphasis. Appendix F lists additional helps and supports, including the offer for you to phone the Business Development Institute, if required, for "free" assistance.

Your third objective should be to effectively carry out those plans, achieve the desired results, and obtain the resulting "championship" benefits.

There are some cautions to be considered in carrying out this process. Keep what you do simple, straightforward, and easy to understand. Don't try to be too clever or complicated. If you do, you're almost certain to fail. Don't ignore ideas just because they appear too obvious. Sometimes the most obvious, best approaches are ignored for reasons that seem ill-founded or downright strange until they are examined carefully. Don't go overboard. Start small. Do one thing well and when that works, add to it. Aim for leadership, at being the best in what you choose. Plan for the present. Don't make the mistake of concentrating only on what will provide results in the future. Build on your strengths. If the approach doesn't "feel like you," it probably isn't for you.

B² FORMULA

The formula $B^2 = S$ (Basics x Brilliance = Success) applies to championship selling as well as to other endeavors.

High jumpers need to do the basics well. They need to build their conditioning. They need to take the right number of approach steps and with a rhythmic pattern. They need to gain momentum as they approach the bar. They need to follow through on their jump.

All these basics are important to being good. However, if they discover something different and better to do that other jumpers don't do, they can become the best.

At one time all high jumpers used the scissors kick. The first jumper who became excellent at rolling over the bar set a world's record. The "roll" or "flop" was a different and much superior way to high jump, which of course everyone uses today. Discovering the rolling high jump was "brilliant."

In your selling, you need to build your conditioning, gain momentum, and follow through. But you also need to find your "roll" if you are going to become a champion.

The first B stands for the basics. To apply the first B, review all the basic principles and practices of successful selling, such as those presented in the Appendixes, discussed in this book, and in other materials you have read or listened to. Choose the few where it is most important for you to improve. Concentrate on improving in the "most important" practice or skill. After you have mastered it, move to the second, then to the third, and so on.

To apply the second B, brilliance, find the one way (or the very few ways) you can sell differently and better than your competitors and other "good" salespeople. Perhaps it is using just one of the 27 championship selling strategies and skills discussed in this book. If so, implement it with brilliance.

The following strategic approach presented in the book's text may be helpful. You can apply it to the championship selling strategy or skill you select for concentration.

(1) **Situation Summary.** List the what, who, when, where, why, and how concerning that strategy or skill.
(2) **Baber's Law Analysis Conclusion.** Decide on what to concentrate for most effective results (on which part or aspect of that strategy or skill).
(3) **Objective(s).** List what specifically you plan to accomplish.
(4) **Strategy(ies)** (for achieving the objective[s]). Lay out how you plan to do it; your overall approach for implementing that strategy or skill.
(5) **Plan(s)** (for implementing the strategy[ies]). List the steps to be taken, when and by whom, to accomplish that strategy for achieving the objective(s).

In selecting your area(s) of concentration and in developing your objectives and strategies, remember to think outside the box of traditional thinking. Be practical and sensible. But be creative, innovative, and big thinking.

Your "brilliant" strategy or skill may require considerable time and resources for total implementation. Joe Gandolfo spent years in selling the new way, and he returned to college to supplement his expertise and experience in tax shelter consulting. Of course, he earned millions of dollars as a result.

And you may want to test it in two ways before totally implementing it.

The first way would be to present your idea and how you might implement it to a group of knowledgeable, skeptical associates. Have them try to shoot it down. Then evaluate their negative comments as to how you can overcome them.

The second way is to develop a strategy and plan, and try it out in a small way—say in a small segment or with a few smaller, less significant accounts. This should take less time and have fewer negative consequences if you are wrong, or if as a result of the test you decide to modify the approach to improve it, which you probably will.

According to Baber's Law very few people become selling champions. In part, this is because they lack the willpower to try. But those who do try and really apply the ideas in this book will generate great results. They may generate results for their customers, their companies, and themselves that are phenomenal. The goal is worthy of the effort.

As the saying goes, "It is better to shoot for the stars and hit the moon than to shoot for a bird and hit a rock." As someone else said, "Hitting the moon ain't all that bad." Vision without action is just a dream. Action without vision is just passing time. Vision with action can change the world.

I believe you can change your world forever for the good by developing a vision and taking effective action based on one or more of the championship selling strategies and skills discussed in this book. It worked for the selling champions discussed in these pages. If you do, and I believe you can, let me hear from you. I'd like to tell your story in the updated version of *How Champions Sell.*

Appendix A

Championship Selling Fundamentals

Performing the fundamentals of selling with excellence—including gathering information, prospecting, making appointments, developing relationships, finding and solving problems, communicating benefits, confirming the order, and servicing the customer, all with an attitude and approach of delivering great value to the customer.

Most selling champions sell in a professional, customer-serving way. This is exemplified by the following approach.

(1) Deliver extraordinary service
(2) Gather background data and information
(3) Prospect and obtain referrals
(4) Prepare to sell
(5) Make appointments/Arrange meetings
(6) Meet, greet, and develop relationships
(7) Gather information, analyze, and prepare presentation
(8) Make the selling presentation and answer questions
(9) Confirm the contract or sale
(10) Deliver extraordinary service

The steps are discussed below, with some of the actions champions take in carrying them out. Additional, related, and creative actions are discussed in other appendixes.

1. Deliver Extraordinary Service

Work with the people in your organization to provide outstanding service to existing accounts—clients, customers, patients, guests—those who pay for what you provide. As a result, you give them the products and services they want, the way they want them—in a friendly, effective, and hassle-free manner. (Giving them what they need can be different from giving them what they want. Try to give them both.)

You then have happy clients. You deserve to expand your business with them and ask for business from others. You get positive referrals and testimonials.

2. Gather Background Data and Information

Gather data and information on target industries, existing accounts, and important prospects. This helps you identify what the trends are, where the business is, and where you should be placing your emphasis for selling.

Gather information, such as who is growing, who is changing, which managers have changed positions, and who is having problems. Review available data such as in periodicals and online resources. Talk with customers and prospects themselves. Don't just depend on the opinions of people inside your organization. Chapter 9 discusses some of the information to gather and analyze.

Identify potential problems and opportunities to address and potential people to contact. Gather information, such as who is satisfied with your present quality of products and level of service and who is not, by how much, why, and how you can make present customers and key personnel even more satisfied.

Determine who is friends with whom. Who is likely to give you referrals and who is not and why? Who has influence on whom? What are the strengths and weaknesses of competition? What is important to present to prospective customers and clients? What competitive companies are currently working with present and prospective accounts and how? What changes have occurred and are occurring? And determine what problems and opportunities those changes indicate for potential customers and for your company.

3. Prospect and Obtain Referrals

Be alert to subtle comments, actions, and events that could indicate the existence of problems or lead to new business, referrals, or agreeable prospects. Examples include an indication that a customer is happy or unhappy with his level of service, that a happy customer contact knows another department manager or a manager from another company particularly well, or that a potential prospect has something in common with you or a key person in your company.

Ask happy customers for referrals both directly and indirectly.

Perform direct mail marketing and networking to make you and your company visible in a positive way.

Proactively search for sensible excuses to communicate with potential prospects—such as sending them some information you know would interest them or meeting them through a mutual acquaintance.

Network through being active in key industry organizations and other appropriate organizations and activities.

Physically visit potential prospects to obtain information or to meet and get acquainted with them.

Read industry and company periodicals, looking for information that indicates a change is occurring related to a company. A change often opens up an opportunity, such as when a top manager is changed or when a new technology is being investigated.

More information on prospecting is presented in Chapter 24.

4. Prepare to Sell

Develop a positive personal selling attitude and approach. Do this through knowing your products, services, and added value, and their potential advantages and benefits to the customer (as compared to competition and as compared to self-performance of services by the customer).

Develop your self-confidence and self-image.

Be friendly and outgoing.

Develop enthusiasm for your products, services, and company.

Know what questions to ask, how to ask them, and how to listen effectively.

Be persistent because you really believe in what you offer. And truly attempt to serve the customer's best interests.

Develop an effective selling approach and supportive selling tools, such as presentation cards, evidence to back up your claims of service superiority, and persuasive pre- and post-visit literature.

Be aware of the types of problems and opportunities your company most frequently solves successfully.

Become informed about and develop expertise in areas related to known customer and prospect interests, opportunities, and problems.

Develop a list of questions that you need answered by the prospect before you can properly prepare a proposal or make a recommendation.

Anticipate and prepare effective answers to questions and objections from the prospect.

Analyze available data to determine which types of prospects (industries, companies, departments, people, problem areas) are most likely to be successfully converted into clients and customers, and how to best approach each.

Determine the kind of information you need concerning the account's or prospect's situation. Gather as much as possible from outside sources (such as periodicals, referrals, and online bulletin boards) and from friendly people inside account organizations before making appointments with key contacts or decision makers. This is for two purposes. First, to impress the account with your preparation. Second, to leave as much time as possible available for information gathering on problems, opportunities, and other important information needs.

5. Make Appointments/Arrange Meetings

Develop an effective appointment- or meeting-generating process through study, experimentation, and preparation.

Utilize referrals to obtain appointments when possible.

Know clearly why the prospect would be foolish to not at least talk to you.

Develop relationships with secretaries and associates who can assist you in obtaining an appointment with the prospect or decision maker.

Prepare the potential prospect through actions such as calling and mailing ahead, being professional and positive during the appointment phone call, and developing innovative ways to obtain appointments.

6. Meet, Greet, and Develop Relationships

Develop a meeting-greeting-relationship development process that works for you and with your personality.

Attempt to learn about the prospect—company, department, problem area, or person—before the visit so you appear informed and can relate effectively.

Be friendly but businesslike.

Be friendly and respectful to the secretary and everyone else who might influence your success now and later.

Relate effectively to the prospective customer's personality style. For instance, getting down to business quickly and avoiding tedious details with a bottom-line oriented driver style; relaxing, being gentle and personal, and taking it slow with a tentative amiable style; sharing stories and having some fun with an outgoing expressive style; or having some detailed facts with supporting evidence to share early with a numbers-oriented analytical style.

Meet and develop a relationship with all decision makers and decision influencers.

Strategize to develop relationships at the highest, most influential level as early as possible.

Offer a genuine compliment. Use that as a basis to explain why you wanted to meet with the prospective customer and how you might be able to help them. Perhaps use an enthusiastic, professional, businesslike, large benefit claim to generate their interest.

Explain that you need some additional information to know exactly how you can benefit the prospect and ask permission to ask some questions.

Invite them to share a mutual interest or sport, such as a golf game or tennis outing. Then have fun and pretty much forget business during the outing.

7. Gather Information, Analyze, and Prepare Presentation

Ask appropriate questions of the prospective account.

Listen respectfully and effectively, taking written notes as appropriate. Avoid the appearance of asking machine-gun questions or probing in sensitive areas (while probing in sensitive areas in a subtle and skillful manner— which requires experience and practice).

Look for areas that are of particular importance to the prospect.

Look for areas of present satisfaction and dissatisfaction.

Look for personal motivations that might in some way be supported by selecting your company as a product and/or service provider.

Be prepared to explain why you need the answers to specific questions if asked.

Appear and be both expert and professional at developing customer-serving sales proposals.

Know the importance of the questions asked so the information received can be used effectively in preparing a persuasive, honest selling proposal or recommendation.

Know how to make a sales proposal or recommendation professional, impressive, and persuasive. Know how to prepare effective, clear, and persuasive audiovisuals, such as display boards and videotapes.

Use a questioning process that leads the customer to identify problems, implications, and solution benefits. The SPIN questioning format explained in Chapter 17 accomplishes these goals.

8. Make the Selling Presentation and Answer Questions

Utilize effective meeting and presentation skills.

Utilize a selling team if appropriate. Bring in other appropriate team members and partners. Coordinate and train the team before the presentation. Perhaps practice the presentation with a stand-in team of prospects.

Be sensitive to prospect questions during the presentation even when they are not vocalized.

Draw out and answer questions confidently and respectfully.

Involve the prospect in the presentation so it is more of a discussion than a one-way conversation.

Plan for and ask questions of the prospect during the presentation—especially those questions that cause the prospect to sell himself.

Clarify questions asked and objections received as appropriate so you don't make mistakes in responding to them.

Remain in control of the presentation and don't allow it to get off track unnecessarily.

Be prepared to offer evidence to back up any claims made.

Be internally enthusiastic and display confidence that you really can help the account in a significant way.

Demonstrate how purchasing your product or service helps the prospect personally, as well as his organization.

Present as many explicit benefits as possible, based on information revealed by the customer when he was answering implication and need-payoff questions. Explicit benefits are those that the prospect has indicated he needs or should act on, not those you think he should need.

9. Confirm the Contract or Sale

Avoid the use of closing techniques and gimmicks.

Never appear to be pushing the prospect before he is ready to decide, but never forget to "ask for the order" when it is appropriate.

Be sensitive to when the prospect is favorably impressed with your company and presentation, and when he might respond favorably to a confirming question. Then ask for the order when appropriate.

Don't be tentative or appear to wonder whether the prospect should make a positive buying decision.

Use trial confirmation (trial closing) statements such as "How do you feel about that?" or "If you were to decide to go ahead with this would you want to start immediately or wait until the beginning of next quarter?"

Admit to any obvious truth—including when that truth keeps you from getting the business. That builds your reputation as an honest straight shooter. It also demonstrates your character and honesty.

Nudge the prospect toward a decision that is in his best interest. And make every effort to make your sales proposal fit both his and your best interest.

Be prepared to efficiently complete all paperwork once a positive decision is made by the prospect.

10. Deliver Extraordinary Service

Start with service; end with service. (This includes maintaining relationships, and proactively seeking referrals, and expanded business).

Work within your own organization to make sure everything you promised the customer is delivered—properly and on time.

Develop positive relationships within your organization so you have a network of powerful and cooperative friends who trust and respect you and will respond positively to your queries and requests on behalf of your customers.

Continue to offer competent, professional service once the purchase is made.

Over-communicate with the customer.

Work at more-than-effectively fulfilling both organizational and personal wants and needs for the customer.

Ask satisfied customers, when appropriate, for the names of potential prospects, and plan ahead as to how to do this most effectively.

Continually gather information about the company and marketplace from numerous sources.

Network through customers, contacts, and friends on a planned basis.

Generate lots of profitable business with happy customers.

Appendix B

Creatively Defining Customer Benefits

$ Value Determination

Estimating and presenting the total $ value (the estimated total *economic consequences) of your proposed solution.*

The $ *value* is a new concept to most salespeople. It usually is higher, and can be many times higher, than what the customer (and most salespeople) think it is. This helps to increase its importance. It is higher because it includes many elements, many of which most salespeople ignore. $ value includes the obvious economic benefits from the salesperson's problem solution. This comes from solving the problem and the associated implications, and providing the need-payoffs—see SPIN questioning, Chapter 17. It includes added values supplied. It includes an informed estimate (sometimes called a "SWAG") of the associated and down-the-line (often soft) benefits and consequences. Frequently these are much larger than the obvious benefits.

For instance, a salesperson may be selling a solution for the problem of a division's computer going down, where the computer provides inventory and sales data to a number of branches around the country on a real-time basis. The solution (service or product sold) might be software or a fast data storage drive.

The $ value of the solution includes saving not only the cost of replacement parts, repair time, and overtime for the data processing department when the computer goes down. But, in addition, it includes the estimated economic consequences—the lost effectiveness in data processing the following days because of department employees being overtired from working the overtime. It includes the lost sales during the downtime, the loss of confidence in the company by the customers affected and prospects who hear of the problem, the associated wasted time of sales leaders and inside and outside salespeople, and the wasted time of corporate management personnel who were contacted to help deal with the situation.

Plus, it includes other negative economic effects, such as the inability to hire championship salespeople who don't care to work for a company they believe doesn't properly support its sales force. In addition, included in the purchase price of the solution (whether it be hardware, software, or services) may be certain added value such as free software and consulting services, or assistance with related problems or challenges—all of which provide additional $ value.

Understanding the $ value of the proposed solution, by itself, often can cause the customer to decide for the value-selling salesperson's proposed solution. It also can help the salesperson improve the solution and its resulting value to the customer.

Determining $ value can help salespeople with one of their biggest challenges: developing a meaningful relationship with the customer's upper management. Many upper level managers today are concerned with EVA (economic value added). EVA was developed by Stern, Stewart & Company and is described in "The Real Key to Creating Wealth," *Fortune*, September 20, 1993. Those who are not familiar with EVA should be and may welcome a competent introduction to EVA. A $ value–understanding salesperson can talk in terms of EVA and how $ value helps with EVA. This is talk that many in upper management will find interesting.

PERSONAL BENEFITS

The personal benefits to each customer contact from solving a personal need, ministering to a dominant buying motive, and/or providing a personal result win. The "result win" is how the contact personally benefits from the company's purchase, such as gaining desired recognition or having her job become easier as a result. Thus, each customer contact understands how she personally will benefit from choosing the salesperson's solution.

As a salesperson you not only call on and sell to accounts (companies), you call on and sell to individuals (people) in those accounts. Those individuals can be decision makers. They can be decision influencers such as the buyer, the user, upper management, or a technical inside consultant. It is important to determine how each one of these can benefit personally from choosing to work with you.

People make decisions and encourage the company to make certain purchases or select one supplier in preference to another because it benefits the company. They also make decisions and encourage the company to make certain purchases or select one supplier in preference to another because it benefits them personally.

There are three ways they can benefit personally: personal needs, motives, and result wins.

Personal Needs

First, all people have certain personal needs. As a starter, they are in one or more of the five levels of the Maslow need hierarchy in regard to this purchase decision.

The lowest level is the physiological need, the need for food, shelter, and clothing.

The next level is the need for security. They might be at this level if they feared losing their job or getting demoted. They would thus respond positively to anything you could provide that would make them appear more competent.

The next level is personal relationship need. You might fulfill this by being a good friend. Or by caring about them or being one of the few people in the world who listens to them in a personal, interested way. You might fulfill this by helping them develop a better relationship with others in their company, perhaps because of purchasing from you and what that purchase will do for others in the company.

Next comes ego need; the need for recognition; the need to feel important or that they have made a great contribution.

The highest Maslow level is self-actualization, where the person is doing something to feel self-fulfilled (such as painting or writing a book) or to make a contribution to humanity.

Thus, people have specific personal needs you might help fulfill. They might have a need for a closer relationship with a friend or relative. They might feel a need in their life to have meaning or to make a positive contribution to the world before they die. If they can see that working with you will fulfill their Maslow hierarchy need, they are more likely to want to do business with you.

Motives

Second, people operate from their own personal motives. There are six basic buying motives.

The first is desire for gain (as by receiving a raise or a small memento).

The second is fear of loss. Many people are more motivated to not lose what they have than to gain more.

The third is desire to be loved or accepted. This could be to be loved or accepted by you, by fellow associates, or by someone else.

The fourth is the desire to be important. Everyone wants to be important and to feel that what they are doing is worthwhile. You can make people feel important through sincere compliments. You can make them feel important by being a good, attentive listener or by showing them meaningful respect. Or you can arrange circumstances so that working with you makes them feel or look important in the eyes of peers or upper management. If you do, and they have this motive, they are going to be inclined to want to do business with you.

The fifth buying motive is pride. They may take pride in beating down the supplier and getting the lowest possible price. If so, you may look for a competitive win for them other than price—like increased added value. Or they might decide to do business with you because you have a high reputation in the industry and it makes them look good to be doing business with you as compared to your "nobody" competitor. If this were the buying motive of a number of key people in a market segment, you might want to spend time becoming a "celebrity" in that segment. See Chapter 22, which presents Industry-Specific Self Marketing.

The sixth motive is love. They may make a buying decision because it brings benefits to someone or something they care about. If so, and you know who or what they care for and design your approach to benefit that person or cause, you increase your chances of getting business.

Determine the customer contact's buying motives and present yourself and your solution as being consistent with those motives.

Result Wins

Third, people make buying decisions because of the result wins those decisions bring them. Determine how each decision maker and decision influencer can win from doing business with you and design your proposal to give them that result win. A result win is specific. Some examples are having more time to spend with their family; increasing their chances for a promotion or raise; looking like an innovative, out-of-the box thinker; or having their department become recognized in some positive way.

Find out how you can provide each key account contact one or more personal benefits and you increase your chances of getting the business and having a happy client or customer.

Appendix C

Creatively Performing the Selling Process

THE SALES CALL PROCESS FOR THE SMALL OR REPEATING SALE

Effectively meeting and greeting the prospect or account, information gathering, making the appropriate presentation, gaining commitment for the right purchase arrangement, and following up on the sale to make sure it is serviced properly.

There are two guidelines to the sales call process for the small or repeating sale.

The first guideline is to focus on preventing rather than handling objections. This is accomplished by being prepared, and doing an effective job of information gathering so you know where prospects have problems and opportunities, and can lead them to know how important they are. It means getting them interested in something before you present anything, and having evidence to support your claims. It means being sincerely passionate about the value you can bring them if they make the purchase, which they sense and respond to positively. It may mean using SPIN questioning (see Chapter 17).

The second guideline is to focus on both the rational and the emotional aspects of the sale. For instance, you appeal to the rational when you talk about needs, results for the company, benefits, and added value received, and have them see the implications of their problems and the tremendous need-payoff from solving them. You appeal to their emotions when you talk about wants, result wins for them, fulfilling personal needs and motives, and are enthusiastic, friendly, caring, and interested in their views. Frequently people buy for emotional reasons and justify the decision to themselves and others with rational explanations and evidence.

1. Meeting and Greeting

The first of the five steps to the sales call process for the small or repeating sale is meeting and greeting. You walk in the door for the first or umpteenth time. You need to say hello, make the prospect feel comfortable with your being there, and get him interested in the purpose of your call. Otherwise he just won't listen, or he wonders why you are wasting your and his time.

There are three parts to the meeting and greeting process: building rapport, obtaining prospects' attention, and generating interest.

You build rapport by talking to prospects briefly about something in which they are interested, usually themselves. This is the time to talk about the lawn out front, something nice you heard about them or their company, their weekend golf game, or their family. Unless it is necessary to do otherwise, this should take just a minute or two. After all, both you and they are professionals and busy.

Have you ever been greeted in the hallway and been told that the prospect is busy and would you please say what you have to say right there? At that point you don't even have his business attention. You should have an important sales call objective or you shouldn't be making the sales call. It is the rare "important" sales call objective that can be accomplished in a hallway.

Your prospects may have had a problem at home, or they may be thinking about all the work they have to do that day. Until you get their attention (the second part of meeting and greeting) off those things and onto you and your business, you shouldn't proceed.

There are ten commonly known mechanisms for getting the prospect's attention. They follow the acronym, SAM CRINGES. They are in order: the startling statement, asking a question bearing on a need, the mystery opener (like holding something relating to business in a box and glancing at it until you are asked about it), a sincere compliment, a referral (probably the most powerful of all), an incident of successful use of your product or service or a category of your product or service, a famous name, a gift—appropriate to the occasion, an exhibit, and providing a valuable service of some kind.

Third, generate their interest. Generate their interest by making a big claim they can believe, making a big possible claim (like, our gadget has helped a number of other companies increase productivity by as much as 100% and perhaps it can do that for you. Could I ask you a few questions?) or by asking questions that cause them to develop interest.

One of the biggest mistakes salespeople make is making their sales presentation before they have gotten the prospect interested in anything.

2. *Information Gathering*

After getting the prospect's attention, and just before or after generating interest, you proceed to ask questions and gather information that tells you whether there is a meaningful reason for the two of you to do business, and probably how much value you can provide the prospect.

It is important that you be a good vvk listener to gather information properly. VVK stands for visual, verbal, and kinesthetic. Visual listening is listening through observation; observing what they have displayed on their desk and their facial expression, among other things. Verbal listening is normal listening through the ears. Kinesthetic listening is received through touch and inner feelings. It is what your emotions and "gut" tell you, and what emotions the prospect is displaying.

You need to ask questions properly during information gathering. The following are some points to keep in mind.

- Limit the number of "situation questions" (see Chapter 17)
- Make lists of, and practice, "implication" and "need-payoff" questions
- Ask permission to ask sensitive questions
- Delay sensitive/threatening questions until a positive relationship is developed
- Take notes as appropriate
- Delay writing down answers to "threatening" questions or sensitive comments until a later time when something non-threatening is being discussed

Make a list of business and personal concerns that need to be addressed before the sales call. The following are examples of business concerns.

- Who the decision maker is
- Specific problem questions based on your industry knowledge and research
- How serious a problem each could become (from implication questions)
- What could make it better or worse
- What solutions they have considered already and why

The following are examples of personal concerns.

- Correct spelling of names and titles
- Whose opinions they value
- Special events and people in their lives (such as birthdays and their children)
- What has brought them great joy
- What has brought them great frustration/irritation
- Personal interests and hobbies

3. Presentation

The presentation can be made in many forms and ways. It can be a formal audio or multi-media presentation to a large group of people. It can be one-on-one. The presentation may be entirely separate, coming after information gathering and before obtaining commitment. Or it may happen along with information gathering, either planned or unplanned. In almost all cases, it should not be a one way flow of information, but should be a discussion, with the customer usually doing more of the talking than the salesperson.

In the presentation step, you present the features and benefits of those aspects of your product or service that match the prospect's wants, needs, and opportunities as determined during the information gathering step. You totally ignore the other features and benefits, unless they are extraordinarily important or sell you or your company in some important way.

The following are some general concerns to keep in mind when planning the presentation step.

- ► The concern (major problem) that is agreed to before solution presentation begins
- ► Your best solution
- ► Features of your solution
- ► The most exciting features (to the prospect)
- ► Advantages of those "exciting" features
- ► Explicit benefits mentioned (with emotion) by the prospect (see Chapter 17)
- ► Evidence supporting those advantages and explicit benefits
- ► Supporting stories/incidents
- ► Supporting analogies
- ► Supporting metaphors.

4. Commitment

At this point you ask for the prospect to make a favorable buying decision. This is also called the closing step. It is discussed in the third section of this appendix.

5. Follow-Up and Service

After making a sale, make sure that you and everyone else in your company does what they should do to deliver and back up the product or service sold with excellence. Appendix D presents more information of interest regarding this step.

THE SALES CALL PROCESS FOR THE LARGE OR COMPLEX SALE

The sales call events looked at from the standpoint of the customer's concerns and actions. After account entry this involves four phases:

recognition of needs, evaluation of options, resolution of concerns, and implementation.

The large or complex sale generally represents a substantial risk for the buyer. Consequently, the buyer makes the purchase more slowly and goes through a more involved decision-making process than with the lower risk, small or repetitive purchase discussed just above.

Listed below are five phases to the large or complex sale. For this type of sale there usually are a number of decision makers or influencers involved. You need to be in contact with each. You might use team selling, with specialists on the team being the prime contacts for corresponding specialists at the customer (see Chapter 19).

Each of the decision makers and influencers move through these five phases at a different pace. In other words, one may be ready to make a purchase decision (being at the end of the "resolution of concerns" phase) while another (too often the decision maker or focus of power) isn't yet through the "recognition of needs" phase. This process is discussed further in the book *Major Account Sales Strategy* by Neil Rackham.

Phase 0. Account Entry

You identify a significant selling opportunity and find a way to penetrate the prospective account. You find, reach, and deal with the "focus of receptivity," the "focus of dissatisfaction," and the "focus of power" or decision maker.

You make contact with the decision maker and key decision influencers in the prospect company. Frequently, the easiest entry point is at the focus of receptivity. This may be people who are entirely out of the product/ service use and buying cycle. However, they have an interest in new or cutting edge ideas, or in the particular approach or technology represented by your company. They are intrigued, and are interested in talking with you. Perhaps they answered an ad, or contacted you because of an article you wrote. Perhaps you were referred to them when you talked to the account's receptionist.

The focus of receptivity can be a great source of information about the prospect, the various needs and opportunities, and the key contacts in the company. They often can serve as a referral or introduction to the user (frequently the focus of dissatisfaction) or the decision maker (the focus of power). They may serve as your coach at the account. They may help you to start identifying needs so you can get a start on Phase 1.

Phase 1. Recognition of Needs

During Phase 1 the prospective account (each of the decision makers and influencers individually) comes to realize that a need exists and it should be solved. In this phase you effectively uncover areas of dissatisfaction. You develop the dissatisfaction. You selectively channel the dissatisfaction to those areas where your product, service, or system is strong.

Before anything else can happen the decision maker and key influencers must recognize that there is a need for change. You can bring them to this understanding through your information gathering and questioning. SPIN questioning, discussed in Chapter 17 on preventing rejection and objections, can be helpful in finding problems or needs and then building their importance in the minds of the buyers with implication questions.

A typical strategic error is to start discussing solutions or moving to the evaluation of options phase before the buyer completes the recognition of needs phase, and clearly understands that a change needs to occur.

Phase 2. Evaluation of Options

The account evaluates available options. You uncover decision criteria, influence the decision criteria to favor your product, service, or system, and maximize the perceived fit of your product, service, or system with the decision criteria.

When buyers decide that a change probably is needed and start to examine ways or criteria for solving the problem or making the change, they have entered the evaluation of options phase. If there will be a bid, it is during this phase that the specifications for the bid are determined, the bid is let, and leading contenders are chosen. It also is during this phase that you have the opportunity to start establishing that a bid might not be a good idea, and start setting the stage for a negotiated arrangement, or even start negotiations.

A common mistake is to fail to realize that the buyer has recognized a need and has entered Phase 2. Thus, the salesperson continues to try to convince the buyer that she has a problem, when the buyer is already looking for a way to solve the problem. Phase 2 requires a different selling strategy from Phase 1.

It is critically important in this phase to clearly understand the buying criteria, and even influence it in your direction if you can. If you are selling "administrative convenience" and the buyer is primarily interested in "speed of delivery," you very well may miss the sale. Or suppose your company has great expertise in delivering administrative convenience and your competitor has greater expertise at speed of delivery. Unless you can lead all key decision makers and decision influencers to understand the importance of administrative convenience as opposed to speed of delivery, you may miss the sale.

Phase 3. Resolution of Concerns

The account realizes they have certain "consequence concerns" and then resolves them. You identify that consequence concerns exist that may block or affect your selling success. You uncover and classify the consequence concern issues, and help the customer resolve concern issues and to take positive action.

When buyers are about to make a final or purchase decision, they frequently have something similar to buyer's remorse. Last minute fears start popping up, sometimes with the assistance of your competitor.

Is the supplier properly capitalized? Has it failed to deliver in similar situations? Did we get a low enough price? What if the quality doesn't measure up to their promises? These and many related concerns are likely to come into the buyer's mind just before he is ready to sign that big contract.

It is important to stay close to all buying influences during these final stages. Look for concerns and questions that you need to answer or deal with. Look for a change in behavior or plans at the last minute. Then react quickly to put out any "concern fires" before they become a conflagration.

On the other hand, if the competitor seems to be in the stronger position, then you might want to fan some consequence concerns about the competitor to delay an unfavorable decision and give you time to regroup and attempt to change the sale in your direction.

After concerns are resolved, and assuming you have convinced the account that your proposal gives them the greatest value, you get the order.

Phase 4. Implementation

Your solution is implemented, but not in total immediately.

The account starts to implement your solution, finds that everything doesn't work perfectly at first, and seeks your assistance and reassurance. You don't go away if you're smart. You stay in contact to provide the assurance, make sure the assistance is rendered properly, and later receive the credit and referrals from a satisfied customer.

After a purchase decision is made in your favor, you effectively lead the customer through the toy stage, the learning stage, and the effectiveness stage. You thereby produce a happy customer who gives you repeat business, references, and referrals.

Once the decision is made, too frequently the salesperson relaxes and goes on vacation, or on to sell to another prospect. But it is at this point that the buyer is under the most pressure. He wants to see a positive result from this expensive and "risky" decision in your favor. If you aren't around, he gets very nervous.

Once the purchase is made, the toy stage is entered. That is a happy stage in which the product or service is first delivered or installed and no one expects anything to work perfectly. The buyer has fun playing with the new "toy."

Then comes the learning stage, when everyone at the buying account gets serious about implementing the purchase and learning how to make it work properly. Of course, at first it doesn't. Then something else doesn't work as planned. It is important that the salesperson and/or his proper representative be on hand to solve the problems and to assure the buyer that everything will work out well.

Once the purchase becomes effectively implemented, and customer service is great, the buyer becomes a salesperson for your company. It is then that you go after and get testimonial letters and prospect referrals. You use those referrals to enter Phase 0, account entry, with a new prospect, or on a new project with this account, and the cycle of success starts again.

OBTAINING A COMMITMENT DECISION

Knowing at what point in the selling process or presentation to ask for or hint at a customer commitment (sale, closing), taking action when and only when the customer is ready to take action, and understanding what has to happen before it is appropriate to take action and ask for the buying commitment.

In old selling terminology, this is "closing the sale" or "asking for the order." In new selling terminology, this is "confirming the sale," or "obtaining a commitment decision." The difference may seem semantic, but it is fundamental.

Once you know something about the prospect's industry you have a good idea of what questions to ask to determine what the problems or opportunities that relate to your product or service are, and how important they are to the buyer. Then it is a matter of asking those questions, and others that come up during the conversation, and getting the buyer to agree (1) that there is an important problem or opportunity, (2) that together you have found a solution, (3) that the solution brings him great value and far more than the cost, (4) that he should act on it by purchasing from or working with you, and (5) how and when he should do so.

One of the most valuable skills in getting a final commitment from a client (to make a purchase) is the skill and process of asking the "trial close" commitment question. This is especially helpful for an associate who is not an experienced salesperson and is somewhat intimidated by this process. The trial close is a question you ask the customer that doesn't ask him to buy or make a buying decision, but asks his opinion on something. One example of a trial close is, "How does this sound to you so far?" Another type of trial close is the "either-or" trial close; such as, "If you were going to go ahead with this idea, would you want to do this or that?" For instance, "If you were going to go ahead with this idea, would you want to go ahead and do it today or would you prefer for me to drop by tomorrow?"

It is important to have the "right" sales call objective to attempt to confirm. There are five potential objectives, and results, from a sales call: the right order, the wrong order, an advance, a continuation, and no-sale. Only two should be considered a success—the right order and an advance. Let's discuss each of the five in turn.

The "right order" is a confirmation of what should have been your sales call objective. It, in effect, is the order that maximizes both the value you provide the customer and the long term profit you obtain by providing that value. It is the best, or close to the best, you could expect to achieve on that particular sales call. The wrong order is something less.

Many times when I travel with salespeople I see them ask for and take an order that is many times smaller than that potentially available to them. They take the "wrong order."

An "advance" is a legitimate sales call objective and result other than a purchase decision. An advance is a specific positive movement toward the right order. For instance, suppose you need to run a test or have the prospect meet a specialist to have a chance at a large order. Then a sales call that confirms an agreement to hold the test, or makes an appointment for the specialist to come in and meet the prospect, is an advance.

A "continuation," on the other hand, is not a legitimate sales call objective or result. Too many salespeople make a call to maintain a relationship. Generally, that may be a valid customer service objective, but it is not a valid sales call objective. First, they probably didn't need to make the call to maintain the relationship. It could have been maintained in a simpler, less costly way. They probably just didn't plan for the call, and just went in to the account to do nothing of great value. In fact, they probably didn't plan for the account or the sales call. They probably don't plan well for most sales calls. A "continuation" maintains the status quo. That is not a valid sales call objective. It should at least be replaced with an "advance."

The fifth potential objective and result is "no sale." This is not a positive sales call result. It didn't take a rocket scientist to figure that out.

Have a positive, assumptive attitude. Assume that the prospect or customer likes and respects you and wants your help. In fact, approach the selling process in almost exactly the same way you would if the prospect had phoned you and asked you to help solve an unclear problem. Assume the customer will act favorably if she understands what the problem is, how you can solve it, and how it is to her benefit to do so. This has a positive emotional effect on you both.

Don't have an attitude that you must "close a sale." Instead, your attitude should be that you want to help the customer solve a problem or take advantage of an opportunity.

Don't be in a hurry; at least don't appear to be. Proceed when the time is right, but not before. The time is right when the customer is comfortable with you, he understands his need and your solution to that need, he understands how big the need is, both you and he believe that it is an appropriate solution, and he has no further important unanswered questions.

Do ask for a commitment. Too often the customer or prospect is willing to act, is never asked to act, and doesn't.

Appendix D
Creatively Serving the Customer

EXTRAORDINARY CUSTOMER SERVICE

Providing customers what they want, when they want it, without hassle. Participating proactively, and helping others to participate in effectively learning customer expectations, solving customer-related problems, and taking actions to serve customer needs and expectations.

A study was performed in the early 1980s for the White House Office of Consumer Affairs by TARP (Technical Assistance Research Programs, Inc.) that came to the following conclusions:

- For every customer who complains to your company, there are 26 who are unhappy but do not complain.
- The average unhappy customer tells 9–10 other people about it, and as a result,
- For every complaint your company receives, there are about 250 people who think you performed poorly, and who may hesitate to do business with your company.

The study also indicated that every time you or one of your people do something good which catches the customer's attention, that customer tells 3–5 other people about your good performance. You can see why so much is being made these days about good customer service.

Four Overriding Considerations

In working with your people to deliver outstanding customer service, there are four overriding considerations to deal with.

The first is attitudes—such as thinking positively toward customers, being proactive as compared to just reactive, being perpetually dissatisfied, and continually looking for ways to better serve customers.

The second is values—such as customers are important, associates are important, empathy, and teamwork.

The third is innovation—a creative and results orientation in which new and different and even strange ideas are valued, and ideas are solicited from everyone and then acted on.

The fourth is management leadership—the realization that managers must be leaders who inspire as well as coach people. Good managers respect and encourage people. They empower them and they "cause" effective performance.

Obviously, much more information is available on each of these, plus the points below. However, with this as a starting point, you can develop many of the concepts you need to use by thinking about them and discussing them with your associates.

Four Areas of Performance

There are four key areas of customer service performance—performance that supports and provides effective customer service. The first two are delivered primarily by frontline people. The second two are delivered primarily by management.

The first is interpersonal communications—who you are: such as being friendly, caring, flexible, and warm.

The second is personal actions—what you do: such as being dependable, responsive, efficient, and listening.

The third is application of resources—what you give: such as building renovations, equipment associates use to do their jobs, training, customer research, and systems design.

The fourth is organizational operations criteria—how you operate: such as your company or organization's strategy, leadership style, communications systems and policy, and organizational structure.

Implementation

There are eleven steps to implementing an effective customer service program.

(1) See a vision (analyze the environment and develop a vision of extraordinary customer service),

(2) Communicate (communicate the vision, supporting values, and the implementation process to the people),

(3) Organize (organize for extraordinary customer service perform-

ance with generalized job descriptions, performance standards, and supporting systems),

(4) Staff (staff for sales and customer service, realizing that some people don't and never will have a customer-serving attitude),

(5) Train (train and develop people, keeping sessions fresh and exciting),

(6) Specialize (introducing specialized, differentiated, quality products and services),

(7) Set up systems and support (establishing sales and customer service systems and support, such as communication meetings, supporting publications, and employee motivation),

(8) Appoint frontline leadership (selecting and developing frontline leaders who really lead),

(9) Gear up (gearing up for extraordinary customer service with individual and department customer service goals and action plans, specific job descriptions, performance standards),

(10) Measure and reward (measure, reward and nudge customer service performance in the many ways available), and

(11) Re-evaluate and improve (continuing to survey customers, performing internal and external customer service audits, developing new objectives and plans, involving all associates in the process).

Integrated Business Leadership Through Cross-Marketing, by M. Baber, contains considerable information on implementing effective customer service and satisfaction.

You as an effective, value-producing, customer-serving salesperson can take the lead in moving your organization in the direction of extraordinary customer service. This causes all customers to want to do business with your company and therefore to do business with you.

The Customer-Driven Dozen

The following is a list of twelve personal characteristics that support extraordinary customer service.

(1) Dependability—doing what you say you will

(2) Communications—supplying needed information in a clear/convenient way

(3) Consistency—service one day being like service other days

(4) Friendliness—positive and supportive human relations interaction between employees and customers

(5) Fairness—trying honestly to do what is in the customer's best interest, keeping the interest of your company in mind

(6) Flexibility—willing to adjust and bend policies to fit customer needs
(7) Responsiveness—moving quickly and effectively to meet customer needs and requests
(8) Respectfulness—trying hard to not waste the customer's time, being respectful, listening without interruption
(9) Sincerity—being honestly and truly concerned with serving customer needs
(10) Speciality—designing systems and procedures to meet specialized needs of particular customers and groups of customers
(11) Sensitivity—treating customers as important persons, caring, and being alert to specialized needs and concerns
(12) Solving Problems—taking action quickly and decisively to right a wrong or fulfill a need

Customer Service Mistakes

There are 25 mistakes you and your people should avoid as you proceed toward offering "extraordinary customer service." They are discussed in *Integrated Business Leadership Through Cross-Marketing* by M. Baber. You should avoid these mistakes and take proactive action to prevent them from occurring. Your organization should develop policies and systems to support you and your associates in accomplishing this objective.

(1) Being unappreciative
(2) Not being interested
(3) Not listening
(4) Unfriendliness
(5) Lack of empathy
(6) Ignoring customer input
(7) Not asking questions
(8) Forgetting customer benefits
(9) Jumping the gun
(10) Lack of sympathy
(11) Keeping customers waiting
(12) Being pushy
(13) Being discourteous
(14) Arguing with customers
(15) Not admitting you are wrong
(16) Allowing distractions
(17) Rushing the customer
(18) Being insensitive to behavior styles
(19) Being undependable
(20) Being inconsistent

(21) Allowing customers to be embarrassed
(22) Criticizing customers
(23) Becoming angry
(24) Expecting customers to be fair
(25) Wasting the customer's time

Many of these customer service ideas you as a salesperson can implement or encourage. Many require management involvement.

But often, you can educate and nudge management to do what it should be doing to better serve customers—and establish the environment to help you build sales.

Appendix E
Creatively Managing Yourself

GENERATING "ELECTRIC" PERSONAL POWER

Demonstrating confidence, friendliness, enthusiasm and a high level of expertise, while discussing with customers and prospects the powerful ways your product or service might benefit them—and as a result "stirring up" the customers emotionally, and getting them thinking of the benefits of working with you and your company.

If you are friendly, if you are self-confident, if you know your business, if you really believe you can help the client in a major and important way and show it, then this is going to come through to the prospect. The prospect is going to want to do business with you, or at least listen to what you have to say and give it major consideration.

Suppose you aren't this kind of person. Suppose you are sort of withdrawn, and you are far from being a high energy, "electric" type of person with personal power. What could you do to improve in this area?

One thing you could do is to consider taking the Dale Carnegie Course. Another is to join Toastmasters. Toastmasters is a public speaking club that gives you frequent opportunities to give short speeches and presentations.

Another thing you might do is to go into your own bedroom, look into a mirror, and talk with great power and great personality and great friendliness and great enthusiasm, and force yourself to present more of all these qualities than you normally do. At first it may not work—at all. But eventually, if you keep doing it, like magic, it will.

You can put yourself in front of a small group of people—your family, or a small group of work associates—and practice before one another, and evaluate and coach (nudge, instruct, and encourage) each other to develop these qualities.

There are a number of selling practices and characteristics that help champions, the top sales people in the country, to be successful. At least seven of these characteristics are related to generating "electric" personal power.

These seven are discussed below briefly.

Once you understand the importance of each of the seven, you can determine which, if any, you need to improve on. Then you can make a determined effort to do so.

1. Aggressiveness

"Proactively, forcefully, purposefully, and tenaciously taking action to achieve benefits on behalf of the customer. Not easily dissuaded, rejected, or unnecessarily delayed in taking action." Note: one can be aggressive and soft spoken at the same time. Some people prefer the word *assertiveness*. But aggressiveness is assertiveness plus some "pushiness," in this case because you believe so strongly in the benefits of the products and services you sell.

Aggressiveness is both how you think and what you do. Aggressiveness gets things done. It also demonstrates to others your enthusiasm and belief in your product, service, and customer solutions, which in turn tends to convince them of their worth. Large obstacles are overcome or bypassed when normally they might have seemed insurmountable.

2. High Energy

"A condition of feeling vigorous, with more than ample physical and emotional resources to produce day after day. This results in a sense of power and inner excitement when faced with important needs and favorable possibilities."

Energy is the physical and psychological resource that helps you to overcome objections, obstacles, and disappointments and keep thinking positively. It provides the power to think intelligently and continue working effectively even after long hours. It supports enthusiasm and an uplifted spirit.

You can list habits and actions in a number of areas (such as diet, exercise, life style, and recuperation) that build your energy level. For instance, physical exercises such as push-ups, stomach crunches, and jogging build your stamina. You then can select the most important to implement first. You can complete an action plan to do so.

3. Enthusiasm

"Powerful, positive, internal excitement and anticipation that strongly encourages vigorous positive action."

Your enthusiasm influences you to keep moving forward toward your goals despite obstacles. It influences your customer or prospect to try your product or service and to give you the benefit of the doubt—because you seem to believe so strongly in it.

Twenty motivational beliefs are discussed in the book, *Integrated Business Leadership Through Cross Marketing,* by M. Baber. An example is (really and powerfully) "believing in your product and the benefits therefrom." Choose from the list the belief or beliefs that are most critical to your having a powerful, positive attitude. Think of all the facts and evidence that support the chosen belief. Then continually remind yourself of that belief and the supporting facts and evidence.

4. Effectiveness in Personal Relationships

"The ability and knowledge to understand, relate to, and positively influence people, and the effective application thereof. The ability to make people feel comfortable with you and to like, trust, and respect you."

Selling requires persuasion, and persuasion is based on developing positive personal relationships. Positive personal relationships combined with the finding and solving of customer problems, and follow-up service, generate short-term sales and long-term business relationships. These in turn lead to increased business, referrals to other potential customers, and joint efforts leading to new business opportunities.

5. Communications

"Effectively transferring the right information in the right way to and from the right people."

When accurate information is transferred to and from the customer, and between you and your associates on a timely basis, accurate decisions are made when they should be made and misunderstandings are avoided. This generates effective results and makes the customer feel secure and happy. Happy customers remain customers, buy more, and recommend you to other potential customers.

6. Being an Expert

"Becoming specialized in an industry or an area of business or technology that is directly related to serving critical customer needs—developing enough knowledge and experience in that area that you are, and are considered by the customer to be, a very important consultative resource."

Your expertise helps you better serve customer needs. As a result, your customer is inclined to purchase from you just to receive the benefit of your expertise. Your expertise also gives you more confidence in yourself and in what you can do for the customer. It helps you to be more aggressive in sharing your ideas and asking the customer to do business with you.

7. *Making Things Happen*

"Intelligently and assertively taking action and 'going after' your objectives. Being the kind of person who looks like and acts like she is action and results oriented."

You develop the reputation of, and achieve the results of, an achiever. Customer contacts, peers and upper management tend to look your way when they want an important-but-difficult job done.

The following are some additional ideas to keep in mind when generating "electric" personal power.

- ► A primary basis of electric personal power is enthusiasm, based on a firm belief in your company, the value of your product or service, and in your ability to facilitate the delivery of that product or service. Build a "business case" to prove the value of your product and build your level of belief in that value. (See Chapter 10.) Enthusiasm is an internal, almost spiritual, quality. It comes from how positively you think and feel. It might or might not be demonstrated with physical excitement. But it always can be sensed as emotional excitement.
- ► Being around positive people can lift you up. Being around negative people can and will pull you down. Stay away from negative, complaining, unhappy people.
- ► Fill your mind with hope and positive thoughts. Read, watch, and listen to positive, up-lifting materials.
- ► Be a learner. Learn as much as you can about your own business, the business and technologies of your customers and customer industries, and the technological bases of your products and services. Become a consultant in ability if not in fact.
- ► Feed and build yourself up physically, mentally, emotionally, and spiritually.

TIME AND TERRITORY MANAGEMENT

Understanding where your time goes, managing your time effectively, concentrating on the most important, most results-generating activities, and determining where you should be, when, and how to get there.

Many books have been written on time management and personal effectiveness. Peter Drucker's *The Effective Executive* is one of the best.

The Scales of Self Management

According to Drucker, there are five "scales" of self-management that every executive and professional salesperson needs to master. The five scales are: (1) know where your time goes and manage your time, (2) focus on outward contribution—in your case what you can do to provide value to the customer and deserve more business and a higher price, (3) build on strengths—yours and those of your company, (4) concentrate on the few areas where superior performance produces outstanding results (another way to state Baber's Law—do first things first; do second things never), and (5) make effective decisions—judgments based on dissenting opinions, not a compromise between the opinions offered.

The Effective Executive discusses these five scales in detail.

Time Management

All salespeople need to measure in detail where they are spending their time, and then find what to eliminate, what to reduce, what to delegate, what to find better ways to handle, and on what to concentrate. This is discussed briefly in Chapter 9.

The following are ten of the most frequent time wasters that have come out of time management studies.

(1) Priorities: Lack of objectives and well clarified priorities, and constantly switching priorities

(2) Dispersion: attempting too much at once; inability to estimate time; inability to say "No!"

(3) Crisis: continually recurring crises, emergencies, and fire-fighting

(4) Paperwork, memoitis, reports, reading, and inadequate filing systems

(5) Leaving tasks unfinished, jumping from one thing to another

(6) Interruptions, telephones, drop-in visitors, distractions

(7) Being involved in too much detail

(8) Meetings; especially ineffectively run ones

(9) Ineffective communication; lack of feedback

(10) Procrastination; indecision; lack of self-discipline.

To these the average salesperson might add unproductive travel time, waiting to see prospects, inability to arrange appointments at convenient times, visiting customers to correct product and service problems, unnecessarily calling on smaller accounts, and completing paperwork for management. If these are at the top time wasters for you, then you need to creatively find ways to solve them. But first, you need to measure where your time is going and determine where your time is being wasted and is less productive than it should be.

One effective way to do this is to record everything you do and how long it takes for a week, or a time long enough to include all the cycles of your business. (This may mean repeating the process one or more times during the year.) Stop every two hours or so and record every major activity you did and how long it took (1 hr., 3 minutes, etc.—as best you can judge). At the end of the time period, then separate your activities by category (such as wasted travel time, productively spent travel time, waiting time at the account, meeting and greeting, information gathering, planning, unproductive time in meetings, or productive time in meetings). Add the total times spent by category. Calculate percentages. Decide which categories are wasted time, which ones should be taking less time, which ones should be receiving more effort, and which should be delegated.

Territory Management

Separate your accounts by account potential into A+, A, B, C, and C- categories, or something equivalent. Include both existing customers and prospects in the categorization. Then adjust the ratings by adding in other factors, such as present purchase volume, difficulty of getting the business, odds of getting the business, and additional benefits of doing business with the customer (such as referral to other customers).

Plan to spend the bulk of your time focused on A+ and A accounts without ignoring the needs of the other accounts.

Develop a creative and effective way of dealing with C and especially C- accounts. C- accounts are those with small sales or potential that will never have a substantial potential. Perhaps you deal with these by phone and mail, with only an occasional visit if any. Perhaps you allow yourself to lose some or many of these, to provide the time to invest in obtaining a much larger amount of profitable business from the larger potential accounts. This goes against the grain for many salespeople. However, in many cases it is necessary, to free up the time that is needed to spend on higher potential accounts and projects.

Schedule your travel time effectively. The common method is some version of "clover leaf scheduling" in which you make four continuous loops, without doubling back, through each of four quadrants. If you were to draw your path on a map, it would look somewhat like a four leaf clover. The point is to develop a method to prevent wasted travel time.

Make every sales call an important sales call. Don't just call it important. (Don't just say it is important without understanding why it is, and specifically what you need to accomplish.) Make it important by setting an important objective for the call and making a plan to accomplish the objective. Most important sales calls deserve an appointment. So, unless you find a compelling reason otherwise (compelling not only to you, but to your associates, to whom you should be able to defend your decisions) make a practice of working by appointment.

If you will be even slightly late for an appointment, stop and call ahead. This gives the correct impression to the prospect that the meeting is important, and you consider their time to be important.

It is important that the prospect or customer you are calling on consider your visit to be an important occasion. Use creative thinking to devise other ways to continually lead them to that conclusion. Make all your sales calls important to the account and to you.

WAYS TO IDENTIFY YOUR CHAMPIONSHIP STRATEGIES AND SKILLS

Making lists of all the potential ways you might use to considerably improve your selling performance and selecting the most powerful and useful to you from that list.

The following is a list of potential methods for identifying the strategies or skills that should yield the most positive results for you. They also contain approaches you might use in evaluating those which seem to have the most potential. Select those that you believe will be most helpful to you.

This list should be helpful, only if the method suggested in the book's introduction and conclusion, and in "How to Use This Book," did not generate satisfactory results for you. It, in essence, is the process the author used in gathering the material for this book.

- List each of the 27 championship strategies and skills that have been discussed, and write out a comment on how you might apply each one.
- For this list, or any other list, evaluate each item on the list for it's potential for effectiveness in your selling.
- Select the most important or most helpful idea or ideas from each of the lists you make. After evaluating all lists, make a master list of the most important ideas, strategies, or skills. Then evaluate each for its potential. Narrow the list to the one or the few best items.
- Read this book from cover to cover, noting (making a list of) each idea discussed that you might use. You may end up with hundreds of ideas.
- While reading the book from cover to cover, write down any additional thoughts that come to your mind, which might help you to sell more effectively.
- Interview sales trainers and sales managers for ideas.

- Interview friends and acquaintances who seem to be effective in selling.
- Ask everyone appropriate you can think of, what is the most valuable book and article on selling they ever read? Read those books and articles and record ideas from them.
- Find a list of periodicals that focus on selling (such as *Sales & Marketing Management, Sell!ng, Sales & Marketing Training Magazine*). Go to the library or go online and review the titles, authors, and excerpts of a number of issues. Look for ideas and for names of highly successful salespeople, and their companies or affiliations.
- Contact personally or by phone as many successful salespeople as you can. Get their ideas on why they are successful and what you can learn from their experiences.
- Find books that discuss highly successful corporations. Examples include *In Search of Excellence,* by Peters & Waterman, *The Winning Performance,* by Clifford & Cavanagh, *Innovation & Entrepreneurship,* by P. Drucker, *Thriving on Chaos,* by T. Peters, and *The Discipline of Market Leaders,* by Treacy & Wiersema. Read them for ideas that might apply to your selling and your industry.
- Find magazines that discuss highly successful corporations and people (such as *Inc, Forbes, Business Week, The Wall Street Journal,* and *Fortune*). Review back issues for articles on successful companies and people that might relate to your selling and industry.
- Join an online discussion group or bulletin board that relates to your selling (such as your industry, your technology, or your profession). (See Chapter 11 on technology for a discussion about going online.) Monitor the discussions and posted information. Ask appropriate questions of the group and on the bulletin board.
- Contact associations representing major industries you serve. Talk to the appropriate expert. Or get referred to industry experts. Phone them to discuss industry problems, needs, trends, and opportunities.
- Contact magazine editors for the periodicals that address your key industries—about appropriate industry problems, needs, trends, and opportunities.
- Survey key customers in your major industries for problems, needs, and opportunities. Do this in such a way as to encourage and not aggravate them.
- Brainstorm with key associates on industry trends, problems, needs, and opportunities.
- Brainstorm with key associates on selling strategies and skills that might generate the most positive selling results. Include in your sessions some out-of-the-box thinkers and some people who don't have a stake in how you do things now.

► Do self-brainstorming and make lists of potentially helpful ideas. I do my best self-brainstorming while taking long walks alone, note pad and pen in hand. Then relax and take your mind off this project. Let your subconscious mind work and make combinations. Record any ideas that just pop into your head.

► Read the best books you can find on the future and how it relates to business success, marketing success, selling success, and your industries and markets. Keep your mind open while reading for related ideas to flow through your subconscious mind to your conscious mind.

► From all of these sources, make lists of what successful and unsuccessful companies and people did to achieve their results. Then ask yourself what each means to you, if anything, about your selling success and selling success in your industry and key market segments.

► Establish for yourself a board of advisors of people you respect. This is like a personal board of directors. Include on your board people with different perspectives and experience. Meet with them regularly (quarterly?) to report to them and discuss your progress, objectives, and results. Have at least one person on the board who will give you a hard time and hold your feet to the fire.

► List every successful and troubled company, businessperson, and salesperson you can think of for the past 100 years. Answer as best you can why they succeeded or failed and how that applies to you. For instance, Henry Ford was extraordinarily successful from 1910 to 1920. This was because he found a way to concentrate on supplying what the bulk of the market wanted at the lowest price possible. He got into trouble after 1920 because he failed to realize that both the market and his competition's response to it was changing.

► List all the general trends and expected events (demographics, political changes, technology) and how they affect you and your industry.

► List all the trends and expected events affecting your industry and your market segments. Ask what problems and opportunities they bring.

► Analyze how the richest people in the world got that way. Ask what you can learn from their lives and experiences.

► List all the industries that have characteristics in common with yours. List the most successful companies and salespeople in those industries and how they became successful. Ask what you can learn and use from their successes. For instance, suppose your company supports insurance companies. It does this by providing claims management services and having numerous offices around the country. Then you might investigate successful companies that supply support services to other industries and have numerous offices around the country. For instance, RE/MAX and Century 21 have franchised real estate offices in every city. What can you learn from them?

SALES CONSULTING AND LEADERSHIP

(A) A Way to Use This Book as a Leader/Consultant If You Are Not Thoroughly Familiar With Its Contents

Start with Chapter 1 and evaluate the importance to your organization of the approach presented in each of the 27 chapters. Some of the strategies or skills presented will fit your situation, strengths, and/or challenges—with or without modifications that you make. It may be obvious that others do not fit your situation at all. Attempt to determine which one or few chapters or approaches are most important to the selling success of your salesperson or organization.

Let's say you are trying to help a particular salesperson or sales organization increase selling effectiveness. You can start with Part A, asking and answering whether this person has personal power, how much, and whether this is an area that needs significant improvement.

Does he have good personal presence, power, and passion? For instance, does he "really" believe in his company, product, service, added value, and himself? What does he believe is really great about each? Does his answer make sense to you? Will it motivate the customer?

Does he really listen? What is the evidence that supports that answer? How important is this to him?

How effective is he at building partnering relationships? How important is that to his selling success? What major customers does he have partnering relationships with, if any? How is he a partner as compared to merely providing friendly and satisfactory service? What great results for customers and his own company have been achieved by that partnership? How can the salesperson be even more effective in partnering with other large customers and prospects?

Which entrepreneurial attitudes and skills does the salesperson display and make use of? Go through and evaluate each of the 25 in turn. How has each been helpful? Where should he be even more entrepreneurial, and what positive results might be expected if he were?

Now go to Part B, providing customers great value.

What are the key business segments and what are the critical issues for each segment? Does the salesperson know? Has he and can he go through the five step process of "grasping" critical issues? If not, help him to do so.

Can "facilitated problem solving and planning" be of great help to him in positioning himself as a "selling" business consultant? Would this be helpful in his particular situation? Perhaps not. But if it would, it may make a major difference in his selling success.

Where does he stand from the standpoint of finding and offering specific added value? Are there added value opportunities that will place him "on a different planet" as compared to competitive salespeople, in that he offers so much more value that the customer would be crazy to not buy from him? This question can't be answered quickly in the negative. There are so many possibilities available. This area deserves a lot of thinking and analysis for any salesperson or sales organization.

How is he at finding problems and opportunities to solve for the customer or prospect? You might help him develop a system. You might work with him in a role playing exercise. How important is this area to the type of selling that he does? Is it a key area for concentrated improvement?

Asking similar questions, you can move through the strategies and skills related to planning and organization, selling strategically, selling professionally, and performing creative marketing. A quick review of Part F shows that some of the creative marketing approaches might help the salesperson to market more effectively; some are added value for the customer.

Also, as part of your analysis and assistance you can review with him the appropriate ones of the creative fundamentals discussed in the other sections of the Appendix. Perhaps some of those will be of major help to the salesperson or sales organization that you are helping.

(B) A Way to Use This Book as a Leader/Consultant If You Are Thoroughly Familiar With Its Contents

The 27 strategies and skills address five key strategic selling objectives. The first (short) list below states and defines these five objectives. The second list shows which strategies/skills (and the respective chapter number) support each of the five objectives (primarily if listed to the left, secondarily if indented—with some being abbreviated).

Working with a salesperson or organization, determine which objectives are most important in achieving goals or increasing sales performance. Then examine the supporting strategies and skills to develop an overall plan for accomplishing the results desired.

Do your salespeople:

➤ Find ways to generate great value for customers even when others can't?
➤ Position themselves powerfully?
➤ Perform highly effectively in what they do?
➤ Have positive, results-generating personalities and skills?
➤ Find and sell to new business opportunities?

If they do each of these five, they will "destroy" their competition and increase their productivity well over 100% on average. A few may become champions and increase their productivity 500% or more (like Joe Gandolfo, Keith Dillon, Nick DiBari, and Martin Shafiroff).

THE FIVE CHAMPIONSHIP STRATEGIC SELLING OBJECTIVES

1. Great Value (provided to customers)
2. Powerful Positioning (having the customer/prospect see you most favorably)
3. Effectiveness (accomplishing objectives, generating great results, and using resources well)
4. Positive Personality (passion for value delivered, and great character and skills)
5. New Business Development (generating new business and new sales)

THE FIVE CHAMPIONSHIP STRATEGIC SELLING OBJECTIVES AND THE CHAMPIONSHIP STRATEGIES/SKILLS SUPPORTING EACH*

1. Great Value
　　　　(4) Entrepreneurship
　　(5) Critical Issues
　　　　(6) Facilitated Problem Solving and Planning
　　(7) Added Value
　　(8) Finding Problems/Opportunities
　　(18) Being a Sales Consultant
　　　　(19) Team Selling
　　(20) Customer Support Marketing
　　(23) Pull-Through Marketing Assistance
　　(25) New Business Marketing Assistance
　　(27) Frontline Marketing

2. Powerful Positioning
　　　　(3) Building Partnering Relationships
　　(6) Facilitated Problem Solving and Planning
　　　　(10) Business Cases
　　(12) Positioning/Differentiating/Focusing

*The strategies/skills (with corresponding chapter numbers) indented to the right are supportive of the strategic selling objective. The unindented ones to the left are primary.

(13) Major Account Competitive Selling
(14) Cultivating Strategic Relationships
   (15) Leveraging Your Selling
(16) Concept/Philosophy
   (18) Being a Sales Consultant
(21) Industry-Specific Marketing
(22) Industry-Specific Self Marketing

3. Effectiveness
   (2) Really Listening
   (9) Territory/Account Planning
(10) Business Cases
(11) Technology
   (12) Positioning/Differentiating/Focusing
(15) Leveraging Your Selling
(17) Preventing Rejection and Objections
(19) Team Selling
(26) Cross-Marketing
   (27) Frontline Marketing

4. Positive Personality
   (1) Personal Presence, Power, and Passion
   (2) Really Listening
   (3) Building Partnering Relationships

5. New Business Development
   (4) Entrepreneurship
   (24) New Business Marketing
   (25) New Business Marketing Assistance

Appendix F
Additional Resources

EIGHTEEN PROVEN STRATEGIES TO DRAMATICALLY INCREASE YOUR SALES VOLUME AND PROFITS*

Eighteen marketing and sales approaches where Business Development Institute has helped clients to dramatically improve performance.

Marketing

(1) Strategic Marketing and Planning. Evaluating the market situation, developing a powerful, success-generating market strategy, and producing a market plan to effectively implement that strategy.

(2) Added Value Marketing. A system of developing added value for targeted customers and customer segments, both by the corporation and by individual marketing and sales personnel. The "added value" helps to serve customers and increase sales, can be offered to some customers and segments as a fee-based service, and, if proven to be valuable enough, can be spun-off as a highly profitable, separate business.

(3) New Business Marketing. A comprehensive approach to looking for, analyzing, and profitably taking advantage of new product/service and new business opportunities.

(4) Market and Product Management. The education and leadership of market managers and product managers, whereby they understand and effectively implement both the strategic and tactical aspects of their responsibilities.

---

*These 18 strategies are explained in the book, *Mine Your Gold Mine: Eighteen Proven Strategies to Dramatically Increase Your Sales Volume and Profits,* by Michael Baber. Business Development Institute provides consulting, systems development, and training in these 18 areas, all of which are in support of *How Champions Sell.* Some can be implemented by individual salespeople. Others are implemented at the sales manager or corporate level.

Sales Management

(5) Sales Management Leadership. A system and approach whereby sales managers—from the general sales manager to frontline managers—provide effective management to their organizations, and leadership to their organizations and their people.

(6) Entrepreneurial Leadership. Leadership in which leaders are customer driven and innovative; they aggressively and persistently seek out new and better ways to create value for customers and generate profitable business for their organizations.

Major Account Selling

(7) Consultative and Key Account Selling. A consultative selling approach that identifies and concentrates on serving key accounts, and forms value-producing, partnering relationships with those high-income-producing companies.

(8) Competitive Strategic Selling. A key account system to aggressively outsell, outsmart, out-maneuver, out-produce, and totally out-perform your competition.

Selling

(9) Strategic Selling and Planning. A system of territory, resource, personal, and account analysis and planning, resulting in the salesperson working "smart," selling in the most effective way, and concentrating efforts where they provide the most customer value and generate the most profit and business.

(10) Championship Selling Strategies and Skills. A process for helping salespersons to think and act smarter through understanding and selecting from a number of selling strategies and skills that have been used by selling champions to be successful.

(11) Strategic Thinking and Analysis in Selling and Marketing. Strategic thinking and analytical processes and tools that will help any salesperson or marketer to think and act smarter and in a more focused and more flexible, results-generating way.

(12) Six Keys to Championship Selling. Six selling approaches that research indicates are generally employed by the nation's most successful salespeople.

(13) The Profession of Selling. The fundamentals of effective tactical selling, combined with a preliminary understanding of strategic selling, which makes the salesperson efficient by planning for and making value-producing, results-generating sales calls.

(14) Value Selling. A focused, easy-to-implement, tactical sales call process designed to provide outstanding results in determining customer needs, in clearly showing the customer the value of your solution to those needs, and then in communicating to and inspiring individual customers as to how they personally will benefit from selecting your solution.

(15) Relationship Selling. The approach to selling that stresses forming partnering and positive business relationships with customers, both large and not-so-large.

Customer Service

(16) Professional Inside Selling and Service. A process and approach whereby inside sales personnel are truly effective, individually and as team members, in both selling to and servicing customers.

(17) Customer Support Marketing. A customer-driven philosophy and system of marketing designed to focus on those things that will cause great business success for customers and consequently for your company.

(18) Frontline Marketing. A process whereby everyone is in the marketing department, giving total customer service and contributing to the selling effort of the company because they believe in the company and its products and services.

ADDITIONAL INFORMATION

If you identify the area of concentration you believe will take you a long way toward becoming a selling champion; and if you study and apply the ideas and approaches in this book regarding the implementation of that area; and if you still are looking for ideas and methods that can help you even more, then contact the Business Development Institute office in metropolitan Atlanta at (770) 740-9895 for a short session of free advice and consultation. You can also contact the Institute at P.O. Box 2970, Lilburn, GA, 30226 and phone us from outside Georgia at (800) 516-1284.

Bibliography

Alessandra, Tony, Phil Wexler, and Rick Barrera. *Non-Manipulative Selling* (New York: Prentice Hall, 1987).

Baber, Michael. *Henry Ford's Success Plan* (Atlanta: Business Development Institute, 1992).

———. *Integrated Business Leadership Through Cross-Marketing* (St. Louis: Warren H. Green, 1986).

———. *Mine Your Gold Mine* (Atlanta: Business Development Institute, 1996).

Burrus, Daniel. *Techno Trends* (New York: HarperCollins, 1993).

Clifford, Donald K., Jr., and Richard E. Cavanaugh. *The Winning Performance: How America's High-Growth Midsize Companies Succeed* (New York: Bantam, 1985).

Covey, Stephen R. *The Seven Habits of Highly Effective People* (New York: Simon & Schuster, 1989).

Davis, Stanley. *Future Perfect* (Reading, Mass.: Addison-Wesley, 1989).

Davis, Stan M., and Bill Davidson. *2020 Vision* (New York: Simon & Schuster, 1992).

Drucker, Peter. *The Effective Executive* (New York: Harper Business, 1993).

———. *Innovation and Entrepreneurship* (New York: Harper Business, 1993).

———. *Managing for Results* (New York: Harper Business, 1993).

Foster, Richard. *Innovation: The Attacker's Advantage* (New York: Summit, 1986).

Hiam, Alexander, and Charles D. Schewe. *The Portable MBA in Marketing* (New York: John Wiley, 1992).

Laborde, Genie. *Influencing With Integrity* (Redwood City, Calif.: Syntony Publishing, 1988).

Levinson, Jay C. *Guerilla Marketing* (Boston: Houghton Mifflin, 1989).

Levitt, Theodore. *The Marketing Imagination* (New York: Free Press, 1983).

Mackay, Harvey. *Swim With the Sharks Without Being Eaten Alive* (New York: William Morrow, 1988).

McKenna, Regis. *The Regis Touch* (Reading, Mass.: Addison-Wesley, 1985).

Negroponte, Nicholas. *Being Digital* (New York: Random House, 1995).

Peters, Tom. *Thriving on Chaos* (New York: HarperCollins, 1989).

Peters, Thomas J., and Robert H. Waterman. *In Search of Excellence* (New York: Warner Books, 1993).

Rackham, Neil. *Major Account Sales Strategy* (New York: McGraw-Hill, 1989).

———. *SPIN Selling* (New York: McGraw-Hill, 1996).

Rapp, Stan, and L. Collins. *Beyond Maximarketing* (New York: McGraw-Hill, 1995).

———. *Maximarketing* (New York: McGraw-Hill, 1987).

Reilly, Thomas P. *Value Added Selling Techniques* (Chicago: Congdon & Weed, 1989).

Ries, Al, and Jack Trout. *Positioning* (New York: McGraw-Hill, 1986).

Robbins, Anthony. *Unlimited Power* (New York: Fawcett, 1987).

Sandhusen, Richard L. *Marketing.* (New York: Barron's, 1987).

Siebel, Thomas, and Michael Malone. *Virtual Selling* (New York: The Free Press, 1996).

Tapscott, Don, and Art Caston. *Paradigm Shift* (New York: McGraw-Hill, 1992).

Treacy, Michael, and Fred Wiersema. *The Discipline of Market Leaders* (Reading, Mass.: Addison-Wesley, 1995).

Van Doren, Charles. *A History of Knowledge* (New York: Carol Pub. Group, 1990).

Index